KDZ
KG-KH

Y0-CXQ-464

Law of the Americas, Latin America, and the West Indies

Library of Congress Classification
2008

Prepared by the Cataloging Policy and Support Office
Library Services

LIBRARY OF CONGRESS
Cataloging Distribution Service
Washington, D.C.

This edition cumulates all additions and changes to subclasses KDZ and KG-KH through Weekly List 2007/48, dated November 28, 2007. Additions and changes made subsequent to that date are published in weekly lists posted on the World Wide Web at

<http://www.loc.gov/aba/cataloging/classification/weeklylists/>

and are also available in *Classification Web*, the online Web-based edition of the Library of Congress Classification.

Library of Congress Cataloging-in-Publication Data

Library of Congress.
   Library of Congress classification. KDZ, KG-KH. Law of the Americas, Latin America, and the West Indies / prepared by the Cataloging Policy and Support Office, Library Services. — 2008 ed.
      p. cm.
   "This edition cumulates all additions and changes to subclasses KDZ and KG-KH through Weekly list 2007/48, dated November 28, 2007. Additions and changes made subsequent to that date are published in weekly lists posted on the World Wide Web at <http://www.loc. gov/aba/cataloging/classification/weeklylists/> and are also available in *Classification Web*, the online Web-based edition of the Library of Congress classification." — T.p. verso.
   Includes index.
   ISBN-13: 978-0-8444-1189-7
   ISBN-10: 0-8444-1189-2
   1. Classification, Library of Congress. 2. Classification—Books—Law. 3. Classification—Books—America. 4. Classification—Books—Latin America. 5. Classification—Books—West Indies. 6. Law—America—Classification. 7. Law—Latin America—Classification. 8. Law—West Indies—Classification. I. Library of Congress. Cataloging Policy and Support Office. II. Title. III. Title: Law of the Americas, Latin America, and the West Indies.
   Z696.U5K34 2008   025.4'63498—dc22   2007050855

For sale by the Library of Congress Cataloging Distribution Service, 101 Independence Avenue, S.E., Washington, DC 20541-4912. Product catalog available on the Web at **www.loc.gov/cds**.

PREFACE

The first edition of Subclasses KDZ, KG-KH, *Law of the Americas, Latin America, and the West Indies*, was published in 1984. A 2000 edition cumulated additions and changes that were made during the period 1984-2000. This 2008 edition includes additions and changes made since the publication of the 2000 edition.

Classification numbers or spans of numbers that appear in parentheses are formerly valid numbers that are now obsolete. Numbers or spans that appear in angle brackets are optional numbers that have never been used at the Library of Congress but are provided for other libraries that wish to use them. In most cases, a parenthesized or angle-bracketed number is accompanied by a "see" reference directing the user to the actual number that the Library of Congress currently uses, or a note explaining Library of Congress practice.

Access to the online version of the full Library of Congress Classification is available on the World Wide Web by subscription to *Classification Web*. Details about ordering and pricing may be obtained from the Cataloging Distribution Service at

<http://www.loc.gov/cds/>

New or revised numbers and captions are added to the L.C. Classification schedules as a result of development proposals made by the cataloging staff of the Library of Congress and cooperating institutions. Upon approval of these proposals by the weekly editorial meeting of the Cataloging Policy and Support Office, new classification records are created or existing records are revised in the master classification database. Weekly lists of newly approved or revised classification numbers and captions are posted on the World Wide Web at

<http://www.loc.gov/aba/cataloging/classification/weeklylists/>

Jolande Goldberg, law classification specialist in the Cataloging Policy and Support Office, and Paul Weiss, senior cataloging policy specialist, are responsible for coordinating the overall intellectual and editorial content of class K and its various subclasses. Kent Griffiths, assistant editor, creates new classification records and their associated index terms, and maintains the master database.

This printed edition of KDZ, KG-KH must be used in conjunction with the separately published K Tables: Form Division Tables for Law, available for purchase from the Cataloging Distribution Service. This classification schedule includes references to form division tables within the range K1 to K24, which are found only in that publication.

Barbara B. Tillett, Chief
Cataloging Policy and Support Office

December 2007

West Indies. Caribbean Area - Continued

KGT1-499	Jamaica
KGT1001-1499	Martinique
KGT2001-2499	Montserrat
KGU1-499	Navassa Islands
KGV1-8200	Puerto Rico
KGW1-499	Saba
KGW2001-2499	Saint Christopher (Saint Kitts), Nevis, and Anguilla
KGW3001-3499	Saint Lucia
KGW5001-5499	Saint Vincent and the Grenadines
KGW7001-7499	Sint Eustatius
KGW8001-8499	Sint Maarten
KGX1-499	Trinidad and Tobago
KGY1-499	Turks and Caicos Islands
KGZ1-499	Virgin Islands of the United States
KH-KHW	South America (General)
KH1-999	General
KHA1-9800	Argentina
KHC1-8200	Bolivia
KHD1-9900	Brazil
KHF1-9800	Chile
KHH1-9900	Colombia
KHK1-9990	Ecuador
KHL1-9000	Falkland Islands
KHM1-9000	French Guiana
KHN1-9000	Guyana
KHP1-9700	Paraguay
KHQ1-9800	Peru
KHR1-9000	South Georgia and South Sandwich Islands
KHS1-9000	Surinam
KHU1-9800	Uruguay
KHW1-9900	Venezuela

KDZ-KH2 1	Bibliography
KDZ-KH2 16	Official gazettes
KDZ-KH2 35	Statutes
KDZ-KH2 70	Law reports and related materials
KDZ-KH2 102	Law dictionaries. Words and phrases
KDZ-KH2 104	Legal maxims
KDZ-KH2 112	Judicial statistics
KDZ-KH2 118	Directories
KDZ-KH2 130	Trials
KDZ-KH2 150	Legal research. Legal bibliography
KDZ-KH2 206	The legal profession
KDZ-KH2 241	Community legal services. Legal aid
KDZ-KH2 250	Notarial law
KDZ-KH2 272	Public registers
KDZ-KH2 290	History
KDZ-KH2 315	Philosophy. Jurisprudence
KDZ-KH2 320	Criticism. Law reform
KDZ-KH2 354	Conflict of laws
KDZ-KH2 356	General principles and concepts
KDZ-KH2 367	Concepts applying to several branches of the law
KDZ-KH2 387	Private law
KDZ-KH2 389	Civil law
KDZ-KH2 449	Persons
KDZ-KH2 480	Domestic relations. Family law
KDZ-KH2 550	Property. Real rights
KDZ-KH2 660	Trusts and trustees
KDZ-KH2 670	Succession upon death
KDZ-KH2 745	Obligations
KDZ-KH2 822	Contracts
KDZ-KH2 955	Quasi contracts. Restitution
KDZ-KH2 965	Torts
KDZ-KH2 1050	Commercial law
KDZ-KH2 1065	Merchants
KDZ-KH2 1081	Auxiliaries and intermediaries of commerce
KDZ-KH2 1098	Commercial mandate and consignment
KDZ-KH2 1103	Commercial sale
KDZ-KH2 1130	Negotiable instruments. Titles of credit
KDZ-KH2 1141	Banking
KDZ-KH2 1171	Commercial loans and credit
KDZ-KH2 1186	Investments
KDZ-KH2 1195	Carriers. Carriage of goods and passengers
KDZ-KH2 1211	Insurance
KDZ-KH2 1295	Business associations. Commercial companies

KDZ-KH2 3450	Veterinary laws. Veterinary hygiene
KDZ-KH2 3470	Food. Drugs. Cosmetics
KDZ-KH2 3490	Alcohol. Alcoholic beverages. Liquor law
KDZ-KH2 3500	Public safety
KDZ-KH2 3523	Control of social activities
KDZ-KH2 3540	Education
KDZ-KH2 3610	Science and the arts. Research
KDZ-KH2 3700	Economic legislation
KDZ-KH2 3729	Regulation of industry, trade, and commerce. Occupational law
KDZ-KH2 3731	Trade regulaton. Control of trade practices. Consumer protection
	Primary production. Extractive industries
KDZ-KH2 3781	Agriculture. Forestry. Rural law
KDZ-KH2 3900	Fisheries. Fishing industry
KDZ-KH2 3920	Mining. Quarrying. Oil and gas
KDZ-KH2 4000	Manufacturing industries
KDZ-KH2 4020	Food processing industries
KDZ-KH2 4060	Trade and commerce
KDZ-KH2 4120	Public utilities
KDZ-KH2 4160	Transportation and communication
KDZ-KH2 4440	Professions and occupations
KDZ-KH2 4550	Public finance
KDZ-KH2 4574	National revenue
KDZ-KH2 4578	Taxation
KDZ-KH2 4801	Tariff. Customs
KDZ-KH2 4840	State (provincial, etc.) and local finance
KDZ-KH2 4950	Government measures in time of war, national emergency, or economic crisis
KDZ-KH2 5100	National defense. Military law
KDZ-KH2 5110	The military establishment. Armed forces
KDZ-KH2 5246	Military criminal law and procedure
KDZ-KH2 5400	Criminal law and procedure
KDZ-KH2 5411	Criminal law
KDZ-KH2 5800	Criminal courts and procedure
KDZ-KH2 5936	Juvenile criminal law and procedure. Administration of juvenile justice

KDZ-KH3 150	Social legislation
KDZ-KH3 151	Labor law
KDZ-KH3 180	Social insurance
KDZ-KH3 195	Public welfare. Public assistance. Public charities
KDZ-KH3 198	Indians
KDZ-KH3 210	Courts. Procedure
KDZ-KH3 211	Court organization and procedure
KDZ-KH3 222	Civil procedure
KDZ-KH3 260	Constitutional law
KDZ-KH3 268	Constitutional history
KDZ-KH3 273	Individual and state
KDZ-KH3 279	Church and state
	Organs of government
KDZ-KH3 280	The people. Election law
KDZ-KH3 281	The legislature
KDZ-KH3 284	The executive branch
KDZ-KH3 290	The judiciary. Judicial power
KDZ-KH3 293	Local government
KDZ-KH3 298	Civil service
KDZ-KH3 304	Administrative law
KDZ-KH3 305	Administrative organization
KDZ-KH3 308	Administrative acts
KDZ-KH3 310	Judicial functions. Remedies
KDZ-KH3 317	Public property. Public restraints on private property
KDZ-KH3 320	Water resources
KDZ-KH3 323	Public land law
KDZ-KH3 328	Regional and city planning. Zoning. Building
KDZ-KH3 336	Public health. Sanitation. Environmental pollution
KDZ-KH3 342	Medical legislation
KDZ-KH3 343	Veterinary laws. Veterinary hygiene
KDZ-KH3 344	Food. Drugs. Cosmetics
KDZ-KH3 345	Alcohol. Alcoholic beverages. Liquor law
KDZ-KH3 347	Public safety
KDZ-KH3 349	Control of social activities
KDZ-KH3 352	Education
KDZ-KH3 355	Science and the arts. Research
KDZ-KH3 357	Economic legislation
KDZ-KH3 364	Regulation of industry, trade, and commerce. Occupational law
KDZ-KH3 365	Trade regulaton. Control of trade practices. Consumer protection
	Primary production. Extractive industries
KDZ-KH3 367	Agriculture. Forestry. Rural law

OUTLINE OF SUBJECT DIVISION TABLES

KDZ-KH4 1	Bibliography
KDZ-KH4 3	Statutes
KDZ-KH4 4	Law reports and related materials
KDZ-KH4 7.33	Law dictionaries. Words and phrases
KDZ-KH4 7.4	Judicial statistics
KDZ-KH4 7.5	The legal profession
KDZ-KH4 7.65	Notarial law
KDZ-KH4 7.7	History
KDZ-KH4 9	Conflict of laws
KDZ-KH4 11	Civil law
KDZ-KH4 11.2	Persons
KDZ-KH4 12	Domestic relations. Family law
KDZ-KH4 15	Property. Real rights
KDZ-KH4 17	Succession upon death
	Obligations
KDZ-KH4 18	Contracts
KDZ-KH4 20	Torts
KDZ-KH4 21	Commercial law
KDZ-KH4 22	Commercial sale
KDZ-KH4 23	Banking
KDZ-KH4 24	Insurance
KDZ-KH4 25	Business associations. Commercial companies
KDZ-KH4 25.7	Insolvency and bankruptcy
KDZ-KH4 25.8	Commercial courts and procedure
KDZ-KH4 27	Social legislation
KDZ-KH4 27.2	Labor law
KDZ-KH4 28	Social insurance
KDZ-KH4 28.5	Public welfare. Public assistance. Public charities
KDZ-KH4 30	Courts. Procedure
KDZ-KH4 30.2	Court organization and procedure
KDZ-KH4 32	Civil procedure
KDZ-KH4 36	Constitutional law
KDZ-KH4 37.3	Constitutional history
KDZ-KH4 38	Structure of government
KDZ-KH4 38.4	Individual and state
	Organs of government
KDZ-KH4 38.8	The people. Election law
KDZ-KH4 39	The legislature
KDZ-KH4 40	The executive branch
KDZ-KH4 40.7	The judiciary. Judicial power
KDZ-KH4 41	Local government

America. North America
                         Including the entire Western Hemisphere
1-999   General (Table KDZ-KH1)
                         Organization of American States (OAS). Organización de los
                              Estados Americanos (OEA)
                              Class here legal works only
                              For general works on the Organization of American States, see
                                   F1402.A1+
                              For works on the law or legal systems of two or more of the
                                   member states of the OAS see KDZ1+
                              For legislative cooperation, unification, or harmonization of the
                                   laws of states in the region at large see KDZ88
1101   Bibliography
1103   Periodicals
                              For periodicals consisting predominantly of legal articles,
                                   regardless of subject matter and jurisdiction, see K1+
                              For periodicals consisting primarily of informative material
                                   (Newsletters, bulletins, etc.) relating to a special subject,
                                   see the subject and form division for periodicals
1105   Monographic series
1107   Official gazettes
                              For the official gazettes of a particular organ, see the issuing
                                   organ
                         Intergovernmental congresses and conferences
                              see KDZ-KH1 8
                         Official records. Documentation
                              Class here the documentation of the organization as a whole
                              For a particular series of an organ of the OAS, see the issuing
                                   organ
1110   Serials
1112   Monographs. By date
                         Indexes. Guides
1114   Lista general de documentos officiales
1116   Indice analítico
                         Official acts
1120   Indexes and tables. By date
1122   Collections. Compilations. By date
                         Treaties and other international agreements
                              General
                                   see KDZ10+
                              Treaties (Individual and collections) establishing and
                                   expanding the OAS see KDZ1144.2<date>
                              Legal measures
                                   see the issuing organ
1124   Yearbooks
1126   Directories
                         Collected works

	Organization of American States (OAS). Organización de los Estados Americanos (OEA)
	Collected works -- Continued
1130	Several authors
	Festschriften see KDZ1136
1132	Individual authors
1134	General works. Treatises
1136	Addresses, essays, lectures
	Including single essays, collected essays of several authors, Festschriften, etc.
	Organization law
1138	General (Table K8)
	Treaties establishing, expanding, and governing the OAS. Charter of the OAS
1140	Indexes and tables
1142	Collections. By date
	Including either multilateral or bilateral treaties, or both
1144.2<date>	Individual treaties and conventions
	Arrange chronologically by appending the date of signature of the treaty to the number KDZ1142.2 and deleting any trailing zeros. Subarrange each by Table K5
1144.2189	First International American Conference. Treaty establishing the International Union of Amercian Republics, Washington, 1890 (Table K5)
1144.21948	Ninth International American Conference. Treaty chartering the OAS, Bogotá, 1948 (Table K5)
	Including the OAS charter as amended by the Buenos Aires protocol of 1967/70
1146	Constitutional principles (Table K8)
	Foreign (external) relations. International cooperation
	Including membership in international organizations
1148	General
	Relations with the United Nations see KZ5003.A+
	Relations with European regional organizations see KJE
1152	Relations with non-member states
	Intergovernmental relations and cooperation
1154	General (Table K8)
1155	Jurisdiction
	Organs of the OAS
1157	General (Table K8)
1158	Election law (Table K8)
	Privileges and immunities
	see the particular organ and member thereof

Organization of American States (OAS). Organización de los
Estados Americanos (OEA)
Organization law
Organs of the OAS -- Continued
Inter-American Specialized Organizations
see the subject
Courts of Justice. Tribunals

1187	General (Table K8)
1188	Jurisdiction
1189.A-Z	Particular courts, A-Z
1189.A3	Administrative Tribunal. Tribunal Administrativo
1190.A-Z	Other commissions and committees, A-Z
1190.S6	Special Committee to Study the Inter-American System and to Propose Measures for Restructuring It

Civil service

1192	General (Table K8)
1193	Privileges and immunites
1194	Appointment
1194.5	Remuneration. Allowances

Finance. Budget

1195	General (Table K8)
1196	Board of External Auditors (Table K15)
1197.A-Z	Special topics, A-Z

Individual countries

2001-2499.2	Bermuda (Table KDZ-KH3)
	Canada
	see KE
3001-3499	Greenland (Table KDZ-KH3)
4001-4499	St. Pierre and Miquelon (Table KDZ-KH3)
	United States
	see KF

4

Latin America
Including Mexico and Central and South America
1-999   General (Table KDZ-KH1)

3001-3999   Mexico and Central America: General (Table KDZ-KH1)

                    Mexico and Central America: Belize
1-5999   General (Table KDZ-KH2)
9000.A-Z   Cities, A-Z
                       Subarrange each by Table KDZ-KH6

Mexico and Central America: British Honduras
see KGA1+

Mexico and Central America: Canal Zone
see KGH9001+

KG-KGH

	Mexico and Central America: Costa Rica
1-5999	General (Table KDZ-KH2)
	Provinces
6201-6299	Alajuela (Table KDZ-KH4)
6401-6499	Cartago (Table KDZ-KH4)
6601-6699	Guanacaste (Table KDZ-KH4)
6801-6899	Heredia (Table KDZ-KH4)
7001-7099	Limón (Table KDZ-KH4)
7201-7299	Puntarenas (Table KDZ-KH4)
7401-7499	San José (Table KDZ-KH4)
	Cities
8001-8019	San José (Table KDZ-KH5)
9000.A-Z	Other, A-Z
	Subarrange each by Table KDZ-KH6

	Mexico and Central America: El Salvador
1-5999	General (Table KDZ-KH2)
	Departments
6201-6299	Ahuachapán (Table KDZ-KH4)
6401-6499	Cabañas (Table KDZ-KH4)
6601-6699	Chalatenango (Table KDZ-KH4)
6801-6899	Cuscatlán (Table KDZ-KH4)
7001-7099	La Libertad (Table KDZ-KH4)
7201-7299	La Paz (Table KDZ-KH4)
7401-7499	La Unión (Table KDZ-KH4)
7601-7699	Morazán (Table KDZ-KH4)
7801-7899	San Miguel (Table KDZ-KH4)
8001-8099	San Salvador (Table KDZ-KH4)
8201-8299	San Vicente (Table KDZ-KH4)
8401-8499	Santa Ana (Table KDZ-KH4)
8601-8699	Sonsonate (Table KDZ-KH4)
8801-8899	Usulután (Table KDZ-KH4)
	Cities
9601-9619	San Salvador (Table KDZ-KH5)
9641-9659	Santa Ana (Table KDZ-KH5)
9800.A-Z	Other, A-Z
	Subarrange each by Table KDZ-KH6

Mexico and Central America: Guatemala

1-5999	General (Table KDZ-KH2)
	Departments
6101-6199	Alta Verapaz (Table KDZ-KH4)
6201-6299	Baja Verapaz (Table KDZ-KH4)
6301-6399	Chimaltenango (Table KDZ-KH4)
6501-6599	Chiquimula (Table KDZ-KH4)
6701-6799	El Progreso (Table KDZ-KH4)
6901-6999	Escuintla (Table KDZ-KH4)
7001-7099	Guatemala (Table KDZ-KH4)
7101-7199	Huehuetenango (Table KDZ-KH4)
7301-7399	Izabal (Table KDZ-KH4)
7501-7599	Jalapa (Table KDZ-KH4)
7701-7799	Jutiapa (Table KDZ-KH4)
7901-7999	Petén (Table KDZ-KH4)
8101-8199	Quezaltenango (Table KDZ-KH4)
8301-8399	Quiché (Table KDZ-KH4)
8501-8599	Retalhuleu (Table KDZ-KH4)
8701-8799	Sacatepéquez (Table KDZ-KH4)
8901-8999	San Marcos (Table KDZ-KH4)
9101-9199	Santa Rosa (Table KDZ-KH4)
9301-9399	Sololá (Table KDZ-KH4)
9501-9599	Suchitepéquez (Table KDZ-KH4)
9701-9799	Totonicapán (Table KDZ-KH4)
9801-9899	Zacapa (Table KDZ-KH4)
	Cities
9921-9939	Guatemala City (Table KDZ-KH5)
9990.A-Z	Other, A-Z
	Subarrange each by Table KDZ-KH6

	Mexico and Central America: Honduras
1-5999	General (Table KDZ-KH2)
	Departments
6101-6199	Atlántida (Table KDZ-KH4)
6301-6399	Choluteca (Table KDZ-KH4)
6501-6599	Colón (Table KDZ-KH4)
6701-6799	Comayagua (Table KDZ-KH4)
6901-6999	Copán (Table KDZ-KH4)
7101-7199	Cortés (Table KDZ-KH4)
7201-7299	Distrito Central (Table KDZ-KH4)
7301-7399	El Paraîso (Table KDZ-KH4)
7501-7599	Francisco Morazán (Table KDZ-KH4)
7701-7799	Gracias a Dios (Table KDZ-KH4)
7901-7999	Intibucá (Table KDZ-KH4)
8101-8199	Islas de la Bahîa (Table KDZ-KH4)
8301-8399	La Paz (Table KDZ-KH4)
8501-8599	Lempira (Table KDZ-KH4)
8701-8799	Ocotepeque (Table KDZ-KH4)
8901-8999	Olancho (Table KDZ-KH4)
9101-9199	Santa Bárbara (Table KDZ-KH4)
9301-9399	Valle (Table KDZ-KH4)
9501-9599	Yoro (Table KDZ-KH4)
	Cities
9921-9939	San Pedro Sula (Table KDZ-KH5)
9961-9979	Tegucigalpa (Table KDZ-KH5)
9990.A-Z	Other, A-Z
	Subarrange each by Table KDZ-KH6

KG-KGH

Mexico and Central America: Honduras, British
see KGA1+

	Mexico and Central America: Mexico
1-5999	General (Table KDZ-KH2)
	States. Federal District
6201-6299	Aguascalientes (Table KDZ-KH4)
6301-6399	Baja California. Baja California Norte (Table KDZ-KH4)
6401-6499	Baja California Sur (Table KDZ-KH4)
6501-6599	Campeche (Table KDZ-KH4)
6601-6699	Chiapas (Table KDZ-KH4)
6701-6799	Chihuahua (Table KDZ-KH4)
6801-6899	Coahuila (Table KDZ-KH4)
6901-6999	Colima (Table KDZ-KH4)
7001-7099	Durango (Table KDZ-KH4)
	Federal District see KGF7601+
7101-7199	Guanajuato (Table KDZ-KH4)
7201-7299	Guerrero (Table KDZ-KH4)
7301-7399	Hidalgo (Table KDZ-KH4)
7401-7499	Jalisco (Table KDZ-KH4)
7501-7599	México (Table KDZ-KH4)
7601-7699	Mexico City (Federal District) (Table KDZ-KH4)
7701-7799	Michoacán (Table KDZ-KH4)
7801-7899	Morelos (Table KDZ-KH4)
7901-7999	Nayarit (Table KDZ-KH4)
	Nueva Galicia see KGF9401+
8001-8099	Nuevo León (Table KDZ-KH4)
8101-8199	Oaxaca (Table KDZ-KH4)
8201-8299	Puebla (Table KDZ-KH4)
8301-8399	Querétaro (Table KDZ-KH4)
8401-8499	Quintana Roo (Table KDZ-KH4)
8501-8599	San Luis Potosî (Table KDZ-KH4)
8601-8699	Sinaloa (Table KDZ-KH4)
8701-8799	Sonora (Table KDZ-KH4)
8801-8899	Tabasco (Table KDZ-KH4)
8901-8999	Tamaulipas (Table KDZ-KH4)
9001-9099	Tlaxcala (Table KDZ-KH4)
9101-9199	Veracruz (Table KDZ-KH4)
9201-9299	Yucatán (Table KDZ-KH4)
9301-9399	Zacatecas (Table KDZ-KH4)
9401-9499	Nueva Galicia (Table KDZ-KH4)
	Cities
9601-9619	Acapulco (Table KDZ-KH5)
9621-9639	Chihuahua (Table KDZ-KH5)
9641-9659	Ciudad Juárez (Table KDZ-KH5)
9661-9679	Cuernavaca (Table KDZ-KH5)
9681-9699	Culiacán (Table KDZ-KH5)
9701-9719	Guadalajara (Table KDZ-KH5)
9721-9739	León (Table KDZ-KH5)
9741-9759	Mexicali (Table KDZ-KH5)

KG-KGH

	Cities -- Continued
	Mexico City see KGF7601+
9761-9779	Monterrey (Table KDZ-KH5)
9781-9799	Puebla (Table KDZ-KH5)
9821-9839	San Luiz Potosî (Table KDZ-KH5)
9841-9859	Tijuana (Table KDZ-KH5)
9900.A-Z	Other, A-Z
	Subarrange each by Table KDZ-KH6

Mexico and Central America: Nicaragua
1-5999	General (Table KDZ-KH2)
	Departments. Territory
6201-6299	Boaco (Table KDZ-KH4)
6401-6499	Cabo Gracias a Dios (Table KDZ-KH4)
6601-6699	Carazo (Table KDZ-KH4)
6801-6899	Chinandega (Table KDZ-KH4)
7001-7099	Chontales (Table KDZ-KH4)
7201-7299	Estelí (Table KDZ-KH4)
7401-7499	Granada (Table KDZ-KH4)
7601-7699	Jinotega (Table KDZ-KH4)
7801-7899	León (Table KDZ-KH4)
8001-8099	Madriz (Table KDZ-KH4)
8201-8299	Managua (Table KDZ-KH4)
8401-8499	Masaya (Table KDZ-KH4)
8601-8699	Matagalpa (Table KDZ-KH4)
8801-8899	Nueva Segovia (Table KDZ-KH4)
9001-9099	Rio San Juan (Table KDZ-KH4)
9201-9299	Rivas (Table KDZ-KH4)
9401-9499	Zelaya (Table KDZ-KH4)
	Cities
9601-9619	Managua (Table KDZ-KH5)
9800.A-Z	Other, A-Z
	Subarrange each by Table KDZ-KH6

KG-KGH

	Mexico and Central America: Panama
1-5999	General (Table KDZ-KH2)
	Provinces
6101-6199	Bocas del Toro (Table KDZ-KH4)
6301-6399	Chiriquî (Table KDZ-KH4)
6501-6599	Coclé (Table KDZ-KH4)
6701-6799	Colón (Table KDZ-KH4)
6901-6999	Darién (Table KDZ-KH4)
7101-7199	Herrera (Table KDZ-KH4)
7301-7399	Los Santos (Table KDZ-KH4)
7501-7599	Panamá (Table KDZ-KH4)
7701-7799	Veraguas (Table KDZ-KH4)
	Cities
7821-7839	Colón (Table KDZ-KH5)
7841-7859	Panama City (Table KDZ-KH5)
7861-7879	San Miguelito (Table KDZ-KH5)
8000.A-Z	Other, A-Z
	Subarrange each by Table KDZ-KH6

9001-9499   Mexico and Central America: Panama Canal Zone (Table KDZ-
KH3)

1-999   West Indies. Caribbean area: General (Table KDZ-KH1)

KGJ-KGZ

7001-7499   West Indies. Caribbean area: Anguilla (Table KDZ-KH3)
                  Cf. KGW2001+ Saint Christopher (Saint Kitts), Nevis, and
                  Anguilla

1-499   West Indies. Caribbean area: Antigua and Barbuda (Table KDZ-
KH3)
Including Redonda

1001-1499   West Indies. Caribbean area: Aruba (Table KDZ-KH3)

1-499   West Indies. Caribbean area: Bahamas (Table KDZ-KH3)

1001-1499   West Indies. Caribbean area: Barbados (Table KDZ-KH3)

KGJ-KGZ

West Indies. Caribbean area: Barbuda
see KGK1+

2001-2499   West Indies: Bonaire (Table KDZ-KH3)

KGJ-KGZ

3001-3499	West Indies. Caribbean area: British Leeward Islands (General) (Table KDZ-KH3)

4001-4499   West Indies. Caribbean area: British Virgin Islands (General)
                 (Table KDZ-KH3)

5001-5999   West Indies. Caribbean area: British West Indies (General)
(Table KDZ-KH1)

6001-6499   West Indies. Caribbean area: British Windward Islands
                           (General) (Table KDZ-KH3)

KGJ-KGZ

West Indies. Caribbean area: Caicos Islands
see KGY1+

0-499 West Indies. Caribbean area: Cayman Islands (Table KDZ-KH3)

KGJ-KGZ

	West Indies. Caribbean area: Cuba
1-5999	General (Table KDZ-KH2)
	Provinces
6201-6299	Camagüey (Table KDZ-KH4)
6401-6499	Ciego de Avila (Table KDZ-KH4)
6601-6699	Cienfuegos (Table KDZ-KH4)
6801-6899	Granma (Table KDZ-KH4)
7001-7099	Guantánamo (Table KDZ-KH4)
7201-7299	Havana (City) (Table KDZ-KH4)
7401-7499	Havana (Province) (Table KDZ-KH4)
7601-7699	Holguîn (Table KDZ-KH4)
7801-7899	Las Tunas (Table KDZ-KH4)
7901-7999	Las Villas (Table KDZ-KH4)
8001-8099	Matanzas (Table KDZ-KH4)
8101-8199	Oriente (Table KDZ-KH4)
8201-8299	Pina del Rió (Table KDZ-KH4)
8401-8499	Sancti Spîritus (Table KDZ-KH4)
8601-8699	Santiago de Cuba (Table KDZ-KH4)
8801-8899	Villa Clara (Table KDZ-KH4)
	Cities
	Havana see KGN7201+
9601-9619	Holguîn (Table KDZ-KH5)
9641-9659	Santa Clara (Table KDZ-KH5)
9661-9679	Santiago de Cuba (Table KDZ-KH5)
9800.A-Z	Other, A-Z
	Subarrange each by Table KDZ-KH6

1-499   West Indies. Caribbean area: Curaçao (Table KDZ-KH3)

KGJ-KGZ

West Indies. Caribbean area: Désirade
see KGR5001+

2001-2499   West Indies. Caribbean area: Dominica (Table KDZ-KH3)

KGJ-KGZ

	West Indies. Caribbean area: Dominican Republic
1-5999	General (Table KDZ-KH2)
	Provinces. National District
6201-6299	Azua (Table KDZ-KH4)
6301-6399	Bahoruco (Table KDZ-KH4)
6401-6499	Barahona (Table KDZ-KH4)
6501-6599	Dajabón (Table KDZ-KH4)
6601-6699	Durarte (Table KDZ-KH4)
6701-6799	El Seibo (Table KDZ-KH4)
6801-6899	Espaillat (Table KDZ-KH4)
6901-6999	Independencia (Table KDZ-KH4)
7001-7099	La Altagracia (Table KDZ-KH4)
7101-7199	La Estrelleta (San Rafael) (Table KDZ-KH4)
7201-7299	La Romana (Table KDZ-KH4)
7301-7399	La Vega (Table KDZ-KH4)
7401-7499	Maria Trinidad Sánchez (Table KDZ-KH4)
7501-7599	Montecristi (Table KDZ-KH4)
	National District see KGQ8701+
7601-7699	Pedernales (Table KDZ-KH4)
7701-7799	Peravia (Table KDZ-KH4)
7801-7899	Puerto Plata (Table KDZ-KH4)
7901-7999	Salcedo (Table KDZ-KH4)
8001-8099	Samaná (Table KDZ-KH4)
8101-8199	San Cristobál (Table KDZ-KH4)
8201-8299	San Juan (Table KDZ-KH4)
8301-8399	San Pedro de Macoris (Table KDZ-KH4)
	San Rafael see KGQ7101+
8401-8499	Sánchez Ramírez (Table KDZ-KH4)
8501-8599	Santiago (Table KDZ-KH4)
8601-8699	Santiago Rodríguez (Table KDZ-KH4)
8701-8799	Santo Domingo (National District) (Table KDZ-KH4)
8801-8899	Valverde (Table KDZ-KH4)
	Cities
9601-9619	San Cristóbal (Table KDZ-KH5)
9661-9679	Santiago de los Caballeros (Table KDZ-KH5)
	Santo Domingo see KGQ8701+
9800.A-Z	Other, A-Z
	Subarrange each by Table KDZ-KH6

1-499   West Indies. Caribbean area: Dutch Leeward Islands (General)
(Table KDZ-KH3)

KGJ-KGZ

1001-1499   West Indies. Caribbean area: Dutch West Indies (Netherlands
                 Antilles) (General) (Table KDZ-KH3)

2001-2499   West Indies. Caribbean area: Dutch Windward Islands (General)
                          (Table KDZ-KH3)

3001-3499   West Indies. Caribbean area: French West Indies (General)
             (Table KDZ-KH3)

West Indies. Caribbean area: Grande Terre
see KGR5001+

4001-4499   West Indies. Caribbean area: Grenada (Table KDZ-KH3)
                   Including the Grenadine Islands under its jurisdiction

West Indies. Caribbean area: Grenadine Islands
see KGR4001+ ; KGW5001+

KGJ-KGZ

5001-5499	West Indies. Caribbean area: Guadeloupe (Table KDZ-KH3)

Including Grand Terre, Marie Galante, Les Saintes, Désirade, Saint Barthélemy, and Saint Martin

	West Indies. Caribbean area: Haiti
1-5999	General (Table KDZ-KH2)
	Departments
6201-6299	Artibonite (Table KDZ-KH4)
6401-6499	Centre (Table KDZ-KH4)
6601-6699	Grande Anse (Table KDZ-KH4)
6801-6899	Nord (Table KDZ-KH4)
7001-7099	Nord Est (Table KDZ-KH4)
7201-7299	Nord-Ouest (Table KDZ-KH4)
7401-7499	Ouest (Table KDZ-KH4)
7601-7699	Sud (Table KDZ-KH4)
7801-7899	Sud Est (Table KDZ-KH4)
	Cities
8001-8019	Port-au-Prince (Table KDZ-KH5)
9000.A-Z	Other, A-Z
	Subarrange each by Table KDZ-KH6

KGJ-KGZ

1-499   West Indies. Caribbean area: Jamaica (Table KDZ-KH3)

West Indies. Caribbean area: Les Saintes
see KGR5001+

KGJ-KGZ

West Indies. Caribbean area: Marie Galante
see KGR5001+

1001-1499   West Indies. Caribbean area: Martinique (Table KDZ-KH3)

KGJ-KGZ

2001-2499 West Indies. Caribbean area: Montserrat (Table KDZ-KH3)

1-499   West Indies. Caribbean area: Navassa islands (Table KDZ-KH3)
                   Including Swan Islands

KGJ-KGZ

West Indies. Caribbean area: Nevis
    see KGW2001+

	West Indies. Caribbean area: Puerto Rico
1-5999	General (Table KDZ-KH2)
	Cities
8001-8019	Bayamón (Table KDZ-KH5)
8021-8039	Caguas (Table KDZ-KH5)
8041-8059	Carolina (Table KDZ-KH5)
8061-8079	Mayagüez (Table KDZ-KH5)
8081-8099	Ponce (Table KDZ-KH5)
8101-8119	San Juan (Table KDZ-KH5)
8200.A-Z	Other, A-Z
	Subarrange each by Table KDZ-KH6

KGJ-KGZ

West Indies. Caribbean area: Redonda
   see KGK1+

1-499   West Indies. Caribbean area: Saba (Table KDZ-KH3)

KGJ-KGZ

West Indies. Caribbean area: Saint Barthélemy
see KGR5001+

2001-2499   West Indies. Caribbean area: Saint Christopher (Saint Kitts), Nevis, and Anguilla (Table KDZ-KH3)

KGJ-KGZ

3001-3499   West Indies. Caribbean area: Saint Lucia (Table KDZ-KH3)

West Indies. Caribbean area: Saint Martin
see KGR5001+

KGJ-KGZ

5001-5499   West Indies. Caribbean area: Saint Vincent and the Grenadines
                            (Table KDZ-KH3)

7001-7499   West Indies. Caribbean area: Sint Eustatius (Table KDZ-KH3)

KGJ-KGZ

8001-8499   West Indies. Caribbean area: Sint Maarten (Table KDZ-KH3)
                              Cf. KGR5001+ Saint Martin

West Indies. Caribbean area: Swan Islands
    see KGU1+

KGJ-KGZ

1-499	West Indies. Caribbean area: Trinidad and Tobago (Table KDZ-KH3)

1-499   West Indies. Caribbean area: Turks and Caicos Islands (Table
                         KDZ-KH3)

KGJ-KGZ

WEST INDIES. CARIBBEAN AREA: VIRGIN ISLANDS, BRITISH

West Indies. Caribbean area: Virgin Islands, British
  see KGL4001+

1-499   West Indies. Caribbean area: Virgin Islands of the United States
(Table KDZ-KH3)

KGJ-KGZ

1-999   South America: General (Table KDZ-KH1)

KH-KHW

	South America: Argentina
1-5999	General (Table KDZ-KH2 modified)
	Constitutional law
	Sources
	Constitutions
2914	Particular constitutions. By date of constitution

Subarrange each by Table K17

The National Constituent Assembly of Argentina held in 1957 abolished the Peron Constitution of 1949 and reverted to the 1853 Constitution as amended up to 1898. In classifying the Argentina constitution in force since the end of 1957, use 1853 as the date of the constitution

	Provinces. Federal District. National Territory
6201-6299	Buenos Aires (Federal District) (Table KDZ-KH4)
6301-6399	Buenos Aires (Province) (Table KDZ-KH4)
6401-6499	Catamarca (Table KDZ-KH4)
6501-6599	Chaco (Presidente Perón) (Table KDZ-KH4)
6601-6699	Chubut (Table KDZ-KH4)
6701-6799	Córdoba (Table KDZ-KH4)
6801-6899	Corrientes (Table KDZ-KH4)
6901-6999	Entre Ríos (Table KDZ-KH4)
	Eva Perón see KHA7301+
	Federal District see KHA6201+
7001-7099	Formosa (Table KDZ-KH4)
7201-7299	Jujuy (Table KDZ-KH4)
7301-7399	La Pampa (Eva Perón) (Table KDZ-KH4)
7401-7499	La Rioja (Table KDZ-KH4)
7601-7699	Mendoza (Table KDZ-KH4)
7701-7799	Misiones (Table KDZ-KH4)
7801-7899	Neuquén (Table KDZ-KH4)
	Presidente Perón see KHA6501+
7901-7999	Río Negro (Table KDZ-KH4)
8001-8099	Salta (Table KDZ-KH4)
8101-8199	San Juan (Table KDZ-KH4)
8201-8299	San Luis (Table KDZ-KH4)
8301-8399	Santa Cruz (Table KDZ-KH4)
8401-8499	Santa Fe (Table KDZ-KH4)
8501-8599	Santiago del Estero (Table KDZ-KH4)
8601-8699	Tierra del Fuego (Table KDZ-KH4)
8701-8799	Tucumán (Table KDZ-KH4)
	Cities
9601-9619	Bahía Blanca (Table KDZ-KH5)
	Buenos Aires see KHA6201+
9641-9659	Córdoba (Table KDZ-KH5)
9661-9679	La Plata (Table KDZ-KH5)
9681-9699	Mendoza (Table KDZ-KH5)

KH-KHW

	Cities -- Continued
9701-9719	Paraná (Table KDZ-KH5)
9721-9739	Rosario (Table KDZ-KH5)
9741-9759	Santa Fe (Table KDZ-KH5)
9761-9779	Tucumán (Table KDZ-KH5)
9800.A-Z	Other, A-Z
	Subarrange each by Table KDZ-KH6

	South America: Bolivia
1-5999	General (Table KDZ-KH2)
	Departments
6201-6299	Chuquisaca (Table KDZ-KH4)
6401-6499	Cochabamba (Table KDZ-KH4)
6601-6699	El Beni (Table KDZ-KH4)
6801-6899	La Paz (Table KDZ-KH4)
7001-7099	Oruro (Table KDZ-KH4)
7201-7299	Pando (Table KDZ-KH4)
7401-7499	Potosî (Table KDZ-KH4)
7601-7699	Santa Cruz (Table KDZ-KH4)
7801-7899	Tarija (Table KDZ-KH4)
	Cities
8001-8019	Cochabamba (Table KDZ-KH5)
8021-8039	La Paz (Table KDZ-KH5)
8041-8059	Oruro (Table KDZ-KH5)
8061-8079	Potosî (Table KDZ-KH5)
8081-8099	Santa Cruz (Table KDZ-KH5)
8101-8119	Sucre (Table KDZ-KH5)
8121-8139	Trinidad (Table KDZ-KH5)
8200.A-Z	Other, A-Z
	Subarrange each by Table KDZ-KH6

KH-KHW

	South America: Brazil
1-5999	General (Table KDZ-KH2)
	States. Federal District. Federal Territories
6201-6299	Acre (Table KDZ-KH4)
6301-6399	Alagoas (Table KDZ-KH4)
6401-6499	Amapá (Table KDZ-KH4)
6501-6599	Amazonas (Table KDZ-KH4)
6601-6699	Bahia (Table KDZ-KH4)
6701-6799	Brasília (Federal District) (Table KDZ-KH4)
6801-6899	Ceará (Table KDZ-KH4)
6901-6999	Espírito Santo (Table KDZ-KH4)
	Federal District see KHD6701+
7001-7099	Fernando do Noronha (Table KDZ-KH4)
7101-7199	Goiás (Table KDZ-KH4)
7201-7299	Gunabara (Table KDZ-KH4)
	Guapore see KHD8401+
7301-7399	Maranhão (Table KDZ-KH4)
7401-7499	Mato Grosso (Table KDZ-KH4)
	Mato Grosso do Sul see KHD8901+
7501-7599	Minas Gerais (Table KDZ-KH4)
7601-7699	Pará (Table KDZ-KH4)
7701-7799	Paraíba (Table KDZ-KH4)
7801-7899	Paraná (Table KDZ-KH4)
7901-7999	Pernambuco (Table KDZ-KH4)
8001-8099	Piauí (Table KDZ-KH4)
8101-8199	Rio de Janeiro (Table KDZ-KH4)
8201-8299	Rio Grande do Norte (Table KDZ-KH4)
8301-8399	Rio Grande do Sul (Table KDZ-KH4)
8401-8499	Rondônia (Guapore) (Table KDZ-KH4)
8501-8599	Roraima (Table KDZ-KH4)
8601-8699	Santa Catarina (Table KDZ-KH4)
8701-8799	São Paulo (Table KDZ-KH4)
8801-8899	Sergipe (Table KDZ-KH4)
8901-8999	Mato Grosso do Sul (Table KDZ-KH4)
	Cities
9601-9619	Belém (Table KDZ-KH5)
9621-9639	Belo Horizonte (Table KDZ-KH5)
	Brasília see KHD6701+
9641-9659	Curitiba (Table KDZ-KH5)
9661-9679	Duque de Caxias (Table KDZ-KH5)
9681-9699	Fortaleza (Table KDZ-KH5)
9701-9719	Goiânia (Table KDZ-KH5)
9721-9739	Manaus (Table KDZ-KH5)
9741-9759	Nova Iguaçu (Table KDZ-KH5)
9761-9779	Pôrto Alegre (Table KDZ-KH5)
9781-9799	Recife (Table KDZ-KH5)
9801-9819	Rio de Janeiro (Table KDZ-KH5)

	Cities -- Continued
9821-9839	Salvador (Table KDZ-KH5)
9841-9859	São Paulo (Table KDZ-KH5)
9900.A-Z	Other, A-Z
	Subarrange each by Table KDZ-KH6

KH-KHW

	South America: Chile
1-5999	General (Table KDZ-KH2)
	Provinces
6201-6299	Aconcagua (Table KDZ-KH4)
6301-6329	Antofagasta (Table KDZ-KH4)
6401-6429	Arauco (Table KDZ-KH4)
6501-6599	Atacama (Table KDZ-KH4)
6601-6699	Aysén (Table KDZ-KH4)
6701-6799	Bĭo-Bĭo (Table KDZ-KH4)
6801-6899	Caufin (Table KDZ-KH4)
6901-6999	Chiloé (Table KDZ-KH4)
7001-7099	Colchagua (Table KDZ-KH4)
7101-7199	Concepción (Table KDZ-KH4)
7201-7299	Coquimbo (Table KDZ-KH4)
7301-7399	Curicó (Table KDZ-KH4)
	Easter Island (Isla de Pascua) see KHF8601+
7401-7499	Linares (Table KDZ-KH4)
7501-7599	Llanquihue (Table KDZ-KH4)
7601-7699	Magallanes (Table KDZ-KH4)
7701-7799	Malleco (Table KDZ-KH4)
7801-7899	Maule (Table KDZ-KH4)
7901-7999	Ñuble (Table KDZ-KH4)
8001-8099	O'Higgins (Table KDZ-KH4)
8101-8199	Osorno (Table KDZ-KH4)
	Sala-y-Gomez see KHF8601+
	San Ambrosio see KHF8601+
	San Felix see KHF8601+
8201-8299	Santiago (Table KDZ-KH4)
8301-8399	Talca (Table KDZ-KH4)
8401-8499	Tarapacá (Table KDZ-KH4)
8501-8599	Valdivia (Table KDZ-KH4)
8601-8699	Valparaîso (Table KDZ-KH4)
	Including Easter Island (Isla de Pascua), Sala-y-Gomez, San Ambrosio, and San Felix
	Cities
9601-9619	Antofagasta (Table KDZ-KH5)
9621-9639	Concepción (Table KDZ-KH5)
9641-9659	Santiago (Table KDZ-KH5)
9661-9679	Talcahuano (Table KDZ-KH5)
9681-9699	Temuco (Table KDZ-KH5)
9701-9719	Valparaîso (Table KDZ-KH5)
9721-9739	Viña del Mar (Table KDZ-KH5)
9800.A-Z	Other, A-Z
	Subarrange each by Table KDZ-KH6

	South America: Colombia
1-5999	General (Table KDZ-KH2)
	Departments. Intendencies. Commissariats
6201-6299	Amazonas (Table KDZ-KH4)
6301-6399	Antioquia (Table KDZ-KH4)
6401-6499	Arauca (Table KDZ-KH4)
6501-6599	Atlántico (Table KDZ-KH4)
6601-6699	Bogotá (Special District) (Table KDZ-KH4)
6701-6799	Bolívar (Table KDZ-KH4)
6801-6899	Boyacá (Table KDZ-KH4)
6901-6999	Caldas (Table KDZ-KH4)
7001-7099	Caquetá (Table KDZ-KH4)
7101-7199	Casnore (Table KDZ-KH4)
7201-7299	Cauca (Table KDZ-KH4)
7301-7399	Chocó (Table KDZ-KH4)
7401-7499	Córdoba (Table KDZ-KH4)
7501-7599	Cundinamarca (Table KDZ-KH4)
7601-7699	El Cesar (Table KDZ-KH4)
7701-7799	Guainía (Table KDZ-KH4)
7801-7899	Huila (Table KDZ-KH4)
7901-7999	La Guajira (Table KDZ-KH4)
8001-8099	Magdalena (Table KDZ-KH4)
8101-8199	Meta (Table KDZ-KH4)
8201-8299	Nariño (Table KDZ-KH4)
8301-8399	Norte de Santander (Table KDZ-KH4)
8401-8499	Putamayo (Table KDZ-KH4)
8501-8599	Quindío (Table KDZ-KH4)
8601-8699	Risaralda (Table KDZ-KH4)
8701-8799	San Andrés y Providencia (Table KDZ-KH4)
8801-8899	Santander (Table KDZ-KH4)
8901-8999	Sucre (Table KDZ-KH4)
9001-9099	Tolima (Table KDZ-KH4)
9101-9199	Valle de Cauca (Table KDZ-KH4)
9201-9299	Vaupés (Table KDZ-KH4)
9301-9399	Vichada (Table KDZ-KH4)
	Cities
9601-9619	Barranquilla (Table KDZ-KH5)
	Bogotá see KHH6601+
9621-9639	Bucaramanga (Table KDZ-KH5)
9641-9659	Cali (Table KDZ-KH5)
9661-9679	Cartagena (Table KDZ-KH5)
9681-9699	Cúcuta (Table KDZ-KH5)
9701-9719	Ibagué (Table KDZ-KH5)
9721-9739	Manizales (Table KDZ-KH5)
9741-9759	Medellín (Table KDZ-KH5)
9761-9779	Pasto (Table KDZ-KH5)
9781-9799	Santa Marta (Table KDZ-KH5)

KH-KHW

Cities -- Continued

9900.A-Z   Other, A-Z

Subarrange each by Table KDZ-KH6

	South America: Ecuador
1-5999	General (Table KDZ-KH2)
	Provinces
6101-6199	Azuay (Table KDZ-KH4)
6301-6399	Bolívar (Table KDZ-KH4)
6501-6599	Cañar (Table KDZ-KH4)
6701-6799	Carchi (Table KDZ-KH4)
6901-6999	Chimborazo (Table KDZ-KH4)
	Colón see KHK7701+
7101-7199	Cotopaxi (Table KDZ-KH4)
7301-7399	El Oro (Table KDZ-KH4)
7501-7599	Esmeraldas (Table KDZ-KH4)
7701-7799	Galápagos Islands (Colón) (Table KDZ-KH4)
7901-7999	Guayas (Table KDZ-KH4)
8101-8199	Imbabura (Table KDZ-KH4)
8301-8399	Loja (Table KDZ-KH4)
8501-8599	Los Ríos (Table KDZ-KH4)
8701-8799	Manabí (Table KDZ-KH4)
8901-8999	Morona-Santiago (Table KDZ-KH4)
9101-9199	Napo (Table KDZ-KH4)
9301-9399	Pastaza (Table KDZ-KH4)
9501-9599	Pichincha (Table KDZ-KH4)
9701-9799	Tungurahua (Table KDZ-KH4)
9801-9899	Zamora-Chinchipe (Table KDZ-KH4)
	Cities
9921-9939	Guayaquil (Table KDZ-KH5)
9961-9979	Quito (Table KDZ-KH5)
9990.A-Z	Other, A-Z
	Subarrange each by Table KDZ-KH6

KH-KHW

South America: Falkland Islands

1-5999	General (Table KDZ-KH2)
9000.A-Z	Cities, A-Z
	Subarrange each by Table KDZ-KH6

                    South America: French Guiana
1-5999   General (Table KDZ-KH2)
9000.A-Z   Cities, A-Z
                        Subarrange each by Table KDZ-KH6

South America: Guiana, British
see KHN1+

South America: Guiana, French
    see KHM1+

	South America: Guyana
1-5999	General (Table KDZ-KH2)
9000.A-Z	Cities, A-Z
	Subarrange each by Table KDZ-KH6

	South America: Paraguay
1-5999	General (Table KDZ-KH2)
	Departments. Federal District
6101-6199	Alto Paraná (Table KDZ-KH4)
6301-6399	Amambay (Table KDZ-KH4)
6501-6599	Asunción (Federal District) (Table KDZ-KH4)
6701-6799	Boquerón (Table KDZ-KH4)
6901-6999	Caaguazú (Table KDZ-KH4)
7101-7199	Caazapá (Table KDZ-KH4)
7301-7399	Central (Table KDZ-KH4)
7501-7599	Concepción (Table KDZ-KH4)
7701-7799	Cordillera (Table KDZ-KH4)
	Federal District see KHP6501+
7901-7999	Guairá (Table KDZ-KH4)
8101-8199	Itapúa (Table KDZ-KH4)
8301-8399	Misiones (Table KDZ-KH4)
8501-8599	Ñeembucú (Table KDZ-KH4)
8701-8799	Olimpo (Table KDZ-KH4)
8901-8999	Paraguarí (Table KDZ-KH4)
9101-9199	Presidente Hayes (Table KDZ-KH4)
9301-9399	San Pedro (Table KDZ-KH4)
	Cities
	Asunción see KHP6501+
9700.A-Z	Other, A-Z
	Subarrange each by Table KDZ-KH6

KH-KHW

	South America: Peru
1-5999	General (Table KDZ-KH2)
	Departments
6201-6299	Amazonas (Table KDZ-KH4)
6301-6399	Ancash (Table KDZ-KH4)
6401-6499	Apurîmac (Table KDZ-KH4)
6501-6599	Arequipa (Table KDZ-KH4)
6601-6699	Ayacucho (Table KDZ-KH4)
6701-6799	Cajamarca (Table KDZ-KH4)
6801-6899	Callao (Table KDZ-KH4)
6901-6999	Cuzco (Table KDZ-KH4)
7001-7099	Huancavelica (Table KDZ-KH4)
7101-7199	Huánuco (Table KDZ-KH4)
7201-7299	Ica (Table KDZ-KH4)
7301-7399	Junîn (Table KDZ-KH4)
7401-7499	La Libertad (Table KDZ-KH4)
7501-7599	Lambayeque (Table KDZ-KH4)
7601-7699	Lima (Table KDZ-KH4)
7701-7799	Loreto (Table KDZ-KH4)
7801-7899	Madre de Dios (Table KDZ-KH4)
7901-7999	Moquegua (Table KDZ-KH4)
8001-8999	Pasco (Table KDZ-KH4)
8101-8199	Piura (Table KDZ-KH4)
8201-8299	Puno (Table KDZ-KH4)
8301-8399	San Marfin (Table KDZ-KH4)
8401-8499	Tacna (Table KDZ-KH4)
8501-8599	Tumbes (Table KDZ-KH4)
	Cities
9601-9619	Arequipa (Table KDZ-KH5)
9621-9639	Callao (Table KDZ-KH5)
9641-9659	Chiclayo (Table KDZ-KH5)
9661-9679	Cuzco (Table KDZ-KH5)
9681-9699	Lima (Table KDZ-KH5)
9701-9719	Trujillo (Table KDZ-KH5)
9800.A-Z	Other, A-Z
	Subarrange each by Table KDZ-KH6

                       South America: South Georgia and South Sandwich Islands
1-5999   General (Table KDZ-KH2)
9000.A-Z   Cities, A-Z
                               Subarrange each by Table KDZ-KH6

KH-KHW

	South America: Suriname
1-5999	General (Table KDZ-KH2)
	Districts
6201-6299	Brokopondo (Table KDZ-KH4)
6401-6499	Commewijne (Table KDZ-KH4)
6601-6699	Coronie (Table KDZ-KH4)
6801-6899	Marowijne (Table KDZ-KH4)
7001-7099	Nickerie (Table KDZ-KH4)
7201-7299	Para (Table KDZ-KH4)
7401-7499	Paramaribo (Table KDZ-KH4)
7601-7699	Saramacca (Table KDZ-KH4)
7801-7899	Surinamee (Table KDZ-KH4)
9000.A-Z	Cities, A-Z
	Subarrange each by Table KDZ-KH6

	South America: Uruguay
1-5999	General (Table KDZ-KH2)
	Departments
6201-6299	Artigas (Table KDZ-KH4)
6301-6399	Canalones (Table KDZ-KH4)
6401-6499	Cerro Largo (Table KDZ-KH4)
6501-6599	Colonia (Table KDZ-KH4)
6601-6699	Durazno (Table KDZ-KH4)
6701-6799	Flores (Table KDZ-KH4)
6801-6899	Florida (Table KDZ-KH4)
6901-6999	Lavelleja (Table KDZ-KH4)
7001-7099	Maldonado (Table KDZ-KH4)
7101-7199	Montevideo (Table KDZ-KH4)
7201-7299	Paysandú (Table KDZ-KH4)
7301-7399	Río Negro (Table KDZ-KH4)
7401-7499	Rivera (Table KDZ-KH4)
7501-7599	Rocha (Table KDZ-KH4)
7601-7699	Salto (Table KDZ-KH4)
7701-7799	San José (Table KDZ-KH4)
7801-7899	Soriano (Table KDZ-KH4)
7901-7999	Tacuarembó (Table KDZ-KH4)
8001-8099	Treinta y Tres (Table KDZ-KH4)
	Cities
9601-9619	Mercedes (Table KDZ-KH5)
9621-9639	Montevideo (Table KDZ-KH5)
9641-9659	Paysandú (Table KDZ-KH5)
9661-9679	Salto (Table KDZ-KH5)
9800.A-Z	Other, A-Z
	Subarrange each by Table KDZ-KH6

KH-KHW

South America: Venezuela

1-5999	General (Table KDZ-KH2)
	States. Federal District. Territories
6201-6299	Amazonas (Table KDZ-KH4)
6301-6399	Anzoátegui (Table KDZ-KH4)
6401-6499	Apure (Table KDZ-KH4)
6501-6599	Aragua (Table KDZ-KH4)
6601-6699	Barinas (Table KDZ-KH4)
	Barquisimeto see KHW8501+
6701-6799	Bolívar (Table KDZ-KH4)
6801-6899	Carabobo (Table KDZ-KH4)
6901-6999	Caracas (Federal District) (Table KDZ-KH4)
7001-7099	Cojedes (Table KDZ-KH4)
7101-7199	Delta Amacuro (Table KDZ-KH4)
7201-7299	Falcón (Table KDZ-KH4)
	Federal District see KHW6901+
7301-7399	Guárico (Table KDZ-KH4)
7401-7499	Lara (Table KDZ-KH4)
7501-7599	Mérida (Table KDZ-KH4)
7601-7699	Miranda (Table KDZ-KH4)
7701-7799	Monagas (Table KDZ-KH4)
7801-7899	Nueva Esparta (Table KDZ-KH4)
7901-7999	Portuguesa (Table KDZ-KH4)
8001-8099	Sucre (Table KDZ-KH4)
8101-8199	Táchira (Table KDZ-KH4)
8201-8299	Trujillo (Table KDZ-KH4)
8301-8399	Yaracuy (Table KDZ-KH4)
8401-8499	Zulia (Table KDZ-KH4)
8501-8599	Barquisimeto (Table KDZ-KH4)
9201-9299	Federal Dependencies (Table KDZ-KH4)
	Cities
9601-9619	Barquisimeto (Table KDZ-KH5)
9641-9659	Cabimas (Table KDZ-KH5)
	Caracas see KHW6901+
9661-9679	Ciudad Bolívar (Table KDZ-KH5)
9681-9699	Ciudad Guyana (Table KDZ-KH5)
9701-9719	Cumaná (Table KDZ-KH5)
9721-9739	Maracay (Table KDZ-KH5)
9741-9759	San Cristóbal (Table KDZ-KH5)
9761-9779	Valencia (Table KDZ-KH5)
9900.A-Z	Other, A-Z
	Subarrange each by Table KDZ-KH6

<table>
<tr><td></td><td>Class here works on the law of, and treaties between, two or more countries or regional organizations in the region</td></tr>
</table>

1	Bibliography
<3>	Periodicals
	For periodicals consisting predominantly of legal articles, regardless of subject matter and jurisdiction, see K1+
	For periodicals consisting primarily of informative material (Newsletters, bulletins, etc.) relating to a special subject, see the subject and form division for periodicals
4	Monographic series
6	Official gazettes
	Regional organizations
	see the subject
	Organization of American States
	see KDZ1101+
8.A-Z	Intergovernmental congresses and conferences. By name of the congress, A-Z

Under each:
| *.xA15A-.xA15Z* | *Serials* |
| *.xA2* | *Monographs. By date* |

For intergovernmental congresses on a special subject, see the subject

For nongovernmental congresses and conferences see KDZ-KH1 90

Treaties and other international agreements
Class here treaties between countries in the same region
For treaties between countries in different regions, see K524+
For treaties on uniform conflict rules see KDZ-KH1 110+
Collections
Including either multilateral or bilateral treaties, or both

10	General
11.A-Z	Collected treaties of an individual country or organization limited to its region. By country or organization, A-Z, and date

Individual treaties
see the subject
Legislative documents
see J
Statutes and administrative regulations
Texts

17	Serials
18	Monographs. By date
19	Digests. Summaries. Indexes

Presidential proclamations, manifestos, etc.
see J
Law reports and related materials

	Law reports and related materials -- Continued
20	Privy Council Judicial Committee (Table KDZ-KH7)
21	Highest court of appeals. Supreme Court (Table KDZ-KH7)
22	Various courts (Table KDZ-KH7)
	Including highest court and lower courts
24	Encyclopedias
25	Dictionaries. Words and phrases
27	Form books
(28)	Yearbooks
	For publications issued annually, summarizing events, statistics, etc. relating to a special subject, see the subject and form division table for periodicals. For other publications appearing yearly, see K1+
	Judicial statistics
31	General
32	Criminal statistics
33.A-Z	Other statistics. By subject, A-Z
	Directories
35	General
36.A-Z	By specialization, A-Z
	Trials
39	General collections
	Criminal trials
40	General
41.A-Z	Special offenses, A-Z
	Individual trials
	see the subclass for the country of the trial
43	Legal research. Legal bibliography
	Including methods of bibliographic research and how to find the law
	Legal education
46	General (Table K8)
47	Directories
	Study and teaching
	General see KDZ-KH1 46
49.A-Z	Particular subjects, A-Z
51	Law schools
54.A-Z	Law societies, institutes, international regional bar associations and other organizations, A-Z
	Each is subarranged by Table KDZ-KH8
	Class here works on individual societies and institutes and their activities, e.g. administrative reports, minutes, etc.
	For works issued by individual law societies and institutes on particular subjects, see the subject
	For congresses and conferences sponsored by societies see KDZ-KH1 90
54.B3	Inter-American Bar Association (Table KDZ-KH8)

	Law societies, institutes, international regional bar associations and other organizations, A-Z -- Continued
54.I55	Inter-American Institute of International Legal Studies (Table KDZ-KH8)
	Inter-American Juridicial Committee
	see KDZ1182+
	The legal profession
	Including law as a career
58	General
59.A-Z	Particular classes of lawyers and types of careers, A-Z
	Practice of law
60	General
	Directories see KDZ-KH1 35+
62	Attorneys' and legal secretaries' handbooks, manuals, etc.
	Biography of lawyers see KDZ-KH1 81+
65	Bar associations
	Cf. KDZ-KH1 54.A+ International regional bar associations
	Law and lawyers in literature
	see PB-PZ
	Legal anecdotes, wit, and humor
	see K183+
	Notarial law. Public instruments
68	General (Table K8)
69	The notarial profession (Table K8)
70	Public instruments (Table K8)
	History
	For the history of special subjects, see the subject
76	General
	Biography
81	Collective
	For national collections, see the subclass for the country
	Individual
	see the subclass for the country of the biographee
83	Philosophy. Jurisprudence
	Class here works on doctrines peculiar to the legal institutions of the region
	For works on the philosophy of particular branches of the law of the region, see the subject; for works on jurisprudence and philosophy of law in general, see K201+
	Relationship of law to other disciplines, subjects, or phenomena
	see K486+
86	Criticism. Legal reform
	Cf. KDZ-KH1 495 Judiciary
	Cf. KDZ-KH1 961 Administration of criminal justice

KDZ-KH1

88	Regional unification, integration, and harmonization
	Including both substantive unification and unification of conflict rules
	For works limited to the unification of conflict rules, see KDZ-KH1 110+
	For organizations devoted to regional integration, see the subject
	For unification of law on a special subject, see the subject
90	Congresses
	For intergovernmental congresses and conferences see KDZ-KH1 8.A+
	Collected works (nonserial)
	For monographic series see KDZ-KH1 4
92	Several authors
93	Individual authors
95	Casebooks. Readings
	Class here general works only
	For casebooks on subjects, see the subject
96	General works. Treatises
97	Compends. Outlines, syllabi, etc.
99	Addresses, essays, lectures
	Including single essays, collected essays of several authors, etc.
101.A-Z	Works for particular users, A-Z
101.A76	Artists and art collectors
101.B87	Businesspeople. Foreign investors
	Foreign investors see KDZ-KH1 101.B87
103.A-Z	Works on diverse aspects of particular subjects and falling within several branches of the law
103.C65	Computers
	Conflict of laws
	Class intergovernmental congresses and conferences as well as treaties and related general works in KG110 (Latin America) even though participants in congresses or parties to treaties include both Latin American and other countries in the Western Hemisphere
	For conflict of laws between the United States and other countries, see KF416
	For works on conflict rules of branches other than private law and law of procedure (e.g. Tax law, criminal law, etc.), see the subject
110	General (Table K8)
112.A-Z	Special topics, A-Z
	Subarrange each by Table K12
112.P6	Points of contact (Table K12)
	Particular branches and subjects of law
114	Aliens (Table K8)

	Conflict of laws
	Particular branches and subjects of law
115	Arbitration (Table K8)
	Class here works on regional arbitration courts, commissions, and proceedings
	For comparative works on arbitration see KDZ-KH1 525
116.A-Z	Other, A-Z
	Subarrange each by Table K12
116.A25	Actions (Table K12)
116.A35	Adoption (Table K12)
116.B34	Bankruptcy (Table K12)
116.C57	Civil procedure (Table K12)
116.C63	Commercial law (Table K12)
116.C64	Contracts (Table K12)
116.C66	Corporations (Table K12)
	Cf. KDZ-KH1 341 Foreign corporations
	Cf. KDZ-KH1 342 Multinational corporations
	Divorce see KDZ-KH1 116.M35
116.D64	Domestic relations (Table K12)
	Extradition see KDZ-KH1 974+
	Foreign arbitral awards see KDZ-KH1 115
116.F65	Foreign judgments (Table K12)
	Including recognition and execution
116.J82	Judicial assistance (International) (Table K12)
116.L46	Letters rogatory (International) (Table K12)
116.M34	Maritime law (Table K12)
116.M35	Marriage. Divorce. Separation. Matrimonial property (Table K12)
	Matrimonial property see KDZ-KH1 116.M35
	Nationality of women see KDZ-KH1 562.W64
	Separation see KDZ-KH1 116.M35
	Stateless persons see KDZ-KH1 567
125	Private law
	Civil law
127	General (Table K8)
	Juristic facts. Juristic acts
129	General (Table K8)
130	Extinctive prescription (Table K8)
	Persons
	Natural persons
132	General (Table K8)
134	Absence and presumption of death (Table K8)
136.A-Z	Particular groups of persons, A-Z
	Subarrange each by Table K12
	Aliens see KDZ-KH1 114

KDZ-KH1

	Civil law
	Property. Real rights
	Personal property -- Continued
181	General (Table K8)
	Intellectual property see KDZ-KH1 400+
184	Trusts and trustees (Table K8)
	Succession upon death
187	General (Table K8)
	Testamentary succession. Wills
189	General (Table K8)
190.A-Z	Special topics, A-Z
	Subarrange each by Table K12
	Legitime see KDZ-KH1 190.N42
	Mejora see KDZ-KH1 190.N42
190.N42	Necessary heirs. Legitime. Mejora (Table K12)
	Intestate succession
192	General (Table K8)
	Order of sucession
194	Succession of spouse (Table K12)
	Obligations
200	General (Table K8)
	Contracts
202	General (Table K8)
206	Government contracts. Public contracts (Table K8)
	Particular types of contracts
	Agricultural contracts see KDZ-KH1 785
	Sale
208	General (Table K8)
	Conditional sale, installment sale, lease purchase see KDZ-KH1 245
210	Contract of service. Master and servant (Table K8)
	Mandate. Agency
	Cf. KDZ-KH1 240+ Commercial mandate
216	General (Table K8)
217	Power of attorney (Table K8)
219	Security (Table K8)
	Torts
221	General (Table K8)
	Strict liability. Liability without fault
226	General (Table K8)
227.A-Z	Ultrahazardous activities or occupations. By risk, A-Z
	Subarrange each by Table K12
227.N82	Nuclear damages (Table K12)
228	Products liability (Table K8)
	Cf. KDZ-KH1 697 Product safety
229	Government torts (Table K8)

	Commercial law
231	General (Table K8)
233	Merchants (Table K8)
	Auxiliaries and intermediaries of commerce
233.5	Boards of trade (Table K8)
234	Stock exchanges. Marketing of securities (Table K8)
	Independent commercial agents and middlemen
236	Brokers (Table K8)
237	Commercial travelers. Traveling salesmen (Table K8)
	Commission merchants see KDZ-KH1 241
	Commercial contracts
	General works see KDZ-KH1 231
	Commercial mandate and consignment
240	General (Table K8)
241	Consignment of goods. Commission merchants (Table K8)
	Commercial sale
243	General (Table K8)
245	Conditional sale. Installment sale. Lease purchase (Table K8)
246	Export sale. International sale. Overseas sale (Table K8)
	Including C.I.F. and F.O.B. clauses
247	Commercial leases (Table K8)
	Including both real and personal property
	Negotiable instruments. Titles of credit
250	General (Table K8)
	Bills of exchange
252	General (Table K8)
253.A-Z	Special topics, A-Z
	Subarrange each by Table K12
253.P75	Protest. Waiver of protest (Table K12)
	Waiver of protest see KDZ-KH1 253.P75
255	Checks (Table K8)
	Corporate securities see KDZ-KH1 335
	Banking
260	General (Table K8)
	Particular types of banks and credit institutions
262	National banks. Central banks (Table K8)
	International regional banks for development and integration see KDZ-KH1 908.A+
265.A-Z	Other banks, A-Z
	Particular banking transactions
	Bank loans. Bank credit
270	General (Table K8)
272	Letters of credit (Table K8)
274	Commercial loans and credit (Table K8)
	Pledge

	Commercial law
	Commercial contracts
	Pledge -- Continued
277	General (Table K8)
278	Non-possessory pledges. Chattel mortgages. Registered pledges (Table K8)
	Investments
282	General (Table K8)
	Marketing of securities see KDZ-KH1 234
	Corporate securities see KDZ-KH1 335
	Foreign investments see KDZ-KH1 744
	Carriers. Carriage of goods and passengers
285	General (Table K8)
286	Carriage by land and inland waterways (Table K8)
	For motor carriers see KDZ-KH1 865
	For railroads see KDZ-KH1 866
	Carriage by air
	Cf. KDZ-KH1 870 Regulation of commercial aviation
288	General (Table K8)
290.A-Z	Special topics, A-Z
	Subarrange each by Table K12
290.M65	Aircraft mortgages
	Carriage by sea see KDZ-KH1 352+
	Insurance
300	General (Table K8)
	Personal insurance
304	Life insurance (Table K8)
306	Health insurance. Medical care (Table K8)
	Property insurance
308	General (Table K8)
310	Transportation insurance (Table K8)
312	Fire insurance (Table K8)
	Marine insurance see KDZ-KH1 366
315	Reinsurance (Table K8)
	Social insurance see KDZ-KH1 463+
	Business associations. Commercial companies
320	General (Table K8)
	Partnership
322	General (Table K8)
324	Joint ventures (Table K8)
325	Limited liability companies. Private companies (Table K8)
	Business corporations
328	General (Table K8)
330	Supervisors. Auditors (Table K8)
	Corporate finance
333	General (Table K8)

	Commercial law
	Commercial contracts
	Business associations. Commercial companies
	Business corporations
	Corporate finance -- Continued
335	Issuing and sale of securities (General) (Table K8)
	For works on security-exchange transactions see KDZ-KH1 234
337	Shares and shareholders' rights. Stock transfers (Table K8)
339	Debentures. Bonds. Preferred stocks (Table K8)
	Particular types of corporations
341	Foreign corporations (Table K8)
	Including nationality of corporations
342	Multinational corporations (Table K8)
	Private companies see KDZ-KH1 325
344	Cooperative societies (Table K8)
346	Consolidation and merger (Table K8)
347	Government-owned corporations and other business organizations (Table K8)
	Including government monopolies in general
	Maritime law
	Including carriage by sea, marine insurance, and maritime social legislation
	For administrative regulations see KDZ-KH1 875+
351	General (Table K8)
	Carriage by sea
352	General (Table K8)
	Carriage of goods. Affreightment
354	General (Table K8)
355	Ocean bills of lading (Table K8)
357	Maritime loans, credits, and security (Table K8)
	Risk and damages in maritime commerce
359	General (Table K8)
361	Maritime torts. Collision at sea (Table K8)
362.A-Z	Special topics, A-Z
	Subarrange each by Table K12
362.A75	Arrest of ships (Table K12)
	Including immunity of state owned ships from arrest
	Immunity of state owned ships see KDZ-KH1 362.A75
366	Marine insurance (Table K8)
	Maritime social legislation
370	General (Table K8)
372	Maritime labor law. Merchant mariners (Table K8)
376	Social insurance (Table K8)
	Insolvency and bankruptcy. Creditors' rights

	Commercial law
	Insolvency and bankruptcy. Creditors' rights -- Continued
382	General (Table K8)
	Bankruptcy
384	General (Table K8)
386	Composition to avoid bankruptcy (Table K8)
	International commercial arbitration see KDZ-KH1 115
	Comparative commercial arbitration see KDZ-KH1 525
	Intellectual property
400	General (Table K8)
401	Copyright (Table K8)
	Industrial property
409	General (Table K8)
411	Patent law (Table K8)
419	Trademarks (Table K8)
421	Unfair competition (Table K8)
	Social legislation
430	General (Table K8)
	Labor law
432	General (Table K8)
433	Constitutional guarantees (Table K8)
	Labor-management relations
435	General (Table K8)
	Labor unions
436	General (Table K8)
	Collective bargaining. Collective labor agreements
438	General (Table K8)
440.A-Z	Particular industries and occupations, A-Z
	Subarrange each by Table K12
440.E43	Electric industries (Table K12)
	Collective labor disputes
442	General (Table K8)
443	Arbitration. Conciliation (Table K8)
444	Labor courts (Table K8)
446	Strikes. Lockouts. Boycotts (Table K8)
	Labor standards. Labor conditions
448	General (Table K8)
	Employment and dismissal
450	General (Table K8)
451	Free choice of employment (Table K8)
453	Wages. Minimum wage (Table K8)
	Hours of labor. Night work
455	General (Table K8)
456.A-Z	Particular industries and groups of employees, A-Z
	Subarrange each by Table K12
456.A34	Agricultural laborers (Table K12)

KDZ-KH1

	Social legislation
	Labor law -- Continued
458	Protection of labor. Labor hygiene and safety (Table K8)
460.A-Z	Labor law of special industries and groups of employees, A-Z
	Subarrange each by Table K12
460.A34	Agricultural laborers (Table K12)
460.A43	Alien labor (Table K12)
	Social insurance
	Cf. KDZ-KH1 370+ Maritime social insurance
463	General (Table K8)
	Particular branches
465	Workers' compensation (Table K8)
467	Social security. Retirement (Table K8)
	Public welfare. Public assistance. Private charities
473	General (Table K8)
475.A-Z	Particular groups, A-Z
	Almshouses see KDZ-KH1 475.P66
	Charity laws see KDZ-KH1 475.P66
475.C48	Children (Table K12)
	Including day care centers
475.P46	People with disabilities (Table K12)
475.P66	Poor. Charity laws. Almshouses (Table K12)
	Indians
480	History
481	General (Table K8)
483.A-Z	Special topics, A-Z
	Subarrange each by Table K12
483.A36	Adultery (Table K12)
483.C74	Criminal law (Table K12)
483.D64	Domestic relations (Table K12)
	Land tenure. Indian lands see KDZ-KH1 772
483.S93	Suffrage (Table K12)
485.A-Z	Particular groups or tribes, A-Z
	For special topics relating to a particular group or tribe see KDZ-KH1 483.A+
	Courts. Procedure
495	Administration of justice. Organization of the judiciary (Table K8)
	Cf. KDZ-KH1 961 Administration of criminal justice
	Court organization and procedure
497	General (Table K8)
	Foreign judgments see KDZ-KH1 116.F65
498	Judicial assistance (Table K8)
	Cf. KDZ-KH1 116.J82 International judicial assistance
	Cf. KDZ-KH1 116.L46 International letters rogatory
	Cf. KDZ-KH1 974+ Judicial assistance in criminal matters

Courts. Procedure
  Court organization and procedure -- Continued
    Regular courts

500   General (Table K8)
501   Highest courts of appeal. Supreme courts (Table K8)
502.A-Z   Regional courts, A-Z
               Subarrange each by Table K12
               e.g. Corte de Justicia Centro-americana, KG502.C67
           Courts for the protection of human rights see KDZ-KH1
               579.A+
         Civil procedure
               Cf. KDZ-KH1 116.C57 International civil procedure
503   General (Table K8)
504   Constitutional safeguards in civil procedure (Table K8)
               Cf. KDZ-KH1 520+ Constitutional remedies. Judicial
                   review
505   Jurisdiction. Venue (Table K8)
           Trial
508   General (Table K8)
             Evidence
510   General (Table K8)
               Witnesses
512   General (Table K8)
                 International letters rogatory see KDZ-KH1 116.L46
514   Expert evidence. Expert witnesses (Table K8)
516   Judgment (Table K8)
               For recognition and enforcement of foreign judgments
                   see KDZ-KH1 116.F65
           Remedies
518   General (Table K8)
             Constitutional remedies. Judicial review
520   General (Table K8)
521   Amparo (Table K8)
522   Habeas corpus (Table K8)
525   Arbitration and award (Table K8)
               Cf. KDZ-KH1 115 International civil and commercial
                   arbitration
533   Public law (Table K8)
         Constitutional law
           Sources
535   Collections
             Sources other than constitutions
536   Collections
536.5   Particular documents
                 By date of adoption or proclamation

	Constitutional law
	Sources
	Sources other than constitutions -- Continued
537	Constitutional conventions. By initial date of the convention
	Including rejected proposals and related proceedings
	Constitutions
540	Texts. By date
542	Digests. Indexes. By date
	Constitutional history
545	General (Table K8)
546	Peonage. Slavery (Table K8)
	Including emancipation, prohibition, and criminal provisions
548	Constitutional law in general (Table K8)
	Constitutional principles
550	The state. Form of government. Sovereignty (Table K8)
552	Rule of law (Table K8)
554	De facto doctrine (Table K8)
	Structure of government
556	General (Table K8)
557	Federal intervention (Table K8)
	Individual and state
	Nationals. Aliens
559	General (Table K8)
	Nationals. Citizenship
561	General (Table K8)
	Naturalization see KDZ-KH1 565
562.A-Z	Particular groups, A-Z
	Subarrange each by Table K12
562.W64	Women (Table K12)
	Aliens
	Cf. KDZ-KH1 114 Conflict of laws
564	General (Table K8)
565	Immigration and naturalization (Table K8)
567	Stateless persons (Table K8)
569	Control of individuals (Table K8)
	Including internal security and control of subversive activitiess
	Cf. KDZ-KH1 966.P64 Political offenses
	Human rights. Civil and political rights
574	General (Table K8)
	Particular constitutional guarantees
576	Freedom of expression (Table K8)
578.A-Z	Organizations on, or for the protection of, human rights, A-Z
	e.g. Inter-American Commission on Human Rights, KDZ578.I5

	Constitutional law
	Individual and state
	Human rights. Civil and political rights -- Continued
579.A-Z	Courts for the protection of human rights, A-Z
	e.g. Inter-American Court to Protect the Rights of Man, KDZ579.I5
580	Church and state (Table K8)
	Organs of government
583	The people (Table K8)
	Election law
585	General (Table K8)
	Suffrage
588	General (Table K8)
590	Women (Table K8)
	Indians see KDZ-KH1 483.S93
	The legislature. Legislative power
593	General (Table K8)
595	Organization of legislative bodies (Table K8)
597.A-Z	Individual legislative bodies, A-Z
	e.g. Parlamento Latinoamericano, KG597.P3
	The executive branch. Executive power
600	General (Table K8)
	The president. Governor
602	General (Table K8)
603	War and emergency powers. Martial law (Table K8)
606	The prime minister and the cabinet (Table K8)
608	The Judiciary. Judicial power (Table K8)
	Class here constitutional status only
	For courts, administration of justice, and organization of the judiciary see KDZ-KH1 495+
	Local government
611	General (Table K8)
	Municipal government. Municipal corporations
613	General (Table K8)
614	Municipal officials (Table K8)
	Municipal civil service see KDZ-KH1 618
	Civil service
616	General (Table K8)
618	Municipal civil service (Table K8)
619	Police and power of the police (Table K8)
	Administrative law
621	General (Table K8)
623	Administrative organization (Table K8)
	Administrative acts
626	General (Table K8)

KDZ-KH1

	Administrative law
	Administrative acts -- Continued
627	Excess and abuse of administrative power. Ombudsman (Table K8)
	Judicial functions. Remedies
628	General (Table K8)
629	Contentious-administrative jurisdiction and procedure. Administrative tribunals (Table K8)
631	Administrative responsiblity. Indemnifiction for government acts
	Cf. KDZ-KH1 229 Government tort liability
	Cf. KDZ-KH1 645 Expropriation. Eminent domain
	Public property. Public restraints on private property
634	General (Table K8)
635	Roads. Highway law (Table K8)
	Natural resources
	Including conservation, management, and environmental planning
	For environmental pollution see KDZ-KH1 670+
637	General (Table K8)
	Water resources
	Including watersheds, rivers, lakes, and watercourses
639	General (Table K8)
640	Conservation. Water resources development (Table K8)
	Including water power
641	Agricultural and industrial use of water resources (Table K8)
	Including treaties and other works on the use of the water of international rivers
	Cf. KDZ-KH1 789 Field irrigation
	Water pollution see KDZ-KH1 672
642.A-Z	Particular bodies of water, etc., A-Z
	Subarrange each by Table K12
643	Marine resources (Table K8)
	For fish protection see KDZ-KH1 649
645	Expropriation. Eminent domain (Table K8)
	Public land law
647	General (Table K8)
649	Wildlife protection. Game laws (Table K8)
	Including game, bird, and fish protection
	Cf. KDZ-KH1 803 Fisheries
	Regional and city planning. Zoning. Building
652	General (Table K8)
655	Building laws (Table K8)
657	Housing. Slum clearance. City development (Table K8)
	Public health. Sanitation. Environmental pollution
661	General (Table K8)

	Public health. Sanitation. Environmental pollution -- Continued
	Contagious, infectious, and other diseases
663	General (Table K8)
664.A-Z	Particular diseases, A-Z
664.M34	Malaria (Table K12)
666	Immigration inspection. Quarantine (Table K8)
	Environmental pollution
	For environmental planning see KDZ-KH1 637+
670	General (Table K8)
672	Water pollution (Table K8)
673	Air pollution (Table K8)
	Including control of smoke, gases, etc.
675	Medical legislation (Table K8)
	For physicians and related professions see KDZ-KH1 895.P48
	Veterinary laws. Veterinary hygiene
680	General (Table K8)
684	Stock inspection. Quarantine (Table K8)
	Food. Drugs. Cosmetics
687	General (Table K8)
688	Food law (Table K8)
	Drug laws
690	General (Table K8)
691	Narcotics (Table K8)
693	Alcohol. Alcoholic beverages. Liquor laws (Table K8)
	Including wine and wine making
	Public safety
695	General (Table K8)
696	Weapons. Firearms. Munitions (Table K8)
697	Hazardous articles and processes. Product safety (Table K8)
	Cf. KDZ-KH1 228 Products liability
698	Control of social activities (Table K8)
	Cultural affairs
702	General (Table K8)
703	Cultural policy (Table K8)
706	Language (Table K8)
	Including regulation of use, purity, etc.
	Education
710	General (Table K8)
716	Higher education. Colleges and universities (Table K8)
	Educational exchanges see KDZ-KH1 726
	Science and the arts. Research
720	General (Table K8)
721	The arts (Table K8)
723	Museums and galleries (Table K8)

KDZ-KH1

	Cultural affairs
	Science and the arts -- Continued
723.5	Historical buildings and monuments. Archaeological excavations (Table K8)
	Including preservation and protection of cultural property
724	Libraries (Table K8)
725	Archives (Table K8)
726	Educational, scientific, and cultural exchanges (Table K8)
	Economic legislation
	Including regional economic integration and groupings
	Class here only works with legal emphasis
	For non-legal works, see HC
	For works relating to a special subject, see the subject, e.g. Regional banks for development and integration, see KDZ-KH1 908 ; Tariff and trade agreements. Customs, see KDZ-KH1 944+
	Cf. KDZ-KH1 955 Emergency economic legislation
735	General (Table K8)
736.A-Z	Regional and subregional organizations, A-Z
	e.g Andean Group, KG736.A5; Caribbean Common Market (CARIFTA), KG736.C37; Caribbean Community (CARICOM), KG736.C39; Central American Common Market, KG736.C4; Latin American Free Trade Association (LAFTA), KG736.L37; Latin American Integration Association (LAIA), KG736.L38; Organization of Central American States, KG736.O73
	Class here treaties establishing, expanding and governing the organizations, and legal works about the organization
	For works relating to special subjects within the geographic areas of the organizations, see the region and the subject, e.g. Tariff in the Andean Group countries, see KH944 ; Multinational corporations in the Caribbean Community countries, see KGJ342
	Economic assistance
740	General (Table K8)
741	Finance. Subsidies (Table K8)
	For economic assistance to a particular industry, see the industry
742.A-Z	Economic assistance and development for particular regions, A-Z
	Subarrange each by Table K12
	Tax incentive legislation see KDZ-KH1 915
744	Foreign investment (Table K8)
	Cf. JZ1546.3 Drago doctrine
	Cf. KDZ-KH1 341 Foreign corporation
	Cf. KDZ-KH1 342 Multinational corporations
	Regulation of industry, trade, and commerce. Occupational law

	Regulation of industry, trade, and commerce. Occupational law -- Continued
750	General (Table K8)
	Trade regulation. Control of trade practices. Consumer protection
	Cf. KDZ-KH1 409+ Industrial property
	Cf. KDZ-KH1 840+ Foreign trade regulation
	Cf. KDZ-KH1 955 Economic emergency legislation
752	General (Table K8)
754	Advertising (Table K8)
756	Weights and measures. Containers (Table K8)
	Competition. Restraint of trade
758	General (Table K8)
759	Monopolies. Antitrust laws (Table K8)
761	Restrictive and unfair trade practices (Table K8)
	Cf. KDZ-KH1 419 Trademarks
	Cf. KDZ-KH1 421 Unfair competition
	Primary production. Extractive industries
	Agriculture. Forestry. Rural law
765	General (Table K8)
766	Agricultural courts and procedure (Table K8)
767	Public lands (Table K8)
	Land tenure
769	History
770	General (Table K8)
771	Large estates. Feudal land grants (Table K8)
	Including haciendas and encomiendas
772	Common lands. Indian lands (Table K8)
	Agrarian land policy legislation. Land reform
775	General (Table K8)
777	Colonization. Agrarian colonies (Table K8)
779	Land reform. Transformation of the agricultural structure (Table K8)
	Including expropriation, nationalization, purchase of agricultural land holdings and their redistribution, land grants, government-constituted homesteads
785	Agricultural contracts (Table K8)
	Agricultural laborers see KDZ-KH1 460.A34
789	Field irrigation (Table K8)
791	Control of agricultural pests, plant diseases, etc. (Table K8)
	Including control of plant imports
793	Economic legislation. Economic assistance
	Agricultural production
	Including marketing, standards and grading
795	General (Table K8)
797.A-Z	Field crops, A-Z

KDZ-KH1

	Regulation of industry, trade, and commerce. Occupational law
	Primary production. Extractive industries
	Agriculture. Forestry. Rural law
	Agricultural production -- Continued
798	Livestock industry and trade. Cattle raising (Table K8)
	For meat industry see KDZ-KH1 832
	Dairy industry see KDZ-KH1 833
800	Forestry. Timber laws
802	Viticulture (Table K8)
	Cf. KDZ-KH1 693 Wine and wine making
	Game laws see KDZ-KH1 649
803	Fisheries (Table K8)
	Mining. Quarrying
810	General (Table K8)
	Petroleum. Oil and gas
815	General (Table K8)
818	Conservation (Table K8)
820	Submerged land legislation. Tidal oil (Table K8)
822	Oil and gas leases (Table K8)
824	Expropriation. Nationalization. Government ownership (Table K8)
	Manufacturing industries
827	General (Table K8)
828.A-Z	Particular industries, A-Z
	Subarrange each by Table K12
828.A87	Automobile industry (Table K12)
828.B56	Biotechnology industries (Table K12)
828.S74	Steel industry (Table K12)
828.T84	Twine industry (Table K12)
	Food processing industries
830	General (Table K8)
	Particular products and industries
831.A-Z	Agricultural products, A-Z
832	Meat industry (Table K8)
833	Dairy industry (Table K8)
835	Building and construction industry (Table K8)
	For building laws see KDZ-KH1 655
	Trade and commerce
	Cf. KDZ-KH1 231+ Commercial law
	Cf. KDZ-KH1 752+ Trade regulation
836	General (Table K8)
838.A-Z	Particular commodites, A-Z
	Subarrange each by Table K12
838.T62	Tobacco (Table K12)

	Regulation of industry, trade, and commerce. Occupational law
	Trade and commerce -- Continued
	International trade. Export and import controls and regulations
	For trade between individual countries in the region and the United States, see KF1975+
840	General (Table K8)
	Trade agreements see KDZ-KH1 944+
842.A-Z	Particular commodities, A-Z
	Subarrange each by Table K12
842.C64	Coffee (Table K12)
	Export trade
	Including export controls, regulations, and promotion
844	General (Table K8)
845.A-Z	Particular commodities, A-Z
	Import trade
	Including import controls and regulations
847	General (Table K8)
848.A-Z	Particular commodities, A-Z
	Subarrange each by Table K12
	Plants see KDZ-KH1 791
850	Retail trade (Table K12)
851	Services trades (Table K12)
853	Warehouses (Table K12)
	Public utilities
855	General (Table K8)
	Power supply. Energy policy
	Including energy resources and development in general
856	General (Table K8)
857	Electricity (Table K8)
	Atomic power
859	General (Table K8)
860.A-Z	International agencies, A-Z
	e.g. Inter-American Nuclear Energy Commisison, KDZ860.I5
	Transportation and communication
861	General (Table K8)
	Road traffic. Automotive transportation
862	General (Table K8)
	Traffic regulation and enforcement
863	General (Table K8)
864	Highway safety. Traffic signs (Table K8)
865	Carriage of passengers and goods. Motor carrier regulation (Table K8)
866	Railroads (Table K8)
	Aviation

	Regulation of industry, trade, and commerce. Occupational law
	Transportation and communication
	Aviation -- Continued
868	General (Table K8)
870	Commercial aviation. Airlines (Table K8)
	Water transportation. Navigation and shipping
875	General (Table K8)
	Merchant mariners see KDZ-KH1 372
876	Shipping laws. The merchant marine (Table K8)
	Communication. Mass media
878	General (Table K8)
	Postal service
879	General (Table K8)
	Postal unions
879.5	General (Table K8)
879.52.A-Z	Individual unions, A-Z
	e.g. Postal Union of the Americas and Spain (previously Pan American Postal Union), KDZ879.52.P6
880.5	Money orders (Table K8)
880.6	Parcel post (Table K8)
882	Press law (Table K8)
	Telecommunication
884	General (Table K8)
885	Telegraph. Teletype (Table K8)
886	Telephone (Table K8)
	Including radio telephone
	Radio communication
	Including radio and television combined
888	General (Table K8)
890	Radio stations. Radio broadcasting (Table K8)
892	Television broadcasting (Table K8)
	Professions and occupations
894	General (Table K8)
895.A-Z	Particular professions, A-Z
	Lawyers see KDZ-KH1 58+
	Notaries see KDZ-KH1 68+
895.P48	Physicians
	Including the health professions in general
	Public finance
900	General (Table K8)
901	Money. Currency. Coinage (Table K8)
	Including monetary unions
902	Foreign exchange regulations (Table K8)
903	Budget. Government expenditures (Table K8)
904	Expenditure control. Public auditing and accounting (Table K8)
	Public debts. Loans. Bond issues

	Public finance
	Public debts. Loans. Bond issues -- Continued
906	General (Table K8)
	External debts. International loan agreements
907	General (Table K8)
908.A-Z	Regional banks for development and integration, A-Z
	e.g. Interamerican Development Bank (IDB), KDZ908.I5; Central American Bank for Economic Integration, KG3908.C4
	National revenue
910	General (Table K8)
	Taxation
911	General (Table K8)
	Tax administration and procedure
	Including administration and procedure relating to income tax
912	General (Table K8)
912.2	Double taxation (Table K8)
912.4	Tax collection. Procedure. Practice (Table K8)
	Exemptions. Tax reductions and other benefits
914	General (Table K8)
915	Tax incentive legislation (Table K8)
917	Criminal law. Tax evasion (Table K8)
	Particular taxes
918	Direct taxes (General) (Table K8)
	Income tax
919	General (Table K8)
	Administration and procedure see KDZ-KH1 912+
	Income. Exclusion from income
921	General (Table K8)
	Particular sources of income
	Capital investment. Securities
923	General (Table K8)
924	Foreign investments (Table K8)
	Including foreign source income in general and surtaxes on foreign investments
926.A-Z	Particular classes of taxpayers, A-Z
	Income of business organizations
928	General (Table K8)
	Juristic persons. Corporations
929	General (Table K8)
930	Corporation income tax (Table K8)
932.A-Z	Particular lines of business, A-Z
	Including both business organizations and individuals, and works on income tax and other taxes combined
932.B35	Banks
	Property taxes. Taxation of capital

	Public finance
	National revenue
	Taxation
	Particular taxes
	Property taxes. Taxation of capital -- Continued
934	General (Table K8)
935	National taxes affecting real property (Table K8)
936	Personal property taxes (Table K8)
	Other taxes of capital and income
937	Estate, inheritance, and gift taxes (Table K8)
	Taxes on transactions. Taxes on production and consumption. Indirect taxes
939	General (Table K8)
940.A-Z	Particular types of taxes, A-Z
941.A-Z	Particular commodities, services, and transactions, A-Z
	Subarrange each by Table K12
941.S94	Sugar (Table K12)
	Particular methods of assessment and collection
942	Stamp duties (Table K8)
	Tariff. Trade agreements. Customs
	Including favored nation clause and reciprocity
	For multilateral trade agreements and related bilateral agreements not limited to a region, see K4600+
	For bilateral trade agreements with the United States, see KF6665+
	For foreign trade regulations see KDZ-KH1 840+
944	General (Table K8)
	Trade agreements. Particular tariffs
945	General (Table K8)
946.A-Z	Particular commodities, A-Z
	Customs administration
948	General (Table K8)
948.5	Enforcement. Criminal law. Smuggling (Table K8)
948.8	Dumping. Antidumping duties (Table K8)
949.A-Z	Other special topics, A-Z
	Subarrange each by Table K12
	Classification and terminology see KDZ-KH1 949.T47
949.D87	Duty-free transit (Table K12)
	Nomenclature see KDZ-KH1 949.T47
949.O74	Origin, Rules of (Table K12)
949.P74	Preferences, Tariff (Table K12)
949.T47	Terminology and classification. Nomenclature (Table K12)
	State and local finance
950	General (Table K8)
951	State finance (Table K8)

	Public finance
	State and local finance -- Continued
	Local finance
952	General (Table K8)
953	Taxation (Table K8)
955	Government measures in time of war, national emergency or economic crisis (Table K8)
957	National defense. Military law (Table K8)
	Criminal law and procedure
	Including regional comparative and international criminal law and procedure
960	General (Table K8)
961	Administration of criminal justice (Table K8)
	Including reform of criminal law, enforcement, and procedure
	Criminal law
	Cf. K5018+, Philosophy and theory of criminal law
	Cf. HV6001+, Criminology
962	General (Table K8)
962.5	Influence of foreign (e.g. Spanish) law (Table K8)
963	Punishment and penalties (Table K8)
966.A-Z	Particular offenses, A-Z
	Subarrange each by Table K12
966.A26	Abortion (Table K12)
	Bribery see KDZ-KH1 966.M57
	Corruption see KDZ-KH1 966.M57
966.F36	Family violence (Table K12)
	Including wife abuse
966.I57	International offenses (Table K12)
966.M57	Misconduct in office (Table K12)
	Including corruption and bribery
966.N36	Narcotics offenses. Illicit possession of, use of, and traffic in narcotics (Table K12)
966.N37	National economy, industry, and commerce, Offenses against the (Table K12)
966.P64	Political offenses (Table K12)
966.P75	Property, Offenses against (Table K12)
966.S47	Sex crimes (Table K12)
	Wife abuse see KDZ-KH1 966.F36
	Criminal courts and procedure
969	General (Table K8)
969.5	Police magistrates' courts. Justices of the peace (Table K8)
	Including procedure before such courts
	Criminal procedure
971	General (Table K8)
	Judicial assistance in criminal matters see KDZ-KH1 974+
972	Prosecution and defense (Table K8)

KDZ-KH1

Criminal courts and procedure
Criminal procedure -- Continued

973   Compulsory and precautionary measures against suspects
(Table K8)
Cf. KDZ-KH1 521 Amparo and habeas corpus
Extradition
Including judicial assistance in criminal matters in general
974   General (Table K8)
974.5   Right of asylum. Refusal of extradition (Table K8)
975   Rights of suspects (Table K8)
Including protection of human rights in criminal proceedings
975.7   Judicial decisions (Table K8)
Including sentencing and judicial discretion
976   Remedies (Table K8)
For amparo, habeas corpus, and similar remedies see
KDZ-KH1 521
Execution of sentence
978   General (Table K8)
979   Imprisonment. Prison administration (Table K8)
980   Indeterminate sentence (Table K8)
982   Victims of crimes (Table K8)
986   Juvenile criminal law and procedure. Administration of juvenile
justice (Table K8)

	Bibliography
	For manuals on legal bibliography, legal research, and the use of law books see KDZ-KH2 150+
1	General bibliography
4	Library catalogs
6	Sales catalogs
8	Indexes to periodical literature, society publications, and collections
	For indexes to particular publications, see the publication
<10>	Periodicals
	For periodicals consisting predominantly of legal articles, regardless of subject matter and jurisdiction, see K1+
	For periodicals consisting primarily of informative material (Newsletters, bulletins, etc.) relating to a special subject, see the subject and form division for periodicals
	For law reports, official bulletins or circulars intended chiefly for the publication of laws and regulations, see appropriate entries in the text or form division tables
12	Monographic series
16.A2-.A29	Official gazettes
	Arranged chronologically
18	Digests of official gazettes
	Legislative documents
	see J
28	Other materials relating to legislative history
	Including recommended legislation; legislation passed and vetoed
	Legislation
	For legislation on a particular subject, see the subject
	Treaties
	General
	see KZ
	Treaties on international uniform law not limited to a region
	see K
	Treaties on international uniform law of American regions
	see the region in KDZ, KG, KGJ or KH
	Statutes
	Including decree laws (decreto-leyes), and works containing statutes and administrative regulations, or federal and comparative state legislation combined
	Sessional volumes. Annual volumes
	Serials
35.A2-.A29	Official editions
	Arranged chronologically
35.A3-Z	Unofficial editions. By publisher or editor
36	Monographs. By date of initial session
	Compilations. Collections. Revisions

KDZ-KH2

	Legislation
	Statutes
	Compilations. Collections. Revisions -- Continued
	Official editions
38	Serials
40	Monographs. By date
	Unofficial editions
42	Serials
43	Monographs. By date
46	Collected codes

Class here works consisting of both private and public law
codes
For codes on a particular branch of law, see the subject
For works consisting of the civil and commercial codes
see KDZ-KH2 387
For collected public law codes see KDZ-KH2 2900

48	Statute revision commission acts and reports. By date
50	Abridgments and digests of statutes
52	Indexes to statutes

Class indexes to a particular publication with the publication

54	Other bibliographical aids
	Administrative and executive publications

Including statutory rules, orders and regulations; orders in council;
proclamations, etc.
For regulations on a particular subject, see the subject

58	Serials
59	Monographs. By date
61	Digests
62	Indexes
	Presidential proclamations, manifestos, etc.
	see J
	Attorneys General's opinions see KDZ-KH2 3238
64	Digests and indexes to state legislation
	Law reports and related materials

Subarrange courts represented by a whole number by Table KDZ-
KH9
Do not further subarrange courts represented by a Cutter number
Including federal reports and reports of two or more states, and
federal and state reports combined
Reports of particular states are classed with the law of the
respective jurisdiction
For reports relating to a particular subject, see the subject
For reports of civil and commercial decisions combined see
KDZ-KH2 387
Cf. KDZ-KH2 324+ Collected opinions
Federal (National) courts

	Law reports and related materials
	Federal (National) courts -- Continued
70	Highest court of appeals. Supreme Court (Table KDZ-KH9)
	Lower courts
72	Various courts (Table KDZ-KH9)
	Including highest court and lower courts, or federal courts and courts of two or more states combined
	Intermediate appellate courts. Federal courts of appeal
74	Collective (Table KDZ-KH9)
75.A-Z	Particular courts, A-Z
	For decisions of federal courts of appeal for federal districts, see the appropriate federal district, e.g., KHA6205, Buenos Aires (Federal District)
	Courts of first instance. District courts
78	Collective (Table KDZ-KH9)
79.A-.Z	Particular courts, A-Z
	For decisions of federal district courts for federal districts, see the appropriate federal district, e.g. KHA6206, Buenos Aires (Federal District)
81.A-Z	Decisions of federal courts in, or of cases before federal courts arising in individual states. By state, A-Z
	For federal decisions and decisions of the courts of an individual state combined, see the respective state
	For decisions of federal district courts for federal districts, see the appropriate federal district, e.g. KHA6206, Buenos Aires (Federal District)
	State courts
	Including courts of federal districts and national territories
83	Reports covering all states or selected states (Table KDZ-KH9)
	Reports covering federal decisions and decisions of the courts of two or more states combined see KDZ-KH2 72
	Reports of individual states
	see the respective state
85	Decisions of federal administrative agencies (Table KDZ-KH9)
	For decisions of particular agencies, see the subject
100	Encyclopedias
102	Dictionaries. Words and phrases
	For bilingual and multilingual dictionaries, see K52+
	For dictionaries on a particular subject, see the subject
104	Maxims. Quotations
106	Form books
	Class here general works only
	For form books on a particular subject, see the subject

KDZ-KH2

(110)	Yearbooks
	For publications issued annually, containing information, statistics, etc. relating to a special subject, see the subject and form division for periodicals. For other publications appearing yearly, see K1+
	Judicial statistics
112	General
	Criminal statistics
114	General
115	Juvenile crime
116.A-Z	Other. By subject, A-Z
	Directories
	General
118	National
119.A-Z	By state, A-Z
120.A-Z	By county or city, A-Z
122.A-Z	By specialization, A-Z
	Trials
130	General collections
	Criminal trials
	For courts-martial see KDZ-KH2 5282+
	Collections
131	General
133.A-Z	Particular offenses, A-Z
	Assassination see KDZ-KH2 133.M85
133.H45	Heresy. Witchcraft
133.M85	Murder. Assassination
133.P64	Political offenses
	Witchcraft see KDZ-KH2 133.H45
135.A-Z	Particular trials. By defendant or best known name, A-Z
	Including records, briefs, commentaries, and stories on particular trials
	For individual amparo cases see KDZ-KH2 2714.A+
	Civil trials. Arbitration proceedings
137	Collections
138.A-Z	Particular trials and proceedings. By plaintiff, A-Z
	Including records, briefs, commentaries and stories on particular trials
	Class individual trials with "Particular cases" or "Particular companies" under subject only if specifically provided for in the schedule, e.g. 1850.P842, Public utilities labor disputes; 2714, Individual amparo cases; 3097.3+, Contested elections
	Legal research. Legal bibliography
	Including methods of bibliographic research and how to find the law
150	General (Table K11)

Legal research. Legal bibliography -- Continued
Electronic data processing. Information retrieval
152   General (Table K11)
153.A-Z   By subject, A-Z
                    Subarrange each by Table K12
158   Legal composition and draftsmanship (Table K12)
                    For legislative drafting see KDZ-KH2 3084
                 Classification of the law see KDZ-KH2 356.C55
                 Legal education
170   Bibliography
172   Periodicals
174   Yearbooks. Annual and periodical surveys
175   Directories
176   Society publications
178   Congresses. Conferences
180.A-Z   Law school catalogs and bulletins. By name of school, A-Z
182   General works. Treatises
183   Addresses, essays, lectures
185   Continuing legal education
                 Study and teaching
                    General works see KDZ-KH2 182
187.A-Z   Particular subjects, A-Z
                    Subarrange each by Table K12
187.A34   Administrative law (Table K12)
187.A36   Agricultural law (Table K12)
187.C45   Civil procedure (Table K12)
187.C63   Commercial law (Table K12)
                 Comparative law
                    see K103.C6
                 Conflict of laws
                    see K103.C6
187.C64   Constitutional law (Table K12)
187.C74   Criminal law (Table K12)
187.C75   Criminal procedure (Table K12)
187.D65   Domestic relations (Table K12)
                 International law
                    see JZ1237+
187.P45   Persons (Table K12)
187.T35   Tariff (Table K12)
189   Teaching methods (Table K11)
193   Students' guides and textbooks
                    For introduction to legal literature (legal bibliography) see
                       KDZ-KH2 150+
                    For introductory surveys of the law see KDZ-KH2 327
196   Law students (Table K11)
                    Including sociology and psychology of law students

	Legal education -- Continued
201.A-Z	Particular law schools. By name, A-Z
	Subarrange each by Table KDZ-KH10
203.A-Z	Law societies and institutes. By name, A-Z
	Subarrange each society or institute by Table KDZ-KH11
	Class here works on individual societies and institutes and their activities, e.g. administrative reports, minutes, etc.
	For works issued by individual law societies and institutes on particular subjects, see the subject
	For law societies incorporated to regulate the profession see KDZ-KH2 233+
	For congresses, conferences, and other meetings sponsored by law societies and institutes see KDZ-KH2 322
	The legal profession
	Including law as a career
206	General (Table K11)
206.5	General special (Special aspects of the subject as a whole)
207	The lawyer and society (Table K11)
209	Procurators (Table K11)
210.A-Z	Particular classes of lawyers and types of careers, A-Z
	Subarrange each by Table K12
210.C73	Creole lawyers (Table K12)
210.G67	Government service (Table K12)
210.W64	Women lawyers (Table K12)
	Practice of law
211	General (Table K11)
	Directories see KDZ-KH2 118+
	Biography of lawyers see KDZ-KH2 300+
213	Admission to the bar. Bar examinations (Table K11)
	Legal ethics and etiquette
	Cf. KDZ-KH2 2560.6 Judicial ethics
215	General (Table K11)
	Discipline. Disbarment. Unauthorized practice
218	General (Table K11)
219.A-Z	Particular cases. By attorney, A-Z
	Attorney and client
221	General (Table K11)
	Privileged (confidential) communications see KDZ-KH2 2653.5.A86
	Violation of professional secrets see KDZ-KH2 5584
	Economics of law practice
224	General (Table K11)

	The legal profession
	Practice of law
	Economics of law practice -- Continued
225	Fees (Table K11)
	Including schedules of fees of attorneys, procurators, notaries, etc., combined
	Cf. KDZ-KH2 2670 Costs (Civil procedure)
	Cf. KDZ-KH2 5899 Costs (Criminal procedure)
	Law office management
227	General works (Table K11)
228	Secretaries' handbooks. manuals, etc. (Table K11)
	Form books see KDZ-KH2 106
229.A-Z	Special topics, A-Z
	Subarrange each by Table K12
229.L43	Legal assistants. Paralegal personnel (Table K12)
	Retirement pensions see KDZ-KH2 2008.L37
	Bar associations
	Including law societies organized to regulate the profession
	For publications of bar associations on special subjects, see the subject
	For membership directories see KDZ-KH2 118+
233	General works
	Particular types of organizations
235.A-Z	National bar associations. By name, A-Z
	Each association is subarranged by Table KDZ-KH12
	For collective biography see KDZ-KH2 300
	For individual biography see KDZ-KH2 304.A+
237.A-Z	State bar associations. By state, A-Z
	Each association is subarranged by Table KDZ-KH12
	For collective biography see KDZ-KH2 301.A+
	For individual biography see KDZ-KH2 304.A+
239.A-Z	Local bar associations, lawyers' clubs, etc. By county, city, A-Z
	Each association is subarranged by Table KDZ-KH12
	For collective biography see KDZ-KH2 303.A+
	For individual biography see KDZ-KH2 304.A+
	Law and lawyers in literature
	see PB+
	Legal anecdotes, wit and humor
	see K184.7
	For purely fictitious works, see PN6231.L4, and PN6268.L4
	Community legal services. Legal aid. Legal services to the poor
241	General (Table K11)
242.A-Z	Local agencies and legal aid societies. By state or place, A-Z
244.A-Z	Legal aid services to particular groups, A-Z
	Public defenders see KDZ-KH2 5844

KDZ-KH2

	Notarial law. Public instruments
250	General (Table K11)
	The notarial profession
251	History
252	General (Table K11)
253	Organization. Regulation. Discipline (Table K11)
256	Education. Qualification (Table K11)
258	Professional ethics (Table K11)
260	Fees (Table K11)
261.A-Z	Special topics, A-Z
	Subarrange each by Table K12
261.C57	Civil liability (Table K11)
	Confidential communications see KDZ-KH2 2653.5.N66
263	Public instruments (Table K11)
	Including protocolization, certification, authentication, legalization
	and recording of documents
	Cf. KDZ-KH2 2820 Executory suits. Executory instruments
	Consular functions
267	General (Table K11)
268	Consular fees (Table K11)
	Public registers. Registration
272	General (Table K11)
	Civil registry see KDZ-KH2 464
	Registration of juristic persons in civil law see KDZ-KH2 468
	Registration of wills see KDZ-KH2 684
	Commercial registers see KDZ-KH2 1076
276	Registration of miscellaneous titles and documents
	Property registration
277	General (Table K11)
	Land registry see KDZ-KH2 646
	Registered pledges see KDZ-KH2 946.2+
	Mining registration see KDZ-KH2 3936
	Aircraft registration see KDZ-KH2 4256
	Ship registration see KDZ-KH2 4304
278	Registration fees (Table K11)
	History
	For works on the history of a particular subject, see the subject
290	Sources
	General works
292	Comprehensive
	Including works on the history of modern law
	Precolonial see KDZ-KH2 2212+
294	Colonial
	Modern see KDZ-KH2 292
	Biography
	Collective

	History
	Biography
	Collective -- Continued
300	General
301.A-Z	By state, A-Z
303.A-Z	By county, city, etc., A-Z
304.A-Z	Individual, A-Z
	Subarranged by Table KDZ-KH13
306	Influence of foreign law
315	Philosophy. Jurisprudence
	Class here works on doctrines peculiar to the legal institutions of the country
	For works on the philosophy of particular branches of the law (e.g. Constitutional or criminal law), see these subjects
	For works by authors identified with a particular country on jurisprudence and philosophy of law in general, see K202+
	Relationship of law to other disciplines, subjects, or phenomena see K486+
320	Criticism. Legal reform
	Cf. KDZ-KH2 2500+ Judiciary
	Cf. KDZ-KH2 5404 Administration of criminal justice
322	Congresses. By date of congress
	For intergovernmental congresses and conferences, see subclass K and regional subclasses
	Collected works (nonserial)
	For monographic series see KDZ-KH2 12
324	Several authors
325.A-Z	Individual authors, A-Z
	Subarranged by Table KDZ-KH14
	Including collected opinions
326	Casebooks. Readings
	Class here general works only
	For casebooks on particular subjects, see the subject
327	General works. Treatises
328	Compends. Outlines, syllabi, etc.
330	Addresses, essays, lectures
	Including single essays, collected essays of several authors, etc.
333.A-Z	Works for particular users, A-Z
333.B86	Businesspeople. Foreign investors
	Foreign investors see KDZ-KH2 333.B86
333.P64	Police
	Tourists see KDZ-KH2 4103.T67
335.A-Z	Works on diverse aspects of particular subjects and falling within several branches of the law. By subject, A-Z
	Subarrange each by Table K12
335.C65	Computers (Table K12)

KDZ-KH2

	Works on diverse aspects of particular subjects and falling within several branches of the law -- Continued
335.H84	Human body (Table K12)
	Cf. KDZ-KH2 3405 Disposal of the dead
	Cf. KDZ-KH2 3446.D64 Donation, sale and transplantation of human organs, tissues, etc.
335.P82	Public interest law (Table K12)
	Equity. Fairness of law and its application see KDZ-KH2 356.E68
	Usage and custom see KDZ-KH2 356.U8
	Conflict of laws
345	History
346	General (Table K11)
348.A-Z	Special topics, A-Z
	Subarrange each by Table K12
	Choice of law by the parties see KDZ-KH2 348.P35
	Connecting factors see KDZ-KH2 348.P64
348.F65	Formalities. Locus regit actum (Table K12)
	Locus regit actum see KDZ-KH2 348.F65
348.N36	Nationality and domicile as points of contact (Table K12)
	Including applicability to juristic persons
	Cf. KDZ-KH2 482 Domicile with regard to domestic relations
348.P35	Party autonomy. Choice of law by the parties (Table K12)
348.P64	Points of contact. Connecting factors (Table K12)
	For locus regit actum see KDZ-KH2 348.F65
	For nationality and domicile as points of contact see KDZ-KH2 348.N36
348.P82	Public policy. Public order (Table K12)
	Retroactive law. Intertemporal law see KDZ-KH2 353
	Regional unification of conflicts rules
	see KDZ-KH1 110+ in Table KDZ-KH1
	Conflict of laws with the United States of America
	see KF416
350	Domestic (interstate, etc.), conflicts (Table K11)
351.A-Z	Particular branches and subjects of the law, A-Z
	Subarrange each by Table K12
351.A35	Aeronautics (Table K12)
351.A44	Aliens (Table K12)
	Including works on civil and public law status combined
	Cf. KDZ-KH2 558 Alien property
	Cf. KDZ-KH2 2981+ Status of aliens in public law
351.B34	Bankruptcy (Table K12)
351.C57	Civil procedure (Table K12)
351.C63	Contracts. Obligations. Debtor and creditor (Table K12)

Conflict of laws
Particular branches and subjects of the law, A-Z -- Continued
351.C65   Corporations (Table K12)
For foreign corporations see KDZ-KH2 1362
For multinational corporations see KDZ-KH2 1363
Creditor and debtor see KDZ-KH2 351.C63
Criminal jurisdiction see KDZ-KH2 5824
Debtor and creditor see KDZ-KH2 351.C63
Decedents' estates see KDZ-KH2 351.I53
Divorce see KDZ-KH2 351.M36
Execution of foreign judgments and arbitral awards see KDZ-KH2 351.F65
Extradition see KDZ-KH2 5862+
Foreign corporations see KDZ-KH2 1362
351.F65   Foreign judgments and arbitral awards (Table K12)
Including recognition and execution
351.I53   Inheritance and succession (Table K12)
Jurisdiction in civil litigation see KDZ-KH2 351.C57
351.J85   Juristic persons (Table K12)
For corporations see KDZ-KH2 351.C65
351.L32   Labor law (Table K12)
Letters rogatory see KDZ-KH2 2652
Marital property see KDZ-KH2 351.M36

KDZ-KH2

351.M35   Maritime law (Table K12)
351.M36   Marriage. Divorce. Marital property (Table K12)
351.N43   Negotiable instruments (Table K12)
Obligations see KDZ-KH2 351.C63
351.P35   Parent and child (Table K12)
351.P68   Power of attorney (Table K12)
Security for costs from foreign plaintiff see KDZ-KH2 2618.S42
351.S65   Social security (Table K12)
Wills made in foreign countries see KDZ-KH2 351.I53
353   Retroactive law. Intertemporal law (Table K11)
Cf. KDZ-KH2 367.V46 Vested rights
General principles and concepts
Comprehensive works see KDZ-KH2 324+
356.A-Z   Particular principles and concepts, A-Z
Subarrange each by Table K12
Analogy see KDZ-KH2 356.S85
356.C55   Classification (Table K12)
For works on the classification of library collections of legal literature, see Z697.L4
356.C63   Codification (Table K12)
Conflict of jurisprudence see KDZ-KH2 356.C64
356.C64   Conflicting decisions. Conflict of jurisprudence (Table K12)

	General principles and concepts
	Particular principles and concepts, A-Z -- Continued
356.E68	Equity. Fairness of law and its application (Table K12)
	Fairness of law and its application see KDZ-KH2 356.E68
356.I35	Ignorance of law. Mistake of law (Table K12)
	Cf. KDZ-KH2 356.E68 Equity. Fairness of law and its application
	Cf. KDZ-KH2 426 Mistake of fact
	Lacunae in law see KDZ-KH2 356.S85
	Mistake of law see KDZ-KH2 356.I35
356.P73	Precedents (Table K12)
	Cf. KDZ-KH2 356.C64 Conflicting decisions
	Rule of law see KDZ-KH2 2929
356.S85	Statutory construction and interpretation. Lacunae in law. Analogy (Table K12)
356.U8	Usage and custom (Table K12)
	Cf. KDZ-KH2 1062 Usage of trade
367.A-Z	Concepts applying to several branches of law, A-Z
	Subarrange each by Table K12
	Abuse of rights see KDZ-KH2 975
367.A25	Accounting. Auditing. Inventories (Table K12)
	Cf. KDZ-KH2 727+ Inventory (Decedents' estates)
	Cf. KDZ-KH2 1346 Corporation accounting
	Cf. KDZ-KH2 4565+ Public auditing and accounting
	Cf. KDZ-KH2 4607.A25 Tax accounting
	Affirmation see KDZ-KH2 367.O16
367.A76	Artificial insemination (Table K12)
	Auditing see KDZ-KH2 367.A25
	Consanguinity. Affinity see KDZ-KH2 537
	Damages (Civil liability) see KDZ-KH2 768
	Damages (Breach of contract) see KDZ-KH2 795+
	Damages (Torts) see KDZ-KH2 1008+
367.E85	Estoppel (Table K12)
	Cf. KDZ-KH2 2609 Preclusion
	Cf. KDZ-KH2 2669 Res judicata
367.G64	Good faith (Table K12)
	Cf. KDZ-KH2 563 Bona fide possessor
	Inventories see KDZ-KH2 367.A25
367.L34	Lapse (Table K12)
	Cf. KDZ-KH2 698 Lapsing of wills
	Cf. KDZ-KH2 2673 Lapse of lawsuits
	Legal advertising see KDZ-KH2 367.N66
367.L37	Legal documents (Table K12)

General principles and concepts
    Concepts applying to several branches of law, A-Z --
        Continued
367.L5   Liability (Table K12)
                    Cf. KDZ-KH2 767+ Civil liability
                    Cf. KDZ-KH2 795+ Liability for breach of contracts
                    Cf. KDZ-KH2 841 Limited liability clause
                    Cf. KDZ-KH2 1008+ Tort liability
                    Cf. KDZ-KH2 1068 Limited liability of individual
                        merchants
                    Cf. KDZ-KH2 5445+ Criminal liability
367.N43   Necessity (Table K12)
                    Cf. KDZ-KH2 5457.N42 Necessity in criminal law
367.N66   Notice. Legal advertising (Table K12)
367.O16   Oath. Affirmation (Table K12)
                    Cf. KDZ-KH2 5673 Perjury
367.P74   Prescription (Table K12)
                    Class here prescription in private and public law combined
                    Cf. KDZ-KH2 440+ Private law
                    Cf. KDZ-KH2 2621.P74 Pleading
                    Cf. KDZ-KH2 5493 Criminal law
367.P75   Presumption (Table K12)
                    Cf. KDZ-KH2 2642.P73 Presumption as a mode of proof
367.P82   Public policy (Table K12)
                    Cf. KDZ-KH2 348.P82 Conflict of laws
                    Cf. KDZ-KH2 855 Contracts against public policy
                    Cf. KDZ-KH2 2712.P82 Amparo and public policy

367.R44   Representation (Table K12)
                    Cf. KDZ-KH2 703 Intestate succession
                    Cf. KDZ-KH2 712 Personal representatives in inheritance
                        proceedings
                    Cf. KDZ-KH2 926+ Mandate. Agency
                    Cf. KDZ-KH2 2602+ Civil procedure. Judicial mandate
367.T54   Time (Computation of time) (Table K12)
                    Cf. KDZ-KH2 2609 Civil procedure
367.V46   Vested rights (Table K12)
387   Private law (Table K11)
                Class here works on civil and commercial law combined
            Civil law
389   History
401-409   General (Table K9b)
412   Criticism. Law reform (Table K11)
            Juristic facts. Juristic acts
414   General (Table K11)
                Prescription see KDZ-KH2 440+

Civil law
  Juristic facts. Juristic acts
    Juristic acts
      Modalities of juristic acts in general -- Continued
437   General (Table K11)
          Modus see KDZ-KH2 688.6
          Condition see KDZ-KH2 835
        Wrongful acts
438   General (Table K11)
          Obligations arising from wrongful acts see KDZ-KH2
            965+
          Abuse of rights see KDZ-KH2 975
        Prescription
            Class here works including both acquisitive and extinctive
              prescription
440   General (Table K11)
          Acquisitive prescription see KDZ-KH2 584+
          Extinctive prescription
            General see KDZ-KH2 440
            Civil procedure see KDZ-KH2 2621.P74
442   Periods of extinctive prescription in general (Table K11)
              For period of extinctive prescription relating to particular
                subjects, see the subject, e.g. Affiliation, see KDZ-
                KH2 520 ; Usufruct, see KDZ-KH2 628.P73

KDZ-KH2

  Persons
449   General (Table K11)
      Natural persons
        Status. Capacity and disability. Personality
450   General (Table K11)
451   Sexuality. Sexual orientation (Table K11)
          Name
452   General (Table K11)
453   Name of married women (Table K11)
            Business names see KDZ-KH2 1071
455   Domicile. Residence (Table K11)
              Cf. KDZ-KH2 348.N36 Nationality and domicile as
                points of contact
              Cf. KDZ-KH2 482 Domicile with regard to domestic
                relations
457   Absence and presumption of death (Table K11)
          Personal legal documents see KDZ-KH2 464
          Particular groups of persons
            Mentally ill. People with mental or physical disabilities
                Including persons with character, behavior, and
                  intelligence disorders
                For care of the mentally ill see KDZ-KH2 3443

Civil law
  Persons
    Natural persons
      Status. Capacity and disability. Personality
        Particular groups of persons
          Mentally ill. People with mental or physical disabilities -
            - Continued

459	General (Table K11)
460	Mental incompetency proceedings. Interdiction (Table K11)
	Cf. KDZ-KH2 533+ Curatorship
461.A-Z	Particular diseases and impairments, A-Z
	Subarrange each by Table K12
461.A43	Alcoholism (Table K12)
	Cf. KDZ-KH2 3445.A43 Medical legislation
461.A63	Aphasia (Table K12)
461.D4	Deafness (Table K12)
461.E64	Epilepsy (Table K12)
	Criminal liability see KDZ-KH2 5457.I56
462.A-Z	Other, A-Z
	Subarrange each by Table K12
462.A34	Aged. Older people (Table K12)
	Aliens see KDZ-KH2 351.A44
462.B55	Blacks (Table K12)
	Convicts' parental rights see KDZ-KH2 526
	Indians see KDZ-KH2 2204+
462.M54	Minors (Table K12)
	Including civil liability and emancipation
	Cf. KDZ-KH2 530 Guardian and ward
	Older people see KDZ-KH2 462.A34
462.P74	Prodigals (Table K12)
462.S57	Slaves (Table K12)
	Cf. KDZ-KH2 2920.P44 Peonage. Slavery (Constitutional law)
462.U52	Unborn children. Nasciturus (Table K12)
462.W64	Women (Table K12)
	Including works on civil and public law status combined
	For works on women in relation to particular subjects, see the subject, e.g. Civil status of married women, see KDZ-KH2 502 ; Nationality of women, see KDZ-KH2 2980.W64 ; Suffrage of women, see KDZ-KH2 3057.W64
464	Civil registry. Registration of civil status (Table K11)
	Including registers of births, marriages, deaths; birth and death certificates; census; vital statistics, etc.

Civil law
   Persons -- Continued
      Juristic persons
         For juristic persons in public law, see the subject in
            constitutional and administrative law
         Cf. KDZ-KH2 5451 Criminal liability of juristic persons

466	General (Table K11)
468	Registration (Table K11)
469	State supervision (Table K11)
470	Nationality and domicile (Table K11)
	Nonprofit associations see KDZ-KH2 917+
	Partnerships. Civil companies see KDZ-KH2 921+
472	Endowments. Foundations. Charitable trusts (Table K11)
	Business associations. Commercial companies see KDZ-KH2 1295+
	Public-private companies (mixed companies) see KDZ-KH2 1378
	Domestic relations. Family law
480	General (Table K11)
481	Domestic relations courts and procedure (Table K11)
482	Domicile with regard to domestic relations (Table K11)
	Marriage. Husband and wife
484	General (Table K11)
485	Betrothal (Table K11)
486	Marriage impediments (Table K11)
	Cf. KDZ-KH2 496+ Void and voidable marriages
487	Certificates. Premarital examinations (Table K11)
	Performance of marriage
	Including civil and religious celebration
489	General (Table K11)
490	Marriage by proxy (Table K11)
492	Mixed marriages (Table K11)
	Class here works on marriages between persons of different religions
493	Common law marriage. Concubinage (Table K11)
	Including property relationships
	Cf. KDZ-KH2 702.6 Concubine's inheritance rights
494	Remarriage (Table K11)
	Void and voidable marriages
496	General (Table K11)
	Annulment
497	General (Table K11)
498.A-Z	Particular grounds for annulment, A-Z
	Subarrange each by Table K12
498.E75	Error (Table K12)
498.I45	Impotence. Sterility (Table K12)

	Civil law
	Persons
	Domestic relations. Family law
	Marriage. Husband and wife
	Void and voidable marriages
	Annulment
	Particular grounds for annulment
	Sterility see KDZ-KH2 498.I45
498.V44	Venereal diseases (Table K12)
499	Putative marriage (Table K11)
	Rights and duties of husband and wife
501	General (Table K11)
502	Civil status of married women (Table K11)
	Cf. KDZ-KH2 453 Name of married women
	Cf. KDZ-KH2 1067 Legal capacity to trade
	Cf. KDZ-KH2 2980.W64 Nationality
	Property relationships. Conjugal partnership
504	General (Table K11)
	Particular modes of property relationships
505	Community property
506	Separate property
	Family property. Homestead law see KDZ-KH2 538
508	Marriage settlements. Antenuptial contracts (Table K11)
	Divorce. Separation. Matrimonial actions
510	General (Table K11)
511.A-Z	Particular grounds, A-Z
	Subarrange each by Table K12
511.A37	Adultery (Table K12)
511.L44	Legal cruelty (Table K12)
513	Separate maintenance. Alimony (Table K11)
	Parent and child
516	General (Table K11)
	Legitimacy. Legitimation. Paternity
518	General (Table K11)
519	Presumption of legitimacy (Table K11)
520	Illegitimate children. Affiliation (Table K11)
	Including acknowledgment by natural father and investigation of paternity
521	Adoption (Table K11)
	Artificial insemination see KDZ-KH2 367.A76
	Parental rights and duties. Property of minors. Custody
523	General (Table K11)
	Termination or suspension of parental rights
525	General (Table K11)
	Emancipation of minors see KDZ-KH2 462.M54

                          Civil law
                            Persons
                              Domestic relations. Family law
                                Parent and child
                                  Parental rights and duties. Property of minors. Custody
                                    Termination or suspension of parental rights --
                                      Continued
526   Suspension of parental rights of convicts (Table K11)
527   Support. Desertion and nonsupport (Table K11)
                                            For criminal provisions see KDZ-KH2 5537
530   Guardian and ward (Table K11)
                                    Curatorship
533   General (Table K11)
534   Curator bonis (Table K11)
535   Legal representatives (General) (Table K11)
                                        Including parents, guardians, husband and wife as legal
                                          representatives of each other
537   Consanguinity. Affinity (Table K11)
538   Family property. Homestead law (Table K11)
                                        Cf. KDZ-KH2 3844.I54 Government-constituted
                                          homesteads
                              Property. Real rights
550   General (Table K11)

552   Right of property. Constitutional guarantees (Table K11)
                                  Classification of things
554   General (Table K11)
555.A-Z   Particular kinds of things, A-Z
555.F77   Fruits (Table K12)
                                        Including natural, industrial, and civil fruits
                                        Cf. KDZ-KH2 563 Bona fide possessor
555.F84   Fungibles. Specific things (Table K12)
                                      Intangible property see KDZ-KH2 650+
555.P74   Principal and accessory things (Table K12)
                                        Cf. KDZ-KH2 555.F77 Fruits
555.R46   Res extra commercium (Table K12)
                                      Specific things see KDZ-KH2 555.F84
                                  Property considered with respect to its owner
558   Alien property
                                        Including restriction on aliens in acquiring real property
                                    Family property see KDZ-KH2 538
                                    Matrimonial property see KDZ-KH2 504+
                                    Public property see KDZ-KH2 3300+
                                  Possession
562   General (Table K11)
563   Bona fide possessor (Table K11)
                                        Including rights and obligations relating to fruits

Civil law
Property. Real rights
Possession -- Continued
Acquisition and loss of possession
565   General (Table K11)
566   Constitutum possessorium (Table K11)
567   Protection of possession. Possessory actions (Table K11)
           Cf. KDZ-KH2 2826 Summary possessory actions
Ownership
570   General (Table K11)
Right of property. Constitutional guarantees see KDZ-KH2
552
Acquisition and loss of property (real and personal
combined) and real property see KDZ-KH2 578+
Acquisition and loss of personal property see KDZ-KH2
652+
Restrictions upon and limitations of ownership
571   General (Table K11)
572   Restraint of alienation (Table K11)
           Cf. KDZ-KH2 870.R45 Restraint of alienation clause
Family property. Homestead law see KDZ-KH2 538
Concurrent ownership see KDZ-KH2 600+
Rights and interests incident to ownership and/or
possession of real property see KDZ-KH2 610+
Fideicommissum. Fiduciary property see KDZ-KH2 660+
Testamentary trust see KDZ-KH2 688.5
Transfer of ownership as security. Fiducia see KDZ-KH2
943
573   Real actions (Table K11)
Real property. Land law
576   General (Table K11)
Public land law see KDZ-KH2 3328+
Land tenure see KDZ-KH2 3810+
Acquisition and loss of ownership
Including works on real and personal property combined
578   General (Table K11)
Accession
579   General (Table K11)
580   Alluvion. Avulsion. Formation of islands (Table K11)
Including abandoned channels
582   Construction. Plantation (Table K11)
Acquisitive prescription
For acquisition of mine ownership by prescription see
KDZ-KH2 3945
Cf. KDZ-KH2 3819 Squatters
584   General (Table K11)

Civil law
Property. Real rights
Real property. Land law
Acquisition and loss of ownership
Acquisitive prescription -- Continued
586   Interruption of period of prescription (Table K11)
Transfer of title. Conveyancing
587   General (Table K11)
Transfer by will or intestate succession see KDZ-KH2 670+
Auction sale see KDZ-KH2 870.R4
Sale of real property see KDZ-KH2 870.R4
Judicial sale see KDZ-KH2 2692
Tax sales see KDZ-KH2 4607.E53
Restriction on aliens in acquiring real property see KDZ-KH2 558
592   Abandonment (Table K11)
Expropriation see KDZ-KH2 3325
594   Underground space (Table K11)
Cf. KDZ-KH2 614 Underground water
Cf. KDZ-KH2 3944+ Ownership of mines and mineral resources
595   Airspace (Table K11)
Concurrent ownership
Including works on concurrent ownership in real and personal property
600   General (Table K11)
Organized forms of concurrent ownership
601   General (Table K11)
602   Horizontal property. Condominium (Table K11)
604   Housing cooperatives (Table K11)
Common lands see KDZ-KH2 3813+
Party walls see KDZ-KH2 634.P35
606   Partition (Table K11)
Cf. KDZ-KH2 619 Boundaries. Fences
Cf. KDZ-KH2 727+ Partition of decedents' estates
Tenancy. Landlord and tenant see KDZ-KH2 881+
Rights and interests incident to ownership and possession
610   General (Table K11)
Water rights
Cf. KDZ-KH2 580 Alluvion. Avulsion. Formation of islands
Cf. KDZ-KH2 634.W36 Servitudes
Cf. KDZ-KH2 3332 Shore protection. Coastal zone management
612   General (Table K11)

KDZ-KH2

	Civil law
	Property. Real rights
	Real property. Land law
	Rights and interests incident to ownership and possession
	Water rights -- Continued
613	Riparian rights (Table K11)
614	Underground water (Table K11)
	Law of adjoining landowners
618	General (Table K11)
619	Boundaries. Fences (Table K11)
	Including actions to define boundary lines and interdictory summary actions to prohibit violations
	Party walls see KDZ-KH2 634.P35
	Real rights upon things of another. Encumbrances
622	General (Table K11)
624	Emphyteusis (Table K11)
	Usufruct. Use. Habitation
626	General (Table K11)
	Usufruct
627	General (Table K11)
628.A-Z	Special topics, A-Z
	Subarrange each by Table K12
628.P73	Prescription of actions to enter the enjoyment of usufruct (Table K12)
630	Use. Habitation (Table K11)
	Life annuities constituted on real property see KDZ-KH2 934
	Servitudes
632	General (Table K11)
	Real servitudes. Easements
633	General (Table K11)
634.A-Z	Particular kinds of real servitudes
	Subarrange each by Table K12
634.L53	Light and air (Table K12)
	Mine servitudes see KDZ-KH2 3948
634.P35	Party walls (Table K12)
634.R53	Right of way (Table K12)
634.W36	Water use (Table K12)
	Public servitudes
636	General (Table K11)
637	Aviation easements (Table K11)
	Personal servitudes see KDZ-KH2 626+
	Real rights of guaranty on real property
	For real rights of guaranty on real and personal property combined, and on personal property see KDZ-KH2 941+

	Civil law
	Property. Real rights
	Real property. Land law
	Real rights upon things of another. Encumbrances
	Real rights of guaranty on real property -- Continued
640	General (Table K11)
	Mortgages
641	General (Table K11)
642.A-Z	Special topics, A-Z
	Subarrange each by Table K12
642.E98	Extinction of mortgages (Table K12)
642.F65	Foreclosure (Table K12)
	Cf. KDZ-KH2 2820 Executory suits. Executory instruments
	Mortgage guaranty insurance see KDZ-KH2 1280
	Mortgage bonds see KDZ-KH2 1358.M65
	Moratorium on mortgage loans see KDZ-KH2 4960.D42
644	Antichresis (Table K11)
	Privileges. Liens see KDZ-KH2 951
646	Land registry (Table K11)
	For cadasters see KDZ-KH2 4717.5
	Personal property
649	General (Table K11)
	Choses in action. Intangible property
650	General (Table K11)
	Fondo de commercio see KDZ-KH2 1069+
	Negotiable instruments see KDZ-KH2 1130+
	Common stock see KDZ-KH2 1341
	Preferred stock. Debentures. Bonds see KDZ-KH2 1357+
	Intellectual property see KDZ-KH2 1570+
	Acquisition and loss of ownership
652	General (Table K11)
653	Specification (Table K11)
655	Acquisitive prescription (Table K11)
656	Transfer. Tradition. Conveyancing (Table K11)
	Cf. KDZ-KH2 868+ Sale
	Cf. KDZ-KH2 875 Gift
	Cf. KDZ-KH2 1095 Auction sale
	Cf. KDZ-KH2 2692 Judicial sale
	Pledge see KDZ-KH2 945+
	Privileges. Liens see KDZ-KH2 951
	Trusts and trustees
	Including fideicommissum and fiduciary property
660	General (Table K11)
661	Trustees. Trust companies (Table K11)

	Civil law
	Trusts and trustees -- Continued
	Testamentary trusts see KDZ-KH2 688+
	Transfer of ownership as security. Fiducia see KDZ-KH2 943
	Safe-deposit companies see KDZ-KH2 1123
	Investment trusts see KDZ-KH2 1188
664	Pension trusts (Table K11)
	Charitable trusts see KDZ-KH2 472
	Succession upon death
	Class here works on succession upon death and gifts combined
670	General (Table K11)
	Provisions common to testamentary and intestate succession see KDZ-KH2 705+
	Testamentary succession. Wills
672	General (Table K11)
	Texts of wills
	see CS
674.A-Z	Contested wills. By testator, A-Z
	Capacity to make wills
675	General (Table K11)
676	Wills made in lucid intervals (Table K11)
678	Freedom of testation and its limitations (Table K11)
	For necessary heirs see KDZ-KH2 696+
	Form of wills
680	General (Table K11)
	Ordinary wills
680.2	General (Table K11)
680.4	Public wills (Table K11)
680.6	Holographic wills (Table K11)
	Class here works on Brazilian "private wills"
	Special wills. Privileged wills
681	General (Table K11)
681.2	Military wills (Table K11)
681.4	Maritime wills (Table K11)
681.6	Oral wills (Table K11)
	Class here works on Mexican "private wills"
683	Witnesses to wills
	Cf. KDZ-KH2 694 Incapacity to receive by will
684	Registration of wills (Table K11)
	Wills made in foreign countries see KDZ-KH2 351.l53
685	Mutual wills (Table K11)
686	Contracts of inheritance (Table K11)
	Testamentary dispositions
688	General (Table K11)
688.15	Institution of heirs (Table K11)

	Civil law
	Succession upon death
	Testamentary succession. Wills
	Testamentary dispositions -- Continued
688.2	Legacies (Table K11)
688.4	Substitution of heirs or legatees (Table K11)
688.5	Testamentary trusts (Table K11)
688.6	Conditional and modal assignments by wills. Modus (Table K11)
688.7	Disinheritance (Table K11)
	Appointment of executors see KDZ-KH2 712
690	Right of accretion (Table K11)
691	Right of election (Table K11)
692	Interpretation and construction of wills (Table K11)
694	Incapacity to receive by will (Table K11)
	Including exclusion of writer of, and witnesses to, a will
	Necessary heirs. Legitime. Mejora
696	General (Table K11)
	Disinheritance see KDZ-KH2 688.7
	Unworthiness see KDZ-KH2 707
697	Rights of the surviving spouse
	Including usufruct of the surviving spouse
698	Nullity of wills. Revocation and lapsing of wills
	Execution of wills see KDZ-KH2 711+
	Intestate succession
701	General (Table K11)
	Order of succession
	General see KDZ-KH2 701
702	Succession of adopted children (Table K11)
702.3	Succession of ascendants (Table K11)
702.5	Succession of illegitimate children and natural father (Table K11)
702.6	Succession of concubine (Table K11)
702.7	Succession of collaterals (Table K11)
702.9	Succession of the public. Escheat (Table K11)
703	Right of representation (Table K11)
	Collation see KDZ-KH2 728
	Provisions common to testamentary and intestate succession
705	General
	Incapacity to inherit
706	General (Table K11)
707	Unworthiness (Table K11)
	Incapacity to receive by will see KDZ-KH2 694
	Disinheritance see KDZ-KH2 688.7
	Rules of succession in government-constituted small holdings see KDZ-KH2 3844.I54

KDZ-KH2

KDZ-KH2

Civil law
  Obligations
    Effects of obligations
      Effects of obligations between the parties
        Extinction of obligations. Discharge of contracts
          Performance. Payment -- Continued
            Special rules as to payment of money debts
              Cf. KDZ-KH2 908+ Loan of money
              Cf. KDZ-KH2 1162+ Bank loans

781	General (Table K11)
782	Foreign currency debts (Table K11)
	Cf. KDZ-KH2 4555+ Foreign exchange regulations
783	Valuta clause (Table K11)
784	Gold clause (Table K11)
785	Escalator clause (Table K11)
786	Revalorization of debts (Table K11)
787	Interest. Usury (Table K11)
	Including legal interest
	Cf. KDZ-KH2 1418 Marine interest
	Cf. KDZ-KH2 5624 Criminal law
	Breach of contract
791	General (Table K11)
792	Default of payment (mora) (Table K11)
	Cf. KDZ-KH2 1112+ Delay in performance of commercial sales
793	Warranty for eviction and redhibitory vices (Table K11)
	Cf. KDZ-KH2 871.W35 Warranty in sale
	Enforcement of performance through astreintes see KDZ-KH2 2693.5
	Liability for breach of contract. Damages
795	General (Table K11)
796	Dolus. Culpa (Table K11)
	Legal interest see KDZ-KH2 787
	Rescission see KDZ-KH2 807
	Dation in payment see KDZ-KH2 779
801	Accord and satisfaction (Compromise) (Table K11)
	Including compromise to prevent or to terminate a law suit
802	Set-off (Compensation) (Table K11)
803	Confusion of rights (Merger) (Table K11)
805	Remission of debts (Table K11)

Civil law
  Obligations
    Effects of obligations
      Effects of obligations between the parties
        Extinction of obligations. Discharge of contracts --
        Continued
806   Novation. Assignment of rights. Assumption of debts
                     (Table K11)
                     Cf. KDZ-KH2 1516.A85 Assignment for the benefit
                       of creditors
807   Cancellation. Rescission. Renunciation (Table K11)
                     Cf. KDZ-KH2 592 Abandonment of ownership
                     Cf. KDZ-KH2 713+ Renunciation of inheritance
809   Resolution. Occurrence of resolutory condition (Table
                     K11)
                     Including works on resolution and rescission combined
811   Arbitration agreement (Compromissum) (Table K11)
                     For arbitration clause see KDZ-KH2 838
                     For arbitration procedure see KDZ-KH2 2817
813   Supervening impossibility. Rebus sic stantibus (Table
                     K11)
                   Bankruptcy see KDZ-KH2 1471+
                   Extinctive prescription see KDZ-KH2 440.22+
        Effects of obligations as to third persons
816   General (Table K11)
                 Simulation see KDZ-KH2 430
                 Fraud against creditors. Fraudulent conveyances see
                   KDZ-KH2 1492
               Culpa in contrahendo see KDZ-KH2 858
             Nullity of obligations see KDZ-KH2 853+
           Contracts
822   General (Table K11)
824   Capacity to contract (Table K11)
825   Liberty of contract (Table K11)
                 Cf. KDZ-KH2 348.P35 Party autonomy
                 Cf. KDZ-KH2 855 Contracts against public policy
             Classification of contracts
827   General (Table K11)
827.2   Consensual and real contracts (Table K11)
827.4   Gratuitous and onerous contracts (Table K11)
                   Cf. KDZ-KH2 430 Simulation
                   Cf. KDZ-KH2 875 Gifts
                   Cf. KDZ-KH2 1492 Fraudulent conveyances
827.5   Atypical or mixed contracts. Innominate contracts (Table
                   K11)
             Formation of contract

KDZ-KH2

Civil law
Obligations
Contracts
Formation of contract -- Continued
830   General (Table K11)
832   Offer and acceptance (Table K11)
Cf. KDZ-KH2 421+ Intent. Declaration of intention
Cf. KDZ-KH2 953 Offer of reward
834   Causa. Consideration (Table K11)
835   Conditions (Table K11)
Cf. KDZ-KH2 809 Resolution. Resolutory condition
837   Standard clauses. Standard forms. Contracts by
adhesion (Table K11)
838   Arbitration clause (Table K11)
839   Penal clause. Liquidated damages (Table K11)
Cf. KDZ-KH2 2693.5 Astreintes
841   Limited liability clause (Table K11)
Cf. KDZ-KH2 1068 Limited liability of individual
merchants
843   Earnest (Table K11)
Valuta clause see KDZ-KH2 783
Gold clause see KDZ-KH2 784
Escalator clause see KDZ-KH2 785
844   Option (Table K11)
Warranties see KDZ-KH2 871.W35
845   Formalities (Table K11)
Parties to contract. Transfer of contracts
847   General (Table K11)
Joint obligations. Solidarity see KDZ-KH2 754
Assignment of rights see KDZ-KH2 806
850   Subrogation (Table K11)
851   Contracts in favor of third parties (Table K11)
Void and voidable contracts
853   General (Table K11)
Lack of genuine consent see KDZ-KH2 425+
854   Unlawful contracts (Table K11)
Cf. KDZ-KH2 787 Usury
855   Contracts against public policy (Table K11)
Including contracts in restraint of trade
856   Immoral contracts. Unconscionable contracts. Lesion
(Table K11)
Contracts intended to prejudice third persons see KDZ-
KH2 816+
Effects of nullity
857   General (Table K11)
Rescission see KDZ-KH2 807

	Civil law
	Obligations
	Contracts
	Void and voidable contracts
	Effects of nullity -- Continued
858	Culpa in contrahendo (Table K11)
	Class here works on loss suffered by relying upon the existence of a supposed agreement
860	Preliminary contract (Table K11)
	Cf. KDZ-KH2 845 Formalities
	Discharge of contracts see KDZ-KH2 770+
	Breach of contract see KDZ-KH2 791+
	Government contracts. Public contracts
	Including government purchasing and procurement
	Cf. KDZ-KH2 898.P82 Public works contracts
	Cf. KDZ-KH2 3757 Concessions
862	General (Table K11)
863	Municipal contracts (Table K11)
864.A-Z	Particular types of government contracts, A-Z
	Subarrange each by Table K12
864.C65	Computer contracts (Table K12)
865.A-Z	Special topics, A-Z
	Advertising see KDZ-KH2 865.P83
865.B73	Breach of contract (Table K12)
865.B89	Buy national (Table K12)
865.N84	Nullity of public contracts (Table K12)
865.P83	Publicity. Advertising (Table K12)
	Particular commercial contracts see KDZ-KH2 1098+
	Particular types of contracts
	Sale
	Cf. KDZ-KH2 1103+ Commercial sale
868	General (Table K11)
870.A-Z	Particular types of sale, A-Z
	Subarrange each by Table K12
	Conditional sale see KDZ-KH2 1114.C64
	Installment sale see KDZ-KH2 1114.C64
	Lease purchase see KDZ-KH2 1114.C64
870.P74	Preemption clause (Table K12)
870.R4	Real property sale (Table K12)
	Including auction sale of real property
870.R43	Redemption sale (Table K12)
870.R45	Restraint of alienation clause (Table K12)
	Sale by sample see KDZ-KH2 1114.S24
871.A-Z	Special topics, A-Z
	Subarrange each by Table K12
	Actio redhibitoria see KDZ-KH2 871.W35

	Civil law
	Obligations
	Contracts
	Particular types of contracts
	Sale
	Special topics, A-Z
871.D44	Delivery of goods (Table K12)
	Implied warranties see KDZ-KH2 871.W35
871.S24	Sale of another's property (Table K12)
871.W35	Warranties. Implied warranties. Actio redhibitoria (Table K12)
872	Barter (Table K12)
873	Aestimatum (Table K12)
	Cf. KDZ-KH2 1100+ Consignment of goods
875	Gifts (Table K12)
	For works on succession upon death and gifts combined see KDZ-KH2 670+
	Lease and hire
878	General (Table K11)
	Lease of things
879	General (Table K11)
	Lease of real property. Landlord and tenant
	Cf. KDZ-KH2 3810+ Land tenure
881	General (Table K11)
882.A-Z	Special topics, A-Z
	Subarrange each by Table K12
882.A85	Assignment of leases. Subleases (Table K12)
882.E94	Eviction of tenant (Table K12)
	Including summary proceedings
882.R44	Repairs (Table K12)
	Subleases see KDZ-KH2 882.A85
882.T45	Termination of lease (Table K12)
	Particular types of real property leases
	Farm tenancy. Rural partnerships see KDZ-KH2 3848+
	Urban leases
	Including leasing houses for habitation in general
884	General (Table K11)
885	Mixed leases (Table K11)
	Class here works on lease of real property for both habitation and trade or commerce
	Commercial leases see KDZ-KH2 1117+
887	Rent. Rent control (Table K11)
	Mining leases see KDZ-KH2 3952
	Oil and gas leases see KDZ-KH2 3979

	Civil law
	Obligations
	Contracts
	Particular types of contracts
	Lease and hire
	Lease of things -- Continued
888	Lease of personal property
	Cf. KDZ-KH2 907 Loans for use (commodatum)
	Contract of service. Contract for work and and labor
891	General (Table K11)
	Contract of service. Labor contract. Master and servant
	Cf. KDZ-KH2 1504.L32 Effect of bankruptcy on labor contracts
	Cf. KDZ-KH2 1860+ Labor standards
	Cf. KDZ-KH2 1943+ Protection of labor
	Cf. KDZ-KH2 1980+ Social insurance
	General see KDZ-KH2 893
	Individual labor contract
893	General (Table K11)
894.A-Z	Special topics, A-Z
	Subarrange each by Table K12
	Employee leasing see KDZ-KH2 894.S83
894.R45	Rescission of individual labor contract by reason of vis major (Table K12)
894.S83	Subcontracting. Employee leasing (Table K12)
894.T46	Temporary employment (Table K12)
895.A-Z	Particular groups of employees, A-Z
	Subarrange each by Table K12
895.A44	Alien labor (Table K12)
	Apprentices see KDZ-KH2 1949
	Commercial employees see KDZ-KH2 2008.C64
	Household employees see KDZ-KH2 895.S45
895.S45	Servants (Table K12)
	Cf. KDZ-KH2 1962.S45 Servants (Labor law)
	Collective labor agreements see KDZ-KH2 1830+
	Labor courts and procedure see KDZ-KH2 1840+
	Contract for work and labor. Independent contractor
896	General (Table K11)
897.A-Z	Special topics, A-Z
	Subarrange each by Table K12
897.M43	Mechanics' liens (Table K12)
897.S92	Subcontracting (Table K12)
898.A-Z	Particular types of contracts, A-Z

KDZ-KH2

Civil law
Obligations
Contracts
Particular types of contracts
Lease and hire
Contract of service. Contract for work and and labor
Contract for work and labor. Independent contractor
Particular types of contracts, A-Z -- Continued
898.B84   Building and construction (Table K12)
Cf. KDZ-KH2 897.M43 Mechanics' liens
Cf. KDZ-KH2 898.P82 Public works contracts
898.C66   Computer contracts (Table K12)
898.E43   Electric engineering (Table K12)
898.P82   Public works contracts (Table K12)
For railroad construction see KDZ-KH2 4206
898.T72   Transportation contracts (Table K12)
Including travel contracts and package tours
Contracts involving bailments
900   General (Table K11)
Deposit
902   General (Table K11)
Tender of payment and deposit see KDZ-KH2 776
Irregular deposits
Bank deposits see KDZ-KH2 1156+
Deposit of fungible goods in warehouses see KDZ-
KH2 1121+
Loans for consumption see KDZ-KH2 908+
Aestimatum see KDZ-KH2 873
Consignment of goods see KDZ-KH2 1100+
904   Innkeeper and guest. Innkeepers' liens (Table K11)
For regulation of hotel and restaurant trade see
KDZ-KH2 4103.H66
906   Civil carriers (Table K11)
Cf. KDZ-KH2 1195+ Commercial carriers
Cf. KDZ-KH2 1402+ Carriage by sea
907   Loans for use (commodatum) (Table K11)
Loans for consumption (mutuum)
Including loan of money
For commercial loans and credit see KDZ-KH2
1171+
908   General (Table K11)
Rules as to the payment of money debts see KDZ-
KH2 781+
Interest. Usury see KDZ-KH2 787
Pledge see KDZ-KH2 945+

Civil law
Obligations
Contracts
Particular types of contracts -- Continued
Associations
For business associations see KDZ-KH2 1295+
Cf. KDZ-KH2 466+ Juristic persons
915 General (Table K11)
Nonprofit associations
Class here purely civil associations, such as scientific,
literary, or moral associations, clubs, etc., the
common purpose of which is not predominantly
economic
917 General (Table K11)
918.A-Z Particular types of nonprofit associations, A-Z
Subarrange each by Table K12
Endowments. Foundations. Charitable trusts see
KDZ-KH2 472
Friendly societies see KDZ-KH2 1284
Labor unions see KDZ-KH2 1820+
Patriotic societies see KDZ-KH2 918.P82
Professional associations see KDZ-KH2 4442
918.P82 Publicly chartered associations. Patriotic societies
(Table K12)
Religious associations see KDZ-KH2 3034+
Partnerships. Civil companies
Class here only purely civil partnerships and civil
companies, the common purpose of which is
predominantly economic, such as agricultural
companies
For commercial partnerships and companies see
KDZ-KH2 1301+
921 General (Table K11)
923.A-Z Particular types, A-Z
Subarrange each by Table K12
Conjugal partnership see KDZ-KH2 504+
923.D43 De facto companies (Table K12)
Rural partnerships see KDZ-KH2 3848+
Mandate. Agency
Cf. KDZ-KH2 1098+ Commercial mandate
926 General (Table K11)
928.A-Z Special topics, A-Z
Subarrange each by Table K12
928.A25 Account, Duty to (Table K12)
Agency coupled with interest see KDZ-KH2 928.I75

KDZ-KH2

	Civil law
	Obligations
	Contracts
	Particular types of contracts
	Mandate. Agency
	Special topics, A-Z
928.A33	Agent of an undisclosed principal (Table K12)
	Cf. KDZ-KH2 1100+ Consignment of goods.
	Commission merchants
928.C64	Conflict of interests (Table K12)
	De facto officers see KDZ-KH2 928.O85
	Duty to account see KDZ-KH2 928.A25
	Effects of bankruptcy see KDZ-KH2 1504.M34
928.E94	Exceeding power. Ratification by principal (Table K12)
	Cf. KDZ-KH2 956 Negotiorum gestio
928.I75	Irrevocable mandate. Agency coupled with interest (Table K12)
928.O85	Ostensible agent. De facto officers (Table K12)
928.P67	Power of attorney (Table K12)
	Ratification see KDZ-KH2 928.E94
928.T45	Termination of mandate (Table K12)
	Undisclosed principal see KDZ-KH2 928.A33
	Negotiorum gestio see KDZ-KH2 956
	Aleatory contracts
931	General (Table K11)
932	Gambling. Wagering. Speculation (Table K11)
	Insurance see KDZ-KH2 1211+
	Marine insurance see KDZ-KH2 1428+
934	Life annuity contract (Table K11)
	Including life annuities constituted on real property
935	Purchase of hope (Table K11)
	Contango and backwardation see KDZ-KH2 1087.C64
	Security
937	General (Table K11)
	Suretyship. Guaranty
	Cf. KDZ-KH2 1274+ Suretyship insurance
	Cf. KDZ-KH2 1504.C62 Effect of bankruptcy
	obligations of codebtors and sureties
938	General (Table K11)
939	Bonding. Bail bonds (Table K11)
	Real rights of security
	Including real rights of guaranty on real and personal property combined
941	General (Table K11)
943	Transfer of ownership as security. Fiducia (Table K11)

Civil law
  Obligations
    Contracts
      Particular types of contracts
       Security
        Real rights of security
         Mortgages see KDZ-KH2 641+
         Antichresis see KDZ-KH2 644
         Mechanics' liens see KDZ-KH2 897.M43
         Pledge
          Including commercial pledge
          Cf. KDZ-KH2 4098.P37 Pawnbrokers

945	General (Table K11)
	Registered pledges
	General see KDZ-KH2 945
947	Industrial pledges (Table K11)
	Including industrial pledge bonds
	Aircraft mortgage see KDZ-KH2 1200.M65
	Ship mortgages see KDZ-KH2 1417+
	Agricultural pledges and liens see KDZ-KH2 3873.5
	Registration and register of pledges see KDZ-KH2 946.2+
951	Privileges. Liens. Right of retention (Table K11)

         Class particular kinds of privileges with the privileged
          credit and particular kinds of liens with the secured
          obligation, e.g. 723+, Privileged credits against
          decedents' estates; 904, Innkeepers' liens
        For privileges in bankruptcy see KDZ-KH2 1498+
       Accord and satisfaction (compromise) see KDZ-KH2 801

953	Obligations by unilateral declaration of intention. Offer of reward (Table K11)
	Quasi contracts. Restitution
955	General (Table K11)
956	Negotiorum gestio (Table K11)
	Unjust enrichment
957	General (Table K11)
958	Recovery of undue payment (Table K11)
	Civil liability see KDZ-KH2 767+
	Torts. Obligations from wrongful acts (Delicts and quasi delicts)
965	General (Table K11)
966	Privileges. Respondeat superior (Table K11)
967	Causality. Proximate cause (Table K11)
	Cf. KDZ-KH2 5437 Criminal law
	Particular torts

Civil law
  Obligations
    Torts. Obligations from wrongful acts (Delicts and quasi
      delicts)
      Particular torts -- Continued
        Torts in respect to the person
968   General (Table K11)
969   Personal injuries (Table K11)
970   Death by wrongful act (Table K11)
                  Violation of privacy
971   General (Table K11)
972.A-Z   Special topics, A-Z
                    Subarrange each by Table K12
972.L46   Violation of the privacy of letters (Table K12)
                        Cf. KDZ-KH2 5582 Criminal law
972.U5   Unauthorized publication of picture (Table K12)
                  Torts in respect to honor and reputation
974   Libel and slander
                    Cf. KDZ-KH2 5591+ Libel and slander (Criminal law)
974.5   Torts in respect to domestic relations (Table K11)
975   Abuse of rights (Table K11)
976   Abuse of legal process. Chicanery (Table K11)
977   Malicious prosecution (Table K11)
                Fraud (Defects of juristic acts) see KDZ-KH2 428
                Fraud (Criminal law) see KDZ-KH2 5613+
                Unfair competition see KDZ-KH2 1675+
979   Torts affecting property (Table K11)
                    For slander of title see KDZ-KH2 2830
                Negligence
981   General (Table K11)
982   Contributory negligence (Table K11)
                  Liability for condition and use of land, buildings, and
                    other structures
984   General (Table K11)
985   Building accidents (Table K11)
987   Malpractice. Professional liability (Table K11)
                      For malpractice and professional liability of particular
                        professions, see the profession, e.g. KDZ-KH2
                        4447.M34 , Medical malpractice
988.A-Z   Particular types of accidents, A-Z
                    Subarrange each by Table K12
988.A94   Automobile accidents (Table K12)
988.A96   Aviation accidents (Table K12)
                      Cf. KDZ-KH2 4276+ Liability of common air
                        carriers
                  Building accidents see KDZ-KH2 985

Civil law
Obligations
Torts. Obligations from wrongful acts (Delicts and quasi delicts)
Particular torts
Negligence
Particular types of accidents, A-Z -- Continued
Marine accidents see KDZ-KH2 1424

988.S67	Sports accidents (Table K12)
	Cf. KDZ-KH2 5535 Criminal law
	Strict liability. Liability without fault
990	General (Table K11)
991	Damage caused by animals (Table K11)
992.A-Z	Ultrahazardous activities or occupations. By risk A-Z
	Subarrange each by Table K12
993	Products liability (Table K11)
	Cf. KDZ-KH2 3503+ Product safety
993.5	Liability for environmental damages (Table K11)
	Parties to actions in tort
	Juristic persons. Corporations
994	General (Table K11)
995	Municipal corporations (Table K11)
996	Nonprofit corporations (Table K11)
998	Public officials and government employees (Table K11)
999	Joint tortfeasors (Table K11)
	Liability for the torts of others. Vicarious liability
1002	General (Table K11)
	Employers' liability
1004	General (Table K11)
1005.A-Z	Particular groups of employees and industries, A-Z
	Subarrange each by Table K12
1007	Government torts (Table K12)
	Remedies. Damages for torts
1008	General (Table K11)
1009	Compensation for moral damage (Table K11)
1011	Compensation to victims of crimes. Reparation (Table K11)
	Cf. KDZ-KH2 5482 Reparation through criminal sentence
	Civil insolvency see KDZ-KH2 1520+
	Commercial law
	For works on diverse laws in matters affecting business see KDZ-KH2 333.B86
1050	History
1051-1059	General (Table K9b)
1062	Usage of trade (Table K11)

KDZ-KH2

	Commercial law -- Continued
1063	Commercial acts and transactions in general (Table K11)
	Commercial courts and procedure see KDZ-KH2 1530+
	Merchants
1065	General (Table K11)
1067	Capacity to carry on commerce (Table K11)
	Including provisions authorizing married women and minors to trade
1068	Limited liability of individual merchants (Table K11)
	Business associations see KDZ-KH2 1295+
	Business enterprises. Fondo de comercio
1069	General (Table K11)
1070	Goodwill (Table K11)
1071	Business names (Table K11)
	Trademarks see KDZ-KH2 1670+
	Commercial leases see KDZ-KH2 1117+
1073	Transfer of business enterprises (Table K11)
	Registration see KDZ-KH2 1076
	Obligations of merchants
1075	General (Table K11)
1076	Registration. Commercial registers (Table K11)
1077	Commercial bookkeeping. Accounting. Business records (Table K11)
1078	Mandatory publications and announcements (Table K11)
	Including notices, legal advertising, etc.
	Auxiliaries and intermediaries of commerce
1081	Boards of trade
	Stock and commodity exchanges
1082	General (Table K11)
	Stock exchanges
1083	General (Table K11)
1084	Stockbrokers (Table K11)
1085.A-Z	Particular stock exchanges, A-Z
	Subarrange each by Table K12
	Stock exchange transactions. Marketing of securities
1086	General (Table K11)
1087.A-Z	Particular types of transactions, A-Z
	Subarrange each by Table K12
1087.C64	Contango and backwardation (Table K12)
1089	Commodity exchanges (Table K11)
	Independent commercial agents and middlemen
	Brokers
1091	General (Table K11)
	Stockbrokers see KDZ-KH2 1084
	Insurance brokers see KDZ-KH2 1222
	Shipbrokers see KDZ-KH2 1409+

	Commercial law
	Auxiliaries and intermediaries of commerce
	Independent commercial agents and middlement
	Brokers
	Customhouse brokers see KDZ-KH2 4821.5
1093	Commercial travelers. Traveling sales personnel (Table K11)
	Ocean freight forwarders see KDZ-KH2 4339
	Freight forwarders see KDZ-KH2 4368
1095	Auctioneers. Auction houses (Table K11)
	Including auction sales in general
	For auction sale of particular types of property, see the sale of such property, e.g. KDZ-KH2 870.R4 , Sale of real property; KDZ-KH2 1115.C36 , Cattle sale
	Cf. KDZ-KH2 2692 Judicial sale
	Commission merchants see KDZ-KH2 1100+
	Carriers see KDZ-KH2 1195+
	Warehousemen see KDZ-KH2 1121+
1096	Managers and commercial employees (Table K11)
	Commercial contracts
	General see KDZ-KH2 1051+
	Commercial mandate and consignment
	For effect of bankruptcy on commercial mandates see KDZ-KH2 1504.M34
1098	General (Table K11)
	Consignment of goods. Commission merchants
	Cf. KDZ-KH2 873 Aestimatum
1100	General (Table K11)
1102	Del credere (Table K11)
	Managers and commercial employees see KDZ-KH2 1096
	Commercial sale
1103	General (Table K11)
1104.A-Z	Special topics, A-Z
	Subarrange each by Table K12
	Implied warranties see KDZ-KH2 1104.W35
1104.W35	Warranties. Implied warranties (Table K12)
	Including warranties for eviction and redhibitory vices
1106.A-Z	Documents of title, A-Z
	Subarrange each by Table K12
1106.B54	Bills of lading (Table K12)
	Cf. KDZ-KH2 1414 Ocean bills of lading
1106.B55	Bills of sale (Table K12)
	Invoices see KDZ-KH2 1138
1106.W35	Warehouse receipts (Table K12)
	Performance
1108	General (Table K11)

KDZ-KH2

	Commercial law
	Commercial contracts
	Commercial sale
	Performance -- Continued
1110	Overseas sale. C.I.F. clause. F.O.B. clause (Table K11)
	Delay
1112	General (Table K11)
1112.5	Delay of purchaser (Table K11)
1114.A-Z	Particular types of sale, A-Z
	Subarrange each by Table K12
	Cf. KDZ-KH2 870.A+ Particular types of civil law sale
1114.C64	Conditional sale. Installment sale. Lease purchase (Table K12)
	Installment sale see KDZ-KH2 1114.C64
	Lease purchase see KDZ-KH2 1114.C64
1114.S24	Sale by sample (Table K12)
1115.A-Z	Sale of particular kinds of property, A-Z
	Subarrange each by Table K12
	Including their sale on public auction
1115.C36	Cattle sale (Table K12)
	Commercial leases
	Including both real and personal property
1117	General (Table K11)
1119.A-Z	Special topics, A-Z
	Subarrange each by Table K12
1119.I53	Industrial equipment leases (Table K12)
1119.R54	Right of renewal (Table K12)
	Deposit of goods. Warehouses
	For warehouse receipts see KDZ-KH2 1106.W35
	For warehouse regulations see KDZ-KH2 4110
	Cf. KDZ-KH2 1159 Deposit banking
1121	General (Table K11)
1123	Safe-deposit companies (Table K11)
	Innkeeper and guest. Innkeepers' liens see KDZ-KH2 904
	Consignment of goods see KDZ-KH2 1100+
	Negotiable instruments. Titles of credit
	Including commercial instruments and documents
	Cf. KDZ-KH2 1159 Deposit banking
1130	General (Table K11)
1132.A-Z	Special topics, A-Z
	Subarrange each by Table K12
1132.A23	Accommodation indorsement. Guaranty. Aval (Table K12)
1132.A25	Actions and defenses. Exceptions (Table K12)
	Aval see KDZ-KH2 1132.A23
1132.C34	Cancellation (Table K12)

158

Commercial law
  Commercial contracts
    Negotiable instruments. Titles of credit
      Special topics, A-Z -- Continued

1132.D84	Duplicates (Table K12)
	Guaranty see KDZ-KH2 1132.A23
1132.I53	Indorsement (Table K12)
	For accommodation indorsement see KDZ-KH2 1132.A23
1132.L65	Lost, destroyed, and stolen negotiable instruments (Table K12)
1132.P73	Presumptions relating to negotiable instruments (Table K12)

     Particular kinds of negotiable instruments
      Bills of exchange

1133	General (Table K11)
1133.5	Documentary bills and credit (Table K11)
1134.A-Z	Special topics, A-Z
	Subarrange each by Table K12
1134.A25	Actions and defenses. Exceptions (Table K12)
	Effects of bankruptcy see KDZ-KH2 1504.B54
	Exceptions see KDZ-KH2 1134.A25
1134.P73	Extinctive prescription (Table K12)
1134.P75	Protest. Waiver of protest (Table K12)
	Waiver of protest see KDZ-KH2 1134.P75
1135	Promissory notes (Table K11)

      Checks

1136	General (Table K11)
1137.A-Z	Special topics, A-Z
	Subarrange each by Table K12
	Alteration see KDZ-KH2 1137.F65
1137.B34	Banker's checks (Table K12)
1137.C45	Certified checks (Table K12)
1137.F65	Forged checks. Alteration (Table K12)
	Cf. KDZ-KH2 5616 Criminal law
1137.T7	Travelers' checks (Table K12)
	Accounts current see KDZ-KH2 1160
1138	Invoices. Conformed invoices (Table K11)
	Industrial pledge bonds see KDZ-KH2 947
	Bills of lading see KDZ-KH2 1106.B55
	Warehouse receipts see KDZ-KH2 1106.W35
	Corporate securities see KDZ-KH2 1357+
	Ocean bills of lading see KDZ-KH2 1414

    Banking

1141-1149	General (Table K9b)
1151	Management. Directors (Table K11)

KDZ-KH2

	Commercial law
	Commercial contracts
	Banking -- Continued
1152	State supervision (Table K11)
	Particular types of banks and credit institutions
1153	National banks. Central banks. Banks of issue (Table K11)
1154.A-Z	Other banks, credit and savings institutions, A-Z
	Subarrange each by Table K12
1154.A34	Agricultural banks (Table K12)
	Cf. KDZ-KH2 3873+ Farm loans
1154.A35	Agricultural cooperative credit associations (Table K12)
1154.B84	Building and loan associations (Table K12)
1154.C34	Capitalization companies (Table K12)
	Clearinghouses see KDZ-KH2 1169
1154.C64	Cooperative banks. Credit unions (Table K12)
	For agricultural cooperative credit associations see KDZ-KH2 1154.A35
	Credit unions see KDZ-KH2 1154.C64
	Development banks see KDZ-KH2 4572
1154.F65	Foreign banks (Table K12)
1154.I57	Investment banks (Table K12)
1154.M54	Mining banks (Table K12)
1154.M65	Mortgage loan banks (Table K12)
	Safe deposit companies see KDZ-KH2 1123
1154.S27	Savings banks (Table K12)
1154.S7	State and provincial banks (Table K12)
	Trust companies see KDZ-KH2 661
	Particular banking transactions
	Bank deposits
1156	General (Table K11)
1157	Deposit insurance (Table K11)
1157.5	Savings accounts (Table K11)
1159	Deposit banking. Custodianship accounts (Table K11)
1159.5	Discount (Table K11)
1160	Accounts current (Table K11)
	Including both banker's and other accounts current
	Bank loans. Bank credit
1162	General (Table K11)
1164.A-Z	Particular kinds, A-Z
	Subarrange each by Table K12
1164.L46	Letters of credit (Table K12)
1166.A-Z	Special topics, A-Z
1166.L52	Liability (Table K12)
1166.R47	Reserves. Specie (Table K12)
1166.S42	Secrecy, Bank (Table K12)

	Commercial law
	Commercial contracts
	Banking
	Special topics, A-Z -- Continued
	Specie see KDZ-KH2 1166.R47
1167.A-Z	Particular banks, A-Z
	Subarrange each by Table K12
	Auxiliary credit organizations
1169	Clearinghouses (Table K11)
	General deposit warehouses see KDZ-KH2 1121+
	Stock and commodity exchanges see KDZ-KH2 1082+
	Commercial loans and credit
	For debtor and creditor in general see KDZ-KH2 745+
	Cf. KDZ-KH2 781+ Payment of money debts
	Cf. KDZ-KH2 1130+ Negotiable instruments. Titles of
	credit
1171	General (Table K11)
	Interest. Usury see KDZ-KH2 787
1172.A-Z	Particular kinds of loans and credits, A-Z
	Subarrange each by Table K12
	Agricultural credit. Farm loans see KDZ-KH2 3873+
	Bank loans. Bank credit see KDZ-KH2 1162+
1172.C64	Consumer credit. Small loans. Credit cards (Table K12)
	Credit cards see KDZ-KH2 1172.C64
	Small loans see KDZ-KH2 1172.C64
	Cf. KDZ-KH2 4098.P37 Pawnbrokers
1174	Suretyship. Guaranty (Table K11)
	Cf. KDZ-KH2 938+ Suretyship and guaranty (Civil law)
	Cf. KDZ-KH2 1274+ Suretyship insurance
	Cf. KDZ-KH2 1504.C62 Effect of bankruptcy on
	obligations of codebtors and sureties
	Pledge see KDZ-KH2 945+
	Investments
1186	General (Table K11)
	Foreign investments see KDZ-KH2 3725
	Stock exchanges. Marketing of securities see KDZ-KH2
	1083+
	Issuing of securities see KDZ-KH2 1339+
1188	Investment trusts. Investment companies (Table K11)
	Carriers. Carriage of goods and passengers
1195	General (Table K11)
	Forwarding agents. Freight forwarders see KDZ-KH2 4368
1196	Carriage by land and inland waterways (Table K11)
	For motor carriers see KDZ-KH2 4187
	For railroads see KDZ-KH2 4200+

KDZ-KH2

	Commercial law
	Commercial contracts
	Carriers. Carriage of goods and passengers -- Continued
	Carriage by air
	Cf. KDZ-KH2 4265+ Regulation of commercial aviation
1198	General (Table K11)
1200.A-Z	Special topics, A-Z
	Subarrange each by Table K12
1200.A36	Air consignment notes (Table K12)
1200.M65	Aircraft mortgages (Table K12)
	Carriage by sea see KDZ-KH2 1402+
	Insurance
	Including regulation of insurance business
1211-1219	General (Table K9b)
1222	Insurance business. Agents. Insurance brokers (Table K11)
1224	Foreign insurance companies (Table K11)
1225	State supervision (Table K11)
	Insurance contract. Insurance policies
1227	General (Table K11)
1228	Risk (Table K11)
1229	Insurance fraud (Table K11)
	Including false statements and withholding essential information
	Cf. KDZ-KH2 5615 Insurance fraud (Criminal law)
	Particular branches
	Personal insurance
	Life
1231	General (Table K11)
1233	Life insurance companies. Finance. Investment of funds (Table K11)
1234.A-Z	Particular plans and modes of payment, A-Z
	Subarrange each by Table K12
1234.G75	Group life (Table K12)
1234.I52	Industrial insurance (Table K12)
1241	Health. Medical care (Table K11)
	Accident
1243	General (Table K11)
1245	Travelers' insurance (Table K11)
1246	Business insurance (Table K11)
	Property insurance
1247	General (Table K11)
1249	Transfer, assignment, and succession of insurance policy (Table K11)
1250	Subrogation (Table K11)
	Transportation insurance

	Commercial law
	Commercial contracts
	Insurance
	Particular branches
	Property insurance
	Transportation insurance -- Continued
1252	General (Table K11)
	Ocean marine insurance see KDZ-KH2 1428+
	Inland marine insurance see KDZ-KH2 1430
1254	Aviation insurance (Table K11)
1256	Fire (Table K11)
1258.A-Z	Other hazards, A-Z
	Subarrange each by Table K12
1258.B86	Business interruption (Table K12)
	Particular kinds of property
	Agricultural
1259	General (Table K11)
1260	Crops (Table K11)
1261	Livestock (Table K11)
	Bank deposit insurance see KDZ-KH2 1156+
1263	Motor vehicles (Table K11)
	Casualty insurance
1268	General liability (Table K11)
	Particular risks
	Automobile
1270	General (Table K11)
	Safety responsibility. Financial reponsibility laws.
	Compulsory insurance see KDZ-KH2 4175
1271.A-Z	Other, A-Z
	Subarrange each by Table K12
1271.E46	Employers' liability insurance (Table K12)
1271.M35	Malpractice (Table K12)
	Surety and fidelity insurance
	For contracts of suretyship and guaranty see KDZ-KH2 938+
1274	General (Table K11)
1276	Bonding (Table K11)
	Guaranty
1278	General (Table K11)
	Bank deposit insurance see KDZ-KH2 1156+
1279	Credit insurance (Table K11)
1280	Mortgage guaranty insurance (Table K11)
1282	Reinsurance (Table K11)
1284	Fraternal insurance. Friendly societies (Table K11)
	Business associations. Commercial companies
	Including partnerships and incorporated companies

KDZ-KH2

	Commercial law
	Commercial contracts
	Business associations. Commercial companies -- Continued
1295	General (Table K11)
1298.A-Z	Special topics, A-Z
	Subarrange each by Table K12
	Accounting see KDZ-KH2 1077
	Antitrust laws see KDZ-KH2 3758
	Corporate accounting see KDZ-KH2 1346
1298.D57	Dissolution. Liquidation (Table K12)
1298.F65	Foreign business associations (Table K12)
	Cf. KDZ-KH2 1362 Foreign corporations
	Liquidation see KDZ-KH2 1298.D57
	Multinational business enterprises see KDZ-KH2 1363
1298.R42	Receivership (Table K12)
	Partnerships
1301	General (Table K11)
	General partnership
1302	General (Table K11)
1304.A-Z	Special topics, A-Z
	Subarrange each by Table K12
1304.D56	Dissolution. Liquidation (Table K12)
	Liquidation see KDZ-KH2 1304.D56
	Limited partnership. Simple limited partnership
1305	General (Table K11)
1306	Stock-issuing partnership (Table K11)
1306.5	Partnership of capital and industry (Table K11)
1307	Joint ventures (Table K11)
	Limited liability companies. Private companies
1308	General (Table K11)
1309.A-Z	Special topics, A-Z
	Subarrange each by Table K12
1309.A25	Accounting. Auditing (Table K12)
	Auditing see KDZ-KH2 1309.A25
	Business corporations
	Cf. KDZ-KH2 466+ Juristic persons
1311-1319	General (Table K9b)
1321	Special aspects
	e.g. Business corporations and the stock-exchange
1323	Government regulation and control. Licensing (Table K11)
	Foreign corporations. Nationality of corporations see KDZ-KH2 1362
1325	Incorporation. Promoters (Table K11)
	Including prospectus, stock subscription, corporate charters and bylaws

Commercial law
Commercial contracts
Business associations. Commercial companies
Business corporations -- Continued

1327	Nullity of corporation (Table K11)
	Management
1330	General (Table K11)
1331	Board of directors. Officers (Table K11)

Including executives in general
Cf. KDZ-KH2 928.O85 De facto officers

1332	Supervisors. Auditors (Table K11)

Cf. KDZ-KH2 1346 Auditing

1333	Corporate legal departments (Table K11)
	Corporate finance

Including capital and dividends

1337	General (Table K11)
	Issuing and sale of securities in general

For works on stock exchange transactions see
KDZ-KH2 1086+

1339	General (Table K11)
1341	Common stock (Table K11)
	Preferred stock see KDZ-KH2 1357+
	Loaned capital see KDZ-KH2 1357+
1343	Corporate reserves (Table K11)
1346	Accounting. Auditing. Financial statements (Table K11)

Cf. KDZ-KH2 1332 Supervisors. Auditors

Shares and shareholders' rights. Stock transfers

1348	General (Table K11)
	Stockholders' meetings
1350	General (Table K11)
1351	Proxy rules (Table K11)
1352	Voting trusts (Table K11)
1354	Minority stockholders (Table K11)
1356	Stock transfers (Table K11)
	Debentures. Bonds. Preferred stock
1357	General (Table K11)
1358.A-Z	Special kinds, A-Z

Subarrange each by Table K12

1358.M65	Mortgage bonds (Table K12)

Effect of bankruptcy on debentures see KDZ-KH2
1504.D43
Particular types of corporations

1362	Foreign corporations (Table K11)

Including works on nationality of corporations

KDZ-KH2

Commercial law
Commercial contracts
Business associations. Commercial companies
Business corporations
Particular types of corporations -- Continued
1363   Multinational corporations. Multinational business
enterprises (Table K11)
1364   Subsidiary and parent corporations. Holding
companies (Table K11)
1366   Cartels and other combinations (Table K11)
Cf. KDZ-KH2 3758 Antitrust aspects
Private companies see KDZ-KH2 1308+
Government-owned corporations see KDZ-KH2 1377+
Public-private corporations (Mixed companies) see
KDZ-KH2 1378
1368   One-person companies (Table K11)
Cooperative societies
1370   General (Table K11)
Agricultural cooperative credit associations see KDZ-
KH2 1154.A35
Farm producers' and marketing cooperatives see
KDZ-KH2 3866
Farm corporations see KDZ-KH2 3865
Mining corporations see KDZ-KH2 3949+
Public utility corporations see KDZ-KH2 4120+
1372   Dissolution. Liquidation
1373   Consolidation and merger
Cf. KDZ-KH2 3758 Antitrust legislation
Corporate reorganization see KDZ-KH2 1512+
Government-based corporations and other business
organizations
Including government monopolies in general
For government petroleum monopoly see KDZ-KH2
3987
1377   General (Table K11)
1378   Public-private corporations (Mixed companies) (Table
K11)
Municipal corporations see KDZ-KH2 3182+
Maritime law
Including carriage by sea, marine insurance and maritime social
legislation
For administrative regulations see KDZ-KH2 4300+
1400   General (Table K11)
Carriage by sea. Maritime commercial law. Admiralty
1402   History
1403   General (Table K11)

Commercial law
 Maritime law
  Carriage by sea. Maritime commercial law. Admiralty --
   Continued
1404   Admiralty courts and proceedings (Table K11)
        Ships
         For registration, safety regulations, etc. see KDZ-KH2
          4304
1406   General (Table K11)
1407   Ownership. Transfer (Table K11)
        Shipowners and their agents
         Including captains, shipmasters, ship's husbands,
          shipbrokers, etc.
1409   General (Table K11)
1410   Merchant mariners's contracts (Table K11)
          Including works on legal status of officers and merchant
           mariners
          Cf. KDZ-KH2 1433+ Maritime social legislation
          Cf. KDZ-KH2 4335 Officers' examinations,
           qualification, promotion, etc.
        Carriage of goods. Affreightment
1413   General (Table K11)
1414   Ocean bills of lading (Table K11)
1415   Charter parties (Table K11)
        C.I.F. and F.O.B. clauses see KDZ-KH2 1110
        Maritime loans, credits, and security
1416   General (Table K11)
         Ship mortgages. Maritime liens
          Including enforcement of maritime claims
          Cf. KDZ-KH2 4304 Ship registers
1417   General (Table K11)
1418   Bottomry and respondentia (Table K11)
           Including marine interest
1419   Privileged maritime credits. Maritime liens (Table
            K11)
            Cf. KDZ-KH2 1437.W34 Privileges and liens
             securing wages of mariners
            Cf. KDZ-KH2 1499.M35 Privileged maritime
             credits and liens in bankruptcy
         Arrest of ships see KDZ-KH2 1426.A75
1421   Carriage of passengers
           Including carriage of passengers' luggage
        Risk and damages in maritime commerce
1423   General (Table K11)
1424   Maritime torts. Collision at sea (Table K11)

	Commercial law
	Maritime law
	Risk and damages in maritime commerce -- Continued
1425	Average (Table K11)
	Cf. KDZ-KH2 1428+ Marine insurance
1426.A-Z	Special topics, A-Z
	Subarrange each by Table K12
1426.A2	Abandonment (Table K12)
1426.A75	Arrest of ships (Table K12)
1426.A83	Assistance and salvage at sea. Wreck (Table K12)
1426.B35	Barratry (Table K12)
	Charter parties see KDZ-KH2 1415
	Effect of bankruptcy on maritime claims see KDZ-KH2 1499.M35
	Salvage see KDZ-KH2 1426.A83
1426.T67	Towage (Table K12)
	War risk see KDZ-KH2 1429
	Wreck see KDZ-KH2 1426.A83
	Marine insurance
	Including inland marine insurance
1428	General (Table K11)
	Average see KDZ-KH2 1425
	Barratry see KDZ-KH2 1426.B35
	Abandonment see KDZ-KH2 1426.A2
1429	War risk (Table K11)
1430	Inland marine insurance (Table K11)
	Maritime social legislation
1433	General (Table K11)
	Maritime labor law. Merchant mariners
1434	General (Table K11)
	Legal status of mariners see KDZ-KH2 1410
	Labor standards
1436	General (Table K11)
1437.A-Z	Special topics, A-Z
	Subarrange each by Table K12
1437.W34	Wages (Table K12)
	Including privileges and liens securing wages
	For wages of mariners as privileged credit in bankruptcy see KDZ-KH2 1499.M35
1439	Protection of labor. Labor hygiene and safety (Table K11)
	Maritime social insurance
1441	General (Table K11)
1443	Health insurance (Table K11)
	Workers' compensation
1444	General (Table K11)

	Commercial law
	Maritime law
	Maritime social legislation
	Maritime social insurance
	Workers' compensation -- Continued
1446	Labor accidents. Occupational diseases (Table K11)
1448	Social security. Retirement (Table K11)
	Insolvency and bankruptcy. Creditors' rights
1470	History
	General see KDZ-KH2 1471+
	Bankruptcy
	Including works on commercial bankruptcy and civil insolvency combined
	For civil insolvency see KDZ-KH2 1520+
1471-1479	General (Table K9b)
1482	Bankruptcy courts and procedure (Table K11)
1486	Creditors' meeting (Table K11)
1488	Receivers in bankruptcy. Inspectors. Syndics (Table K11)
	The estate in bankruptcy
1490	General (Table K11)
	Avoidance of transfers
	Including actions to recover assets for the estate and to enforce demands of estate
1491	General (Table K11)
1492	Fraudulent sales and conveyances. Actio Pauliana (Table K11)
	Property not included in the bankrupt estate
	Including right of creditors to rescind onerous contracts
1494	General (Table K11)
1494.4	Revendication of property from the bankrupt estate (Table K11)
1494.6	Exempted property (Table K11)
	Priority of credits
1497	General (Table K11)
	Secured and privileged credits
	Including credits secured by mortgage, pledge or liens
1498	General (Table K11)
1499.A-Z	Particular secured and privileged credits, A-Z
	Subarrange each by Table K12
	Including credits preferred on special real or personal property, or both
1499.C65	Costs and fees of bankruptcy proceedings (Table K12)
	Including costs of preservation and liquidation of assets
	Costs in inheritance proceedings see KDZ-KH2 723+
1499.M35	Maritime privileges (Table K12)

KDZ-KH2

Commercial law
  Insolvency and bankruptcy. Creditors' rights
    Bankruptcy
      Priority of credits
        Secured and privileged credits
          Particular secured and privileged credits, A-Z --
            Continued
            Salaries see KDZ-KH2 1499.W34
1499.T38   Taxes and other public debts (Table K12)
1499.W34   Wages. Salaries (Table K12)
            Wages of mariners see KDZ-KH2 1499.M35
1502   Composition to avoid bankruptcy (Table K11)
              For other means of debtors' relief see KDZ-KH2 1510+
1504.A-Z   Effect of bankruptcy on particular types of persons and
              legal relationships, A-Z
              Subarrange each by Table K12
            Bankruptcy of decedents' estates see KDZ-KH2 1504.I53
1504.B54   Bills of exchange (Table K12)
1504.C62   Codebtors and sureties (Table K12)
            Commercial agency see KDZ-KH2 1504.M34
1504.C64   Contracts and other obligations (Table K12)
1504.D43   Debentures (Table K12)
1504.I53   Inheritance and succession. Bankruptcy of decedents'
              estates (Table K12)
1504.L32   Labor contracts (Table K12)
1504.M34   Mandate. Commercial agency (Table K12)
            Maritime privileges see KDZ-KH2 1499.M35
        Types of bankruptcy
1506   General (Table K11)
1507   Culpable and fraudulent bankruptcies (Table K11)
                Cf. KDZ-KH2 1492 Fraudulent sales and
                  conveyances. Actio Pauliana
                Cf. KDZ-KH2 5618 Criminal provisions
    Debtors' relief
1510   General (Table K11)
          Composition see KDZ-KH2 1502
          Corporate reorganization
1512   General (Table K11)
1514.A-Z   Particular types of corporations or lines of business, A-Z
                Subarrange each by Table K12
1516.A-Z   Other forms of debt relief, A-Z
                Subarrange each by Table K12
1516.A85   Assignment for the benefit of creditors (Table K12)
1516.J82   Judicial liquidation. Liquidation without bankruptcy
                (Table K12)
            Liquidation without bankruptcy see KDZ-KH2 1516.J82

	Commercial law
	Insolvency and bankruptcy. Creditors' rights
	Debtors' relief
	Other forms of debt relief
1516.M65	Moratorium (Table K12)
	Cf. KDZ-KH2 4960.D42 War and emergency legislation
	Civil insolvency
	Class here works on insolvency against non-merchants
1520	General (Table K11)
1522.A-Z	Special topics, A-Z
	Subarrange each by Table K12
1522.P74	Prescription (Table K12)
	Commercial courts and procedure
	Cf. KDZ-KH2 2817 Commercial arbitration
1530	General (Table K11)
1531	Commercial courts (Table K11)
	Commercial procedure
	For works on civil and commercial procedure combined see KDZ-KH2 2571+
1533	General (Table K11)
	Intellectual property
1570	General (Table K11)
	Copyright
1571-1579	General (Table K9b)
1584	Formalities. Administration (Table K11)
	Scope of protection
1587	Duration and renewal (Table K11)
1588	Moral rights (Table K11)
1590	Employees' copyright (Table K11)
	Including government employees
	Literary copyright. Authorship
1595	General (Table K11)
	Protected works
1596	General (Table K11)
1596.5.A-Z	Particular types of works, A-Z
	Subarrange each by Table K12
1596.5.C65	Computer programs (Table K12)
1596.5.T55	Titles (Table K12)
	Scope of protection
	General works see KDZ-KH2 1595
1597	Performing rights (Table K11)
1597.3	Broadcasting rights (Table K11)
1597.6	Filming (Table K11)
1597.65	Adaptation (Table K11)
1597.7	Translation (Table K11)

	Intellectual property
	Copyright
	Literary copyright. Authorship
	Scope of protection -- Continued
1597.95	Other special topics (not A-Z)
1599	Duration (Table K11)
	Musical copyright
1601	General (Table K11)
	Protected works
1602	General (Table K11)
1602.5.A-Z	Particular types of works, A-Z
	Subarrange each by Table K12
1602.5.C65	Computer programs (Table K12)
1602.5.T55	Titles (Table K12)
	Scope of protection
	General works see KDZ-KH2 1601
1603	Performing rights (Table K11)
1603.3	Broadcasting rights (Table K11)
1603.6	Filming (Table K11)
1603.65	Adaptation (Table K11)
1603.7	Translation (Table K11)
1603.95	Other special topics (not A-Z)
	Works of art and photography
1605	General (Table K11)
1607	Designs and models (Table K11)
1608	Works of photography (Table K11)
1610	Motion pictures (Table K11)
	Quasi copyright. Neighboring rights
1612	General (Table K11)
1613	Performing artists (Table K11)
	Infringement. Plagiarism. Litigation. Criminal protection
	Including works on infringement, etc. on diverse types of
	intellectual property (e.g. copyright and patent) combined
1614	General (Table K11)
1615	Plagiarism (Table K11)
1618	Author and publisher. The publishing contract (Table K11)
1620	Design protection (Table K11)
	Cf. KDZ-KH2 1607 Design copyright
	Cf. KDZ-KH2 1654 Design patent
	Industrial property
1629	General (Table K11)
	Patent law
1631-1639	General (Table K9b)
1641	Relationship to antitrust laws (Table K11)
1644	Administrative organization. Patent office (Table K11)
1645	Procedure (Table K11)

KDZ-KH2

	Social legislation
	Labor law -- Continued
	Labor courts see KDZ-KH2 1840+
	Labor contract
	General see KDZ-KH2 893+
	Individual labor contract see KDZ-KH2 893+
	Collective labor agreements see KDZ-KH2 1830+
	Alien labor see KDZ-KH2 1962.A44
	Management-labor relations
1810	General (Table K11)
1813	Employers' associations (Table K11)
	Labor unions
1820	General (Table K11)
	Union security
1821	General (Table K11)
1822	Open and closed shop (Table K11)
1825	Union organization (Table K11)
	Collective bargaining. Collective labor agreements
1830	General (Table K11)
	Particular clauses and benefits
	see the subject
1832.A-Z	Particular industries, occupations, and groups of employees, A-Z
	Subarrange each by Table K12
1832.A34	Agricultural laborers (Table K12)
1832.B34	Bank employees (Table K12)
1832.C63	Construction industry (Table K12)
1832.C64	Copper mines and mining (Table K12)
1832.D77	Drug trade (Table K12)
1832.H66	Hotel and restaurant employees (Table K12)
1832.M4	Meat industry (Table K12)
1832.M54	Mining and mineral industries (Table K12)
1832.P47	Petroleum industry (Table K12)
1832.R34	Railways (Table K12)
1832.S34	School employees (Table K12)
	Collective labor disputes
1836	General (Table K11)
1838	Arbitration. Conciliation (Table K11)
	Labor courts and procedure
	Including proceedings in noncollective labor controversies
1840	General (Table K11)
1841.A-Z	Special topics, A-Z
	Subarrange each by Table K12
1841.A66	Appellate procedure (Table K12)
	Citation see KDZ-KH2 1841.S94

Social legisltation
Labor law
Management-labor relations
Labor unions
Collective labor disputes
Labor courts and procedure
Special topics, A-Z -- Continued
Citizen suits see KDZ-KH2 1841.C55
1841.C55   Class action. Citizen suits (Table K12)
1841.C67   Costs. Fees (Table K12)
1841.E93   Evidence (Table K12)
1841.E97   Exceptions (Table K12)
1841.E98   Execution (Table K12)
Fees see KDZ-KH2 1841.C67
1841.J82   Judgments (Table K12)
1841.J83   Judgments by default (Table K12)
1841.J87   Jurisdiction (Table K12)
Notification see KDZ-KH2 1841.S94
1841.N84   Nullity (Table K12)
1841.P37   Parties (Table K12)
1841.P73   Precautionary measures (Table K12)
1841.P75   Prescription (Table K12)
1841.S93   Summary proceedings (Table K12)
1841.S94   Summons. Notification. Citation (Table K12)
Strikes. Boycotts. Lockouts
1845   General (Table K11)
Particular industries see KDZ-KH2 1850.A+
1850.A-Z   By industry, occupation, or group of employees, A-Z
Subarrange each by Table KDZ-KH17
1850.A33-.A332   Agricultural laborers (Table KDZ-KH17)
1850.E43-.E432   Electric industry (Table KDZ-KH17)
1850.L64-.L642   Longshoremen (Table KDZ-KH17)
Public employees
see KDZ-KH2 3200+
1850.P84-.P842   Public utilities (Table KDZ-KH17)
1853   Employees' representation in management (Table K11)
1855.A-Z   Particular industries, occupations, or groups of employees,
A-Z
Subarrange each by Table K12
1855.S34   School employees (Table K12)
Labor standards. Labor conditions
1860   General (Table K11)
Employment and dismissal
For individual labor contracts see KDZ-KH2 893+
1863   General (Table K11)

KDZ-KH2

	Social legislation
	Labor law
	Labor standards. Labor conditions
	Employment and dismissal -- Continued
1865	Free choice of employment. Liberty of occupation (Table K11)
	Including criminal protection
1867	Probationary employment (Table K11)
1869	Discrimination in employment and its prevention (Table K11)
	Dismissal. Resignation. Suspension. Job security
1871	General (Table K11)
1873	Dismissal pay (Table K11)
1875	Reinstatement (Table K11)
1877	Relocation of employees (Table K11)
	Wages. Minimum wage
1885	General (Table K11)
	Wage discrimination. Equal pay for equal work see KDZ-KH2 1869
	Types of wages. Mode of remuneration
1887	General (Table K11)
	Incentive wages
	Including bonus system, profit sharing, employee ownership
1888	General (Table K11)
1889	Cost-of-living adjustment. Escalator clause (Table K11)
1890	Family allowances (Table K11)
1892	Supplementary wages (Table K11)
1894	Overtime payments. Night differentials (Table K11)
	Wages as privileged credits in bankruptcy see KDZ-KH2 1499.W34
1896.A-Z	Particular industries, occupations, and groups of employees, A-Z
	Subarrange each by Table K12
1896.E43	Electric industry. Electric utilities (Table K12)
1896.R34	Railroads (Table K12)
	Nonwage payments. Fringe benefits
1900	General (Table K11)
	Pension and retirement plans
1902	General (Table K11)
	Pension trusts see KDZ-KH2 1902+
1906	Health benefits. Health insurance plans (Table K11)
	Dismissal pay see KDZ-KH2 1873
1908	Other

	Social legislation
	Labor law
	Labor standards. Labor conditions
	Nonwage payments. Fringe benefits -- Continued
1909.A-Z	By industry, occupation, and groups of employees, A-Z
	Subarrange each by Table K12
1909.R34	Railroads (Table K12)
	Hours of labor. Night work
1920	General (Table K11)
	Children see KDZ-KH2 1945
	Women see KDZ-KH2 1946
1922.A-Z	Particular industries and groups of employees, A-Z
	Subarrange each by Table K12
1922.A35	Aeronautics (Table K12)
1926	Vacations. Holidays. Days of rest (Table K11)
1927	Sick leave (Table K11)
	Labor discipline. Work rules
1933	General (Table K11)
1935	Shop committees. Works councils (Table K11)
	Labor supply. Manpower controls
1938	General (Table K11)
1939.A-Z	Special topics, A-Z
	Subarrange each by Table K12
1939.L32	Labor passports (Table K12)
	Seasonal laborers see KDZ-KH2 1962.S4
	Protection of labor. Labor hygiene and safety
1943	General (Table K11)
1945	Child labor (Table K11)
	Including hours of child labor
1946	Woman labor (Table K11)
	Including hours of woman labor
1947	Home labor (Table K11)
1949	Apprentices. Learners (Table K11)
	Labor hygiene and safety. Hazardous occupations. Safety regulations
1954	General (Table K11)
1956	Factory inspection. Labor inspection (Table K11)
1958.A-Z	By industry or type of labor, A-Z
	Subarrange each by Table K12
1958.A35	Agricultural laborers (Table K12)
1958.A86	Atomic industry (Table K12)
1958.C65	Construction industry (Table K12)
1958.M54	Mining industry (Table K12)
1962.A-Z	Labor law of particular industries, occupations, or types of employment, A-Z
	Subarrange each by Table K12

KDZ-KH2

	Social legislation
	Labor law
	Labor law of particular industries, occupations, or types of employment, A-Z -- Continued
1962.A34	Agricultural laborers (Table K12)
1962.A44	Alien labor (Table K12)
	Cf. KDZ-KH2 1939.L32 Labor passports
1962.A76	Artisans (Table K12)
1962.B34	Bank employees (Table K12)
1962.C55	Clerks (Table K12)
1962.C65	Construction industry (Table K12)
1962.F56	Fishing industry (Table K12)
1962.H66	Hotel and restaurant employees (Table K12)
	Household employees see KDZ-KH2 1962.S45
1962.I56	Insurance companies (Table K12)
1962.L64	Longshoremen (Table K12)
	Merchant mariners see KDZ-KH2 1434+
1962.P46	Petroleum industry (Table K12)
1962.P82	Public utilities (Table K12)
1962.R34	Railroads (Table K12)
	Restaurant employees see KDZ-KH2 1962.H66
1962.S24	Sales personnel (Table K12)
1962.S4	Seasonal laborers (Table K12)
	Including temporary admission
1962.S45	Servants (Table K12)
	Cf. KDZ-KH2 895.S45 Master and servant
1962.V65	Volunteers (Table K12)
	Social insurance
1980	General (Table K11)
	Organization and administration
1981	General (Table K11)
1982	Officers and personnel (Table K11)
1984	Finance. Social insurance funds (Table K11)
1985.A-Z	Special topics, A-Z
	Subarrange each by Table K12
1985.J83	Judicial review of administrative acts relating to social insurance (Table K12)
1985.S44	Self-employed and social insurance (Table K12)
1985.W64	Women and social insurance (Table K12)
1986.A-Z	Groups of beneficiaries, A-Z
	Subarrange each by Table K12
1986.A34	Agricultural laborers (Table K12)
1986.5	Criminal provisions (Table K11)
	Particular branches

	Social legislation
	Social insurance
	Particular branches -- Continued
	Health insurance
	Cf. KDZ-KH2 1241 Private health insurance
	Cf. KDZ-KH2 1906 Health benefits as non-wage payments
1987	General (Table K11)
1988.A-Z	Particular industries and groups, A-Z
	Subarrange each by Table K12
	Merchant mariners see KDZ-KH2 1443
1988.P83	Public employees (Table K12)
1989	Maternity insurance (Table K11)
	Workers' compensation
	For employers' tort liability see KDZ-KH2 1004+
1991	General (Table K11)
	Labor accidents. Occupational diseases
1992	General (Table K11)
1993	Labor accidents (Table K11)
1994	Occupational diseases (Table K11)
1995.A-Z	Special topics, A-Z
	Subarrange each by Table K12
1995.D56	Disability evaluation (Table K12)
1996.A-Z	Particular industries and groups of employees, A-Z
	Subarrange each by Table K12
	Merchant mariners see KDZ-KH2 1444+
	Social security. Retirement and disability pensions. Survivors' benefits
2000	General (Table K11)
	For works on particular industries, occupations, or groups of employees see KDZ-KH2 2008.A+
2002	Organization and administration. Social security agency (Table K11)
	For funds (caja) of particular industries, occupations, and groups of employees see KDZ-KH2 2008.A+
2004	Contributions. Social security taxes (Table K11)
	For works on particular industries, occupations, or groups of employees see KDZ-KH2 2008.A+
	For withholding of both income and social security taxes see KDZ-KH2 4672
2008.A-Z	Particular industries, occupations, and groups of employees, A-Z
	Subarrange each by Table K12
2008.A34	Agricultural laborers (Table K12)
	Armed forces see KDZ-KH2 5125.6
2008.B34	Baking industry (Table K12)

KDZ-KH2

	Social legislation
	Social insurance
	Particular branches
	Social security. Retirement and disability pensions. Survivors' benefits
	Particular industries, occupations, and groups of employees, A-Z -- Continued
2008.C47	Charitable institutions (Table K12)
2008.C64	Commercial employees (Table K12)
2008.L37	Lawyers (Table K12)
2008.P48	Physicians (Table K12)
2008.P74	Printing industry (Table K12)
2008.P82	Public utilities (Table K12)
2008.R34	Railroads (Table K12)
	Unemployment insurance
2014	General (Table K11)
2015	Administration (Table K11)
	Public welfare. Public assistance. Private charities
2040	General (Table K11)
2041	Organization and administration (Table K11)
	Particular groups
2047	Maternity and infant welfare (Table K11)
2048	Children. Child welfare. Youth services (Table K11)
2049	People with disabilities. Vocational rehabilitation (Table K11)
2055	The poor. Charity laws. Almshouses (Table K11)
	Cf. KDZ-KH2 4098.P37 Charitable pawnshops
2060	Disaster relief (Table K11)
2063	Birth control. Family planning. Population control (Table K11)
	Cf. KDZ-KH2 5526 Abortion (Criminal law)
	Indians
2200	History
2202	General (Table K11)
	National legislation
	Including collective state law
2204	General (Table K11)
2206	Administration (Table K11)
	Indian lands see KDZ-KH2 3813+
2210.A-Z	Special topics, A-Z
	Subarrange each by Table K12
2210.C74	Criminal law (Table K12)
2210.E38	Education (Table K12)
	Hospitals see KDZ-KH2 2210.M43
2210.M43	Medical care. Hospitals (Table K12)
	Tribal law. Precolonial history
2212	General (Table K11)

Indians

Tribal law. Precolonial history -- Continued

2213.A-Z	Special topics, A-Z
	Subarrange each by Table K12
2213.C75	Criminal law (Table K12)
2213.L33	Labor (Table K12)
2213.L36	Land tenure (Table K12)
2213.T37	Taxation (Table K12)
2213.W37	Water rights (Table K12)
2216.A-Z	Particular tribes, groups, etc., A-Z
	For special topics, relating to a special tribe or group see KDZ-KH2 2213.A+

Courts. Procedure

Administration of justice. Organization of the judiciary

Judicial statistics see KDZ-KH2 112+

2500	History
2501	General works (Table K11, modified)
2501.A65	Directories
2503	Judicial districts (Table K11)
	Department of justice. Attorney General see KDZ-KH2 3147
2505	Judicial councils. Judicial conferences

Court organization and procedure

2508	General (Table K11)
2511	Conduct of court proceedings. Decorum (Table K11)
2512	Congestion and delay (Table K11)
	Cf. KDZ-KH2 2730+ Amparo proceedings
2513	Publicity and proceedings and records (Table K11)
2515	Judicial assistance (Table K11)
	For foreign judgments and their enforcement see KDZ-KH2 351.F65
	For letters rogatory see KDZ-KH2 2652
	Cf. KDZ-KH2 5862+ Judicial assistance in criminal matters

Administration and management

2518	General (Table K11)
2520	Finance. Accounting. Auditing (Table K11)
2521	Records management (Table K11)
2523	Inspection and supervision of courts (Table K11)
	Cf. KDZ-KH2 2505 Judicial councils

Particular courts and procedure in general before such courts

For special subjects, e.g. actions, evidence, see the relevant subject

Cf. KDZ-KH2 2698+ Extraordinary remedies. Judicial review

Cf. KDZ-KH2 2800+ Appellate proceedings

Federal (National) courts

KDZ-KH2

Courts. Procedure
 Court organization and procedure
  Particular courts and procedure in general before such courts
   Federal (National) courts -- Continued

2528	General (Table K11)
	Supreme court
2530	General (Table K11)
2533	Criticism

      For decisions on a special subject, see the subject
      Cf. KDZ-KH2 315 Jurisprudence

2535	Procedure (Table K11)
	Courts of appeals. Circuit courts of appeals
2537	General (Table K11)
2539.A-Z	By circuit, A-Z

      Subarrange each by Table K12
      For federal courts of appeal for federal districts, see the
       district, e.g. KHA6230.3, Buenos Aires (Federal
       District)

	District courts. Courts of first instance
2541	General (Table K11)
2543.A-Z	By district, A-Z

      For federal district courts for federal districts, see the
       district, e.g., KHA6230.55, Buenos Aires (Federal
       District)

	Minor courts see KDZ-KH2 2551+
2545	Older courts (Table K11)
	Courts of special jurisdiction

     Including defunct courts
    Agricultural courts see KDZ-KH2 3795+
    Commercial courts see KDZ-KH2 1530+

2548	Constitutional courts. Courts of extra-ordinary remedies (Table K11)

      e.g. Tribunal de Guarantias Constitucionales (Argentina);
       Tribunal de Recursos Extra-ordinarios (Argentina);
       Tribunal Constitucional (Chile); Tribunal de
       Guarantias Constitucionales y Sociales (Plenary
       session of the Supreme Court in Cuba)

2548.5	Court of claims (Table K11)
	Courts-martial see KDZ-KH2 5282+
	Criminal courts see KDZ-KH2 5801+
	Customs courts see KDZ-KH2 4823
	Domestic relations courts see KDZ-KH2 481
	Electoral courts see KDZ-KH2 3061
	Juvenile courts see KDZ-KH2 5937
	Labor courts see KDZ-KH2 1840+
	Probate courts see KDZ-KH2 709

Courts. Procedure
   Court organization and procedure
      Particular courts and procedure in general before such courts
         Federal (National) courts
            Courts of special jurisdiction -- Continued
               Small claims courts see KDZ-KH2 2660
               Tax courts see KDZ-KH2 4605

2550	State and territorial courts
	Class here general and comparative works only
	Minor courts. Local courts
	Class here general and comparative works only
2551	General (Table K11)
	Particular types of local courts
2552	Justices of the peace
	For criminal jurisdiction see KDZ-KH2 5805
2552.8	Neighborhood courts. 'Audiencias populares' (Table K11)
	Judicial officers. Court employees
2558	General (Table K11)
	Judges
2560	General (Table K11)
	For biography of judges see KDZ-KH2 300+
2560.2	Appointment. Tenure. Retirement (Table K11)
2560.4	Salaries. Pensions (Table K11)
2560.5	Immovability of judges (Table K11)
2560.6	Discipline. Judicial ethics (Table K11)
	Cf. KDZ-KH2 5672 Judicial corruption
	Procedure for removal. Impeachment and trial of judges
	Including special courts for trial of judges
2561	General (Table K11)
2561.3.A-Z	Particular cases. By respondent, A-Z
2562	Civil liability of judges (Table K11)
	Disqualification and challenge of judges in civil procedure see KDZ-KH2 2590
	Government representatives
2563	General (Table K11)
2563.4	Fiscals (Table K11)
	Cf. KDZ-KH2 5838 Fiscals in criminal proceedings
	Public prosecutors see KDZ-KH2 5838
	Justices of the peace (General) see KDZ-KH2 2552
	Justices of the peace (Criminal procedure) see KDZ-KH2 5805
2564.A-Z	Other, A-Z
	Subarrange each by Table K12
2564.B34	Bailiffs (Table K12)
2564.C55	Clerks. Secretaries (Table K12)

KDZ-KH2

	Courts. Procedure
	Court organization and procedure
	Judicial officers. Court employees
	Other, A-Z -- Continued
2564.M37	Court marshals and auxiliaries (Table K12)
	Secretaries see KDZ-KH2 2564.C55
2564.T7	Translators (Table K12)
2569	Procedure (Table K11)
	Class here works on civil and criminal procedure
	For works on civil, commercial and labor procedure combined see KDZ-KH2 2571+
	Civil procedure
	Including works on civil, commercial, and labor procedure combined
	For autonomously regulated commercial procedure see KDZ-KH2 1533+
	For works on procedure and practice in general before particular types of courts or individual courts see KDZ-KH2 2528+
	For handbooks and manuals for justices of the peace and magistrates see KDZ-KH2 2552
2571-2579	General (Table K9b)
	Jurisdiction. Venue
2582	General (Table K11)
	Pleas to the jurisdiction see KDZ-KH2 2618.P55
	Pre-commencement activities
2584	General (Table K11)
2585	Conciliation (Table K11)
	Precautionary measures (granted ex-parte)
2587	General (Table K11)
	Preventive attachment see KDZ-KH2 2694
	Deposition to perpetuate testimony see KDZ-KH2 2834
2589	Powers and duties of the judges (Table K11)
	Including disciplinary powers
2590	Challenges and disqualification of judges and other judicial officers (Table K11)
	Actions
	Including works on the classification of actions
2591	General (Table K11)
2592.A-Z	Particular kinds of actions, A-Z
	Subarrange each by Table K12
	Class action see KDZ-KH2 2600
2592.D42	Declaratory actions (Table K12)
	Frivolous actions see KDZ-KH2 2627
	Interdictal actions see KDZ-KH2 2824+
	Oral actions see KDZ-KH2 2660

Courts. Procedure
　　Civil procedure
　　　Actions
　　　　Particular kinds of actions, A-Z -- Continued
2592.P45　　　　Personal actions (Table K12)
　　　　　Popular or public actions see KDZ-KH2 2768
　　　　　Possessory actions see KDZ-KH2 567
　　　　　Prejudicial actions see KDZ-KH2 2611
　　　　　Real actions see KDZ-KH2 573
　　　　　Summary possessory actions see KDZ-KH2 2826
2593　　　　Joinder of actions (Table K11)
　　　　　　Cf. KDZ-KH2 2597 Joinder of parties
　　　　Parties
2595　　　　General (Table K11)
2596　　　　Personality and capacity of parties (Table K11)
2597　　　　Joinder of parties (Table K11)
　　　　　　Cf. KDZ-KH2 2593 Joinder of actions
2598　　　　Substitution of parties (Table K11)
2599　　　　Third party proceedings. Intervention. Interpleader (Table
　　　　　K11)
　　　　　　Including third party proceedings in executory suits
2600　　　　Class action (Table K11)
　　　　　　Cf. KDZ-KH2 1841.C55 Labor courts and procedure
　　　　The state as a party see KDZ-KH2 2811
　　　　Representation of parties. Judicial mandate
2602　　　　General (Table K11)
2603　　　　Compulsory representation by counsel. Litigants in person
　　　　　(Table K11)
　　　　Legal profession see Table KDZ-KH1 206
2605　　　In forma pauperis (Table K11)
　　　　Procedural acts. Pre-trial proceedings
2607　　　　General (Table K11)
2608　　　　Process and service. Notification. Citation (Table K11)
　　　　　　Including notification by publication
2609　　　　Procedural deadlines. Preclusion. Default (Table K11)
　　　　　　Cf. KDZ-KH2 2668 Judgment by default
2611　　　　Prejudicial actions. Civil effects of penal sentences (Table
　　　　　K11)
　　　　　　Including stay of proceedings until decision of prejudicial
　　　　　　　question
2612　　　　Deposition and discovery. Interrogatories (Table K11)
　　　　　　For letters rogatory see KDZ-KH2 2652
2613　　　　Nullity of procedural acts (Table K11)
　　　　Judicial decisions see KDZ-KH2 2663+
　　　　Costs. Fees see KDZ-KH2 2670
　　　Pleading and motions

	Courts. Procedure
	Civil procedure
	Pleading and motions -- Continued
2615	General (Table K11)
	Defenses and actions. Exceptions
2616	General (Table K11)
2616.5	Confession (Table K11)
	Dilatory exceptions
2617	General (Table K11)
2618.A-Z	Particular exceptions, A-Z
	Subarrange each by Table K12
2618.L56	Lis pendens (Table K12)
	Cf. KDZ-KH2 2628 Transfer of rights litigated
	during pendency of suit
2618.P55	Pleas to the jurisdiction (Table K12)
2618.S42	Security for costs from foreign plaintiff (Table K12)
	Answer. Peremptory exceptions
	Including dilatory exceptions not taken within the time
	period prescribed
2620	General (Table K11)
2621.A-Z	Particular defenses, A-Z
	Subarrange each by Table K12
2621.P74	Prescription (Table K12)
	Cf. KDZ-KH2 442 Periods of prescription
	Res judicata see KDZ-KH2 2669
2623	Counterclaim and cross claim (Table K12)
2625	Joinder of issue (Table K11)
2627	Frivolous pleadings (Table K11)
	Including frivolous actions and remedies
2628	Transfer of rights litigated during pendency of suit (Table K11)
	Hearings. Trial
2633	General (Table K11)
	Trial practice. Trial tactics
2634	General (Table K11)
2635	Confrontation. Cross examination (Table K11)
2636	Forensic psychology (Table K11)
2637.A-Z	Particular types of cases and claims, A-Z
	Subarrange each by Table K12
2637.I56	Insurance (Table K12)
	Evidence
	Including works on both civil and criminal evidence
	For works on evidence pertaining to particular
	proceedings see KDZ-KH2 2815+
2640	General (Table K11)
	Burden of proof

	Courts. Procedure
	Civil procedure
	Hearings. Trial
	Evidence
	Burden of proof -- Continued
2641	General (Table K11)
2642.A-Z	Special topics, A-Z
	Subarrange each by Table K12
	Judicial notice see KDZ-KH2 2642.P82
2642.P73	Presumptions
2642.P75	Proof of foreign law
2642.P82	Public fame. Judicial notice
2644.A-Z	Particular claims or actions, A-Z
	For works on evidence before courts classed with particular subjects, see the subject, e.g. 709, Evidence before probate courts
2644.I56	Insurance
	Negligence see KDZ-KH2 2644.T65
2644.T65	Torts. Negligence
	Particular kinds of evidence
2646	Testimony of the parties. Admissions (Table K11)
2647	Circumstantial (Table K11)
	For techniques of identification (Criminology), see HV8073+
	For techniques of identification (Forensic medicine), see RA1001+
2648	Real evidence (Table K11)
2649	Documentary evidence (Table K11)
2650	Judicial examination or inspection (Table K11)
	Witnesses
2651	General (Table K11)
	Oath and affirmation see KDZ-KH2 367.O16
2652	Letters rogatory (Table K11)
	Including international letters rogatory
	Contempt of court see KDZ-KH2 5670
	Privileged (Confidential) communications
2653	General (Table K11)
2653.5.A-Z	Particular relationships, A-Z
	Subarrange each by Table K12
2653.5.A86	Attorney and client (Table K12)
2653.5.C64	Confessional (Table K12)
2653.5.N66	Notary and client (Table K12)
2653.5.P48	Physician and patient (Table K12)
2654	Hearsay (Table K11)
	Expert evidence. Expert witnesses
2655	General (Table K11)

KDZ-KH2

	Courts. Procedure
	Civil procedure
	Hearings. Trial
	Evidence
	Particular kinds of evidence
	Expert evidence. Expert witnesses -- Continued
2655.3	Medical evidence. Medical witnesses (Table K11)
	Cf. RA1001+, Forensic medicine
2655.5.A-Z	Other, A-Z
	Subarrange each by Table K12
2655.5.A25	Accountants. Auditors (Table K12)
	Auditors see KDZ-KH2 2655.5.A25
2655.5.E63	Engineers (Table K12)
2655.5.S63	Social workers (Table K12)
	Presumptions see KDZ-KH2 2642.P73
	Public fame. Judicial notice see KDZ-KH2 2642.P82
2656	Evaluation of evidence (Table K11)
2660	Minor actions and proceedings (Table K11)
	Including oral actions and proceedings for collection of small claims
	Special proceedings see KDZ-KH2 2815+
	Judicial decisions
2663	General (Table K11)
2664	Orders. Rulings. Resolutions (Table K11)
	Judgment
2665	General (Table K11)
	Civil effects of penal sentences see KDZ-KH2 2611
2667	Declaratory judgment (Table K11)
2667.5	Interlocutory decisions (Table K11)
2668	Judgment by default (Table K11)
	Including remedies
	Cf. KDZ-KH2 2673 Dismissal and nonsuit
2669	Res judicata (Table K11)
2670	Costs. Fees (Table K11)
	Cf. KDZ-KH2 241+ Legal aid
	Cf. KDZ-KH2 2605 In forma pauperis
	Termination of proceedings by means other than final judgment
2672	General (Table K11)
2673	Dismissal and nonsuit (Table K11)
	Including voluntary nonsuit and termination of proceedings through inactivity over a period of time
	Compromise see KDZ-KH2 801
	Conciliation see KDZ-KH2 2585
	Remedies
2677	General (Table K11)

	Courts. Procedure
	Civil procedure
	Remedies -- Continued
2677.5	Remedies against orders of mere practice (Table K11)
2678	Injunctions (Table K11)
	For interdictal actions see KDZ-KH2 2824+
	Remedy from order denying admission of appeal. Queja see KDZ-KH2 2802
	Remedies by civil courts against acts of ecclesiastical courts see KDZ-KH2 3041
	Execution
	Execution of judgment
	General see KDZ-KH2 2690
	Execution against property. Attachment and garnishment
2690	General (Table K11)
	Exemptions
2691	General (Table K11)
2691.5.A-Z	Particular exemptions, A-Z
	Subarrange each by Table K12
	Homesteads (Domestic relations) see KDZ-KH2 538
	Homesteads (Land reform) see KDZ-KH2 3831+
2691.5.W34	Wages (Table K12)
2692	Judicial sale (Table K12)
2693	Imprisonment for debts (Table K11)
2693.5	Enforcement for specific performance. Astreintes (Table K11)
	Enforcement of foreign judgments and arbitral awards see KDZ-KH2 351.F65
2694	Preventive attachment (Table K11)
	Cf. KDZ-KH2 2820 Executory suits. Executory instruments
	Cf. KDZ-KH2 2824+ Summary suits
	Constitutional remedies. Judicial review
	For works on judicial review by means of a particular type of constitutional remedy, see the remedy
	For constitutional courts and independently organized courts of constitutional remedies see KDZ-KH2 2548
	For judicial review in the ordinary course of appellate procedure see KDZ-KH2 2800+
	For judicial review of administrative acts in the ordinary course of proceedings see KDZ-KH2 3263+
2698	General (Table K11)

KDZ-KH2

Courts. Procedure
Civil procedure
Remedies
Constitutional remedies. Judicial review -- Continued
Constitutional remedies of comprehensive scope
For constitutional remedy against violation of
personal liberty only see KDZ-KH2 2772+

2699	General (Table K11)
	Amparo
	For Chilean recurso de amparo, see KHF2772; for Chilean querella de amparo, see KHF2825; for Cuban amparo, see KGN2825
2700	History
2701-2709	General (Table K9b)
	Class constitutional documents other than amparo articles with legislative documents and amparo articles of the constitution with statutes
2711	Constitutional foundation (Table K11)
	For constitutional documents and text of constitution see KDZ-KH2 2701+
2712.A-Z	Particular concepts and relationships, A-Z
2712.H32	Amparo and habeas corpus
2712.I56	International repercussions of amparo
2712.P82	Amparo and public policy
	Relativity of amparo judgments see KDZ-KH2 2750.3
	Strict law rule see KDZ-KH2 2750.5
2714.A-Z	Individual amparo cases. By complainant, A-Z
	Constitutional scope and limits of amparo
2716	General (Table K11)
	Fundamental objects of protection
2717	General (Table K11)
	Protection of individual constitutional guarantees see KDZ-KH2 2722+
2717.4	Judicial defense and control of federal system (Table K11)
2717.6	Judicial defense of sovereignty of states (Table K11)
2718	Expansion of scope through interpretation of the organic act (Table K11)
	Constitutional limits of amparo
2720	General (Table K11)

	Courts. Procedure
	Civil procedure
	Remedies
	Constitutional remedies. Judicial review
	Constitutional remedies of comprehensive scope
	Amparo
	Constitutional scope and limits of amparo
	Constitutional limits of amparo -- Continued
2720.5.A-Z	Particular exclusions, A-Z
	Subarrange each by Table K12
	Including both explicit exclusions and exclusions established through the "jurisprudence" of Supreme Court
2720.5.E95	Expulsion and extradition of aliens (Table K12)
	Landowners affected by decisions in favor of ejidos see KDZ-KH2 2759.A35
2720.5.P64	Political rights (Table K12)
	Class here works on exclusion limited to rights relating to the exercise of suffrage and to the holding of elective or appointive public office
	Attack in amparo against acts of authority violating individual constitutional guaranties
2722	General (Table K11)
	Amparo based on the unconstitutionality of the act itself
	Including judicial and administrative acts
2723	General (Table K11)
	Judicial acts
2724	General (Table K11)
2724.3	Civil amparo (Table K11)
2724.5	Penal amparo (Table K11)
2725	Administrative amparo (Table K11)
	For amparo in contentious-administrative proceedings see KDZ-KH2 2759.C64
	Labor judgments and awards see KDZ-KH2 2759.L32
	Attack in amparo against unconstitutionality of laws
2726	General (Table K11)
	Attack in amparo against the unconstitutionality of the law upon which the act is based see KDZ-KH2 2726+
2727	"Amparo against laws"
	Class here works on attack by indirect amparo against "self-executing laws" in absence of acts of authority

KDZ-KH2

Courts. Procedure
Civil procedure
Remedies
Constitutional remedies. Judicial review
Constitutional remedies of comprehensive scope
Amparo -- Continued
Application of amparo in respect to particular subjects
see KDZ-KH2 2759.A+
Injured parties see KDZ-KH2 2741+
Procedure in amparo. The amparo suit

2730	General (Table K11)
2732	Congestion and delay. Case load (Table K11)
	Cf. KDZ-KH2 2736 Direct amparo jurisdiction
	and its reform
	Jurisprudence of Supreme Court in amparo see
	KDZ-KH2 2760
	Jurisdiction. Venue
	Including jurisdictional distinction between direct and
	indirect amparo
2735	General (Table K11)
2736	Direct amparo (Table K11)
	Including amparo jurisdiction of the Federal
	Supreme Court and of collegial circuit courts
2737	Indirect amparo. Jurisdiction of federal district
	courts (Table K11)
	Cf. KDZ-KH2 2727 "Amparo against laws"
2738	Venue. Territorial competence (Table K11)
	Parties
	Including capacity and personality
2740	General (Table K11)
	Injured parties initiating amparo proceedings
2741	General (Table K11)
	Juristic persons as injured parties
2742	General (Table K11)
2742.5	Public juristic persons (Table K11)
	Class here works on public juristic persons
	affected in their patrimonial interest by the
	complained act
2743	Injured third parties (Table K11)
2744	Responsible authority (Table K11)
2745	Federal public ministry as a party
2746	Evidence. Hearings. Trial
	Suspension of contested acts
2748	General (Table K11)
2748.5	Suspension of civil judgments (Table K11)
2748.6	Suspension of penal sentences (Table K11)

Courts. Procedure
Civil procedure
Remedies
Constitutional remedies. Judicial review
Constitutional remedies of comprehensive scope
Amparo
Procedure in amparo. The amparo suit -- Continued
Judgment
Including issuance of a writ of amparo, denial of the
writ, and dismissal

2750	General (Table K11)
2750.2	Dismissal of amparo action (Table K11)
2750.3	Relativity of amparo judgments (Table K11)
	Cf. KDZ-KH2 2760 Jurisprudence of Supreme Court in amparo
2750.5	Strict law rule (Table K11)
2750.8	Scope of amparo judgment (Table K11)
	Including works on the transgression of the scope
2752	Res judicata in amparo proceedings (Table K11)
2753	Costs and fees of amparo suits (Table K11)
	Execution of amparo judgments
2754	General (Table K11)
2754.3	Responsibility for noncompliance. Sanctions (Table K11)
2754.5	Queja against excesses and defects in execution (Table K11)
	Remedies against amparo judgments
2756	General (Table K11)
2756.3	Appeals (Revisiones) (Table K11)
	Queja
2757	General (Table K11)
2757.5	Correction of the deficiencies of queja (Table K11)
	Queja against excesses and defects in execution see KDZ-KH2 2754.5
2758	Amparo-Cassation (Table K11)
2759.A-Z	Application of amparo in relation to particular subjects, A-Z
	Subarrange each by Table K12
	Administrative amparo see KDZ-KH2 2725
2759.A35	Agrarian amparo (Table K12)
	Including exclusion of landowners affected by decisions granting or restoring communal land from the right of access to amparo suit and partial restoration of this right to small holders

	Courts. Procedure
	Civil procedure
	Remedies
	Constitutional remedies. Judicial review
	Constitutional remedies of comprehensive scope
	Amparo
	Application of amparo in relation to particular subjects, A-Z -- Continued
2759.C64	Amparo in contentious-administrative proceedings (Table K12)
2759.L32	Labor amparo (Table K12)
2759.M54	Military amparo (Table K12)
2759.P66	Possession (Table K12)
2759.R44	Rent. Rent control (Table K12)
	Small holders' access to agrarian amparo see KDZ-KH2 2759.A35
2759.S95	Suretyship and guaranty (Table K12)
2759.T37	Taxation (Table K12)
2760	Jurisprudence of Supreme Court in amparo
	Suspension of amparo in war or other emergency see KDZ-KH2 3128
2762	Writ of security (Table K11)
2768	Popular or public actions. Petition of unconstitutionality (Table K11)
	Extraordinary appeal to Supreme Court from final state court decisions see KDZ-KH2 2807
	Writ of injunction see KDZ-KH2 2678
	Habeas corpus and similar remedies
	Including Chilean recurso de amparo
2772	General (Table K11)
	Amparo and habeas corpus see KDZ-KH2 2712.H32
	Suspension of habeas corpus in war or emergency see KDZ-KH2 3128
	Appellate procedure
	Including appeals from final or interlocutory judgments
2800	General (Table K11)
2802	Remedy from order denying admission of appeal. Queja (Table K11)
	Cf. KDZ-KH2 2757+ Queja against amparo judgments
2805	Appeals for annulment. Cassation (Table K11)
	For amparo-cassation see KDZ-KH2 2758
2807	Extraordinary appeal to Supreme Court (Table K11)
	Including extraordinary appeals from final state court decisions; extraordinary writ (Argentina); and 'extraordinary remedy' (Brazil)

Courts. Procedure
  Civil procedure
    Remedies -- Continued
2810   Suit for revision of final judgment (Table K11)
2811   Proceedings by or against the state (Table K11)
            For tort liability of the state see KDZ-KH2 1007
        Special proceedings
2815   General (Table K11)
         Annulment of marriage see KDZ-KH2 497+
2817   Arbitration and award. Commercial arbitration (Table K11)
            Cf. KDZ-KH2 351.F65 Foreign judgments and arbitral
              awards
            Cf. KDZ-KH2 838 Arbitration clause
            Cf. KDZ-KH2 3854.A72 Agricultural arbitration
         Bankruptcy and insolvency procedure see KDZ-KH2 1482
         Condemnation procedure see KDZ-KH2 3325
         Divorce see KDZ-KH2 510+
2820   Executory suits. Executory instruments (Table K11)
            Cf. KDZ-KH2 642.F65 Foreclosure
            Cf. KDZ-KH2 2599 Third party procedure in executory
              suits
         Mental competency procedure see KDZ-KH2 460
         Probate see KDZ-KH2 709
         Summary suits and procedure. Interdictal actions
2824   General (Table K11)
          Summary proceedings relating to real property
2825   General (Table K11)
2826   Summary possessory actions. Possessory interdicts
            (Table K11)
            Including proceedings to acquire, to retain, or recover
              possession
2828   Actions on account of new or dangerous work (Table
            K11)
           Actions to define boundary lines and prohibit their
            violation see KDZ-KH2 619
2830   Actions of jactitation (Table K11)
             Including substantive law on protection against slander of
              title
           Summary proceedings for eviction of tenants see KDZ-
            KH2 882.E94
         Testamentary and intestate proceedings see KDZ-KH2 709
         Third party procedure see KDZ-KH2 2599
         Workers' compensation see KDZ-KH2 1991+
        Noncontentious (ex-parte) jurisdiction
2832   General (Table K11)
2834   Deposition to perpetuate testimony (Table K11)

KDZ-KH2

	Courts. Procedure
	Civil procedure
	Noncntentious (ex parte) jurisdiction
	Notarial practice and procedure see KDZ-KH2 263
	Judicial assistance see KDZ-KH2 2515
	Negotiated settlement. Compromise see KDZ-KH2 801
2900	Public law (Table K11)
	Constitutional law
	Sources
2902	Bibliography
2903	Collections
	Sources other than constitutions
2905	Collections. By date of publication
2906	Individual documents. By date of adoption or proclamation
	Class here documents not related to constitutional conventions, e.g. declarations of independence, articles of confederation, etc.
	Constitutions
	Collections
	For works containing federal constitutions and constitutions of a particular state, see the state
	For works containing federal and two or more state constitutions see KDZ-KH2 2916+
2910	Texts. By date
2912	Digest. Indexes. By date
	State constitutions and constitutional conventions see KDZ-KH2 2916+
2914	Particular constitutions. By date of constitution
	Subarrange each by Table K17
	State constitutions. State constitutional conventions
	Collective
	Including federal constitutions and constitutions of two or more states combined
2916	Texts. By date
2917	Digests. Indexes
	Constitutions of a particular state
	see the state
	Constitutional history
2919	General (Table K11)
2920.A-Z	Special topics, A-Z
	Subarrange each by Table K12
	For history of a particular subject of constitutional law, see the subject
2920.P44	Peonage. Slavery (Table K12)
	Including emancipation, prohibition, and criminal provisions
	Slavery see KDZ-KH2 2920.P44

Constitutional law -- Continued

2921	Constitutional law in general (Table K11, modified)
2921.Z95	Works comparing constitutions
	Including works comparing federal constitutions with each other or with state constitutions, and comparative works on state constitutions
2923	Interpretaton and construction of constitutional law (Table K11)
2924	Revision and amending process (Table K11)
2926	The state. Form of government. Sovereignty (Table K11)
	Constitutional principles
2929	Rule of law (Table K11)
2930	De facto doctrine (Table K11)
	Separation of powers. Delegation of powers
2932	General (Table K11)
2934	Implied powers (Table K11)
2936	Conflict of interests (Table K11)
	Including incompatibility of offices and ethics in government
	Cf. KDZ-KH2 3095 Legislators
	Cf. KDZ-KH2 5662 Criminal law
	Judicial review of legislative acts see KDZ-KH2 2699+
	Constitutional courts see KDZ-KH2 2548
	Sources and relationships of law
2938	International and municipal law. Treaties and agreements (Table K11)
2939	Statutory law and delegated legislation (Table K11)
	Cf. KDZ-KH2 3230+ Administrative law
	Structure of government
	Including federal and state relations, relations between the states, and jurisdiction
2943	General (Table K11)
	Exclusive and concurrent legislative powers see KDZ-KH2 3071
2945	Federal-state disputes (Table K11)
2947	Federal intervention (Table K11)
	For federal intervention in matters of a particular state, see the state
2948	Federal areas within states (Table K11)
	Relations between states
2950	General (Table K11)
2951	Full faith and credit clause (Table K11)
2953	Disputes between states (Table K11)
2957	National territory (Table K11)
	Including continental shelf and territorial waters
	Cf. KDZ-KH2 3235 Administrative and political divisions. Decentralization
	Foreign relations

KDZ-KH2

	Constitutional law
	Foreign relations -- Continued
2962	General (Table K11)
	Department of foreign affairs see KDZ-KH2 3148+
	Foreign service see KDZ-KH2 3149+
2968	Public policy. Police power (Table K11)
	Individual and state
	Nationals. Aliens
2972	General (Table K11)
	Nationals. Citizenship
2973	General (Table K11)
	Acquisition and loss of citizenship
2975	General (Table K11)
	Naturalization see KDZ-KH2 2983
2977	Option of nationality (Table K11)
2979	Loss of citizenship (Table K11)
2980.A-Z	Particular groups, A-Z
2980.R43	Refugees
	Including asylum seekers
2980.W64	Women
	Aliens
	For civil law status see KDZ-KH2 351.A44
2981	General (Table K11)
2983	Immigration and naturalization (Table K11)
	Cf. KDZ-KH2 3826 Colonization
2985.A-Z	Temporary admission of particular groups, A-Z
	Subarrange each by Table K12
2985.A25	Actors. Artists (Table K12)
	Artists see KDZ-KH2 2985.A25
	Pensioners see KDZ-KH2 2985.R46
2985.R46	Retired and other unoccupied persons. Pensioners (Table K12)
	Seasonal laborers see KDZ-KH2 1962.S4
2985.T67	Tourists (Table K12)
	Cf. KDZ-KH2 2985.T67 Tourist trade
2987	Deportation and expulsion (Table K12)
	Control of individuals
2990	General (Table K11)
	Aliens see KDZ-KH2 5118.A44
2992	Passport. Identification. Registration (Table K11)
	For labor passports see KDZ-KH2 1939.L32
	Internal security. Control of subversive activities
	Cf. KDZ-KH2 5636 Subversive activities (Criminal law)
2994	General (Table K11)
2995.A-Z	Particular groups, A-Z
	Subarrange each by Table K12

198

	Constitutional law
	Individual and state
	Control of individuals
	Internal security. Control of subversive activities
	Particular groups, A-Z -- Continued
2995.C64	Communists (Table K12)
	Human rights. Civil and political rights
	For protection of human rights in criminal proceedings see KDZ-KH2 5866+
3003	General (Table K11)
	Particular constitutional guaranties
	Equality before the law. Antidiscrimination (General)
	Including racial, ethnic, national, and religious minorities in general
3008	General (Table K11)
3009.A-Z	Particular groups, A-Z
	Subarrange each by Table K12
3009.B54	Blacks (Table K12)
3009.G38	Gays (Table K12)
	Indians see KDZ-KH2 2200+
3009.W64	Women (Table K12)
	Including sex discrimination against women
3010	Due process of law (Table K12)
	For due process of law in criminal procedure see KDZ-KH2 5870
3011	Right to life (Table K12)
	Freedom of expression
3012	General (Table K11)
3013	Freedom of speech (Table K11)
	Freedom of the press and of information
3015	General (Table K11)
	Press law see KDZ-KH2 4370+
3016	Press censorship (Table K11)
	Including theater and motion picture censorship
3018	Freedom of assembly and association (Table K11)
	Cf. KDZ-KH2 915+ Associations (Civil law)
3019	Freedom of petition (Table K11)
3021	Freedom of religion and conscience (Table K11)
	Cf. KDZ-KH2 3034+ Church and state
	Freedom of teaching. Academic freedom see KDZ-KH2 3602
3022	Right of privacy and integrity of home (Table K11)
	Cf. KDZ-KH2 5580+ Criminal violation of privacy and the right of secrecy
	Cf. KDZ-KH2 5859 Protection against unreasonable searches and seizures

KDZ-KH2

Constitutional law
  Individual and state
    Human rights. Civil and political rights
      Particular constitutional guarantees
        Prohibition of peonage and slavery see KDZ-KH2
          2920.P44
        Free choice of employment see KDZ-KH2 1865
        Amparo see KDZ-KH2 2700+
        Habeas corpus and similar remedies see KDZ-KH2
          2772+
        Self-incrimination see KDZ-KH2 5882
        Limitation or suspension of civil and political rights in time
          of war or other emergency see KDZ-KH2 3128
        Loss of political rights

3027	General (Table K11)
	Disability imposed by law or criminal sentence see KDZ-KH2 5473
	Constitutional remedies against arbitrary official action see KDZ-KH2 2699+
3029	Resistance to government. Passive resistance (Table K11)
3031	Political parties (Table K11)
	Control of individuals see KDZ-KH2 2990+
	Economic constitution and structure see KDZ-KH2 3702+
	Church and state. Secular ecclesiastical law
	Class here works on the constitutional status and regulation of the Roman Catholic Church and other denominations by civil government
3034	General (Table K11)
	Roman Catholic Church
	Including works on religious associations and state supervision
	Sources
3035.A3	Collections. By date of publication
3035.A35	Concordats. By date of conclusion
	Statutes
3035.A4	Collections. By date of publication
3035.A5	Particular acts. By date of enactment
3035.A6	Digests. Indexes. By date of publication
3037	General works
	Special topics
3038	Clergy (Table K11)
3039	Patronage (Table K11)
	Church property
3040	General (Table K11)
	Church lands see KDZ-KH2 3040+
	Disentailment of mortmains. Nationalization of church lands see KDZ-KH2 3817

	Constitutional law
	Church and state. Secular ecclesiastical law
	Roman Catholic Church
	Special topics -- Continued
3041	Remedies by civil courts against acts of ecclesiastical courts (Table K11)
	Freedom of religion and conscience see KDZ-KH2 3021
	Church and education. Denominational schools see KDZ-KH2 3545
	Confessional communications privileged in secular procedure see KDZ-KH2 2653.5.C64
3042.A-Z	Other denominations, A-Z
	Organs of government
3049	General (Table K11)
	The people
3050	General (Table K11)
3051	Initiative and referendum. Plebiscite. Recall (Table K11)
	Political parties see KDZ-KH2 3031
	Election law
3053	General (Table K11)
3054	Election law and congressional representation of territories (Table K11)
	Representative government see KDZ-KH2 2926
	Suffrage
3055	General (Table K11)
3057.A-Z	Particular groups of voters, A-Z
	Subarrange each by Table K12
3057.S67	Soldiers (Table K12)
3057.W64	Women (Table K12)
3058	Registration. Qualification (Table K11)
3059	Election districts (Table K11)
3061	Electoral courts. Remedies. Appeals (Table K11)
	Election to particular offices
3063	President. Vice president (Table K11)
3064	Congress
3065	Other
	e.g. Local and municipal elections, comparative state law
3067	Campaign funds (Table K11)
3068	Corrupt practices. Illicit political activities (Table K11)
	Cf. KDZ-KH2 5657 Corruption and bribery
	The legislature. Legislative power
3070	General (Table K11)
3071	Exclusive and concurrent legislative powers (Table K11)
3073	Organization of legislative bodies (Table K11)
	Including procedure, and general and comparative state law
3074	Legislative branch employees (Table K11)

KDZ-KH2

	Constitutional law
	Organs of government
	The legislature. Legislative power -- Continued
	The Congress (Parliament, Legislative Council, etc.)
	Including general works on the legislature, if unicameral, or on the body that exercises legislative power if other than a congress, e.g. the Council of Ministers in Cuba
3075	General (Table K11)
3077	Rules and procedure (Table K11)
	Powers and duties
3078	General (Table K11)
3079	Investigative power (Table K11)
	The legislative process
3081	General (Table K11)
3083	Committees (Table K11)
3084	Bill drafting (Table K11)
	Including drafting techniques, editing, and publishing of codes
	Cf. KDZ-KH2 158 Legal composition and draftsmanship
3085	Introduction, discussion, and passage of bills (Table K11)
3086	Publication and promulgation of laws (Table K11)
	Veto see KDZ-KH2 3131
3090	Impeachment power and procedure (Table K11)
	Cf. KDZ-KH2 2561+ Impeachment of judges
	Cf. KDZ-KH2 3136+ Impeachment of the president
	Legal status of legislators
3093	Parliamentary immunity (Table K11)
3094	Salaries, pensions, etc. (Table K11)
3095	Conflict of interests. Incompatibility of offices (Table K11)
	Cf. KDZ-KH2 5662 Criminal law
	Contested elections
3097	General (Table K11)
	Cases
3097.3	Upper house (Senate, etc.)
3097.3.A2	Collections. By date of publication
3097.3.A5-Z	Particular cases. By incumbent, A-Z
3097.6	Lower house (Chamber of deputies, House of representatives, etc.)
3097.6.A2	Collections. By date of publication
3097.6.A5-Z	Particular cases. By incumbent, A-Z
	Upper house (Senate, etc.)
3100	General (Table K11)
3101	Rules and procedure (Table K11)
	Committees

Constitutional law
  Organs of government
    The legislature. Legislative power
      The Congress (Parliament, Legislative Council, etc.)
        Upper house (Senate, etc.)
          Committees -- Continued
3103   General (Table K11)
3103.5.A-Z   Particular committees, A-Z
3104   Powers and duties (Table K11)
        Lower house (Chamber of deputies, House of
            representatives, etc.)
3105   General (Table K11)
3106   Rules and procedure (Table K11)
          Committees
3108   General (Table K11)
3108.5.A-Z   Particular committees, A-Z
3111   Offices and agencies of the Congress (Table K11)
    The executive branch. Executive power
3120   General (Table K11)
3121   State executives. Governors (Table K11)
3122   Monarchs (Table K11)
      The President
3123   General (Table K11)
        Powers and duties
3124   General (Table K11)
3125   Treatymaking power (Table K11)
          War and emergency powers
3127   General (Table K11)
3128   Martial law. State of siege. Military government
                (Table K11)
                Including right to limit or suspend civil rights and
                    constitutional remedies (Amparo, habeas corpus,
                    etc.)
          Legislative power
3130   General (Table K11)
3131   Veto power (Table K11)
3132   Ordinance power (Table K11)
                Cf. KDZ-KH2 3233 Delegated legislation
          Impeachment
3136   General (Table K11)
3137.A-Z   Particular cases. By president, A-Z
          Legal status
3138   General (Table K11)
                Election see KDZ-KH2 3063+
3139   Term of office (Table K11)

	Constitutional law
	Organs of government
	The executive branch. Executive power
	The President
	Legal status -- Continued
3140	Succession. Disability. Vacancy of presidency (Table K11)
3142	Vice President (Table K11)
	The Prime Minister and the Cabinet
3144	General (Table K11)
	Procedures for removal. Impeachment
3145	General (Table K11)
3145.5.A-Z	Particular cases. By respondent, A-Z
	Executive departments and non-departmental organizations
3146	General (Table K11)
	Particular departments
	For the administrative law relating to and applied by a particular department, see the respective branches of the law and the particular subject under the jurisdiction of the department
3147	Department of justice. Attorney general (Table K11)
	Department of foreign affairs
3148	General (Table K11)
	The foreign service
3149	General (Table K11)
3150	Legal status of foreign service personnel (Table K11)
	Including salaries, allowances, pensions, etc.
	Consular fees see KDZ-KH2 268
	Other departments, including proposed departments see the subject
	Independent agencies, special bureaus, etc.
3152	General (Table K11)
3153.A-Z	Particular agencies, etc. (not classed elsewhere), A-Z
	Regulatory agencies see KDZ-KH2 3233
3154	Council of State (Table K11)
	Civil service see KDZ-KH2 3200+
3156	The Judiciary. Judicial power (Table K11)
	Class here constitutional status only
	For courts, administration of justice, and organization of the judiciary see KDZ-KH2 2499.2+
	Cf. KDZ-KH2 2698+ Constitutional remedies against arbitrary official action
	Cf. KDZ-KH2 5404 Administration of criminal justice
3158	Seat of government (Table K11)

3164	National emblem. Flag (Table K11)
	Decorations of honor. Awards. Dignities
3165	Civilian (Table K11)
3165.5	Military (Table K11)
	Local government
3180	General (Table K11)
	Municipal government. Municipal corporations. Municipal services
3182	General (Table K11)
3184	Charters and ordinances. Local law (Table K11)
	Including model ordinances and drafting manuals
	Tort liability see KDZ-KH2 995
	Municipal officials. Organs of local government
3187	General (Table K11)
	Particular officials and organs
3188	Mayors (Table K11)
3189	City councils (Table K11)
3190.A-Z	Special topics, A-Z
	Criminal liability of municipal officials see KDZ-KH2 5655+
	Municipal civil service see KDZ-KH2 3224+
3193	Parishes and other local self-government (Table K11)
3194.A-Z	Other units of local authority, A-Z
	Subarrange each by Table K12
3194.L63	Local councils (Table K12)
3194.M46	Metropolitan areas (Table K12)
	Civil service. Government officials and employees
	National (Federal) civil service
3200	General (Table K11)
	Conditions and restrictions of employment
	Including employment discipline
3205	General (Table K11)
3206	Employment discipline. Disciplinary measures (Table K11)
3208	Types and modes of employment (Table K11)
	Tenure and remuneration
3210	General (Table K11)
3212	Classification of civil service positions (Table K11)
3214	Salaries (Table K11)
3215	Retirement. Pensions (Table K11)
	Particular departments and agencies
	see the departments or agencies
3220	State civil service (Table K11)
	Including general and comparative
	Local civil service
3222	General (Table K11)

KDZ-KH2

	Civil service. Government officials and employees -- Continued
	Municipal civil service
	Including general and comparative
3224	General (Table K11)
3225	Retirement. Pensions (Table K11)
3228	Police and power of the police (Table K11)
	Including comparative works on state, local, and rural police
	Cf. KDZ-KH2 5840 Judicial police
	Administrative law
	For the administrative law of a particular subject, see the subject, e.g., KDZ-KH2 4597+ , Tax administration and procedure
3230	General (Table K11)
	Administrative organization
3232	General (Table K11)
	Ministries. Executive departments see KDZ-KH2 3146+
	Independent agencies. Special bureaus see KDZ-KH2 3152+
3233	Regulatory agencies. Legislative functions. Delegated legislation (Table K11)
3234	Public institutions in general (Table K11)
	Civil service see KDZ-KH2 3200+
3235	Administrative and political divisions. Decentralization (Table K11)
	Local government see KDZ-KH2 3180+
3238	Attorneys General's opinions
	For collected opinions of individual fiscals see KDZ-KH2 325.A+
	Offenses against the public administration see KDZ-KH2 5653+
	Administrative acts
3240	General (Table K11)
	Rule of law see KDZ-KH2 2929
3242	Competent authority (Table K11)
3244	Retroaction of administrative acts (Table K11)
3245	Administrative discretion (Table K11)
3247	Excess and abuse of administrative power. Ombudsman (Table K11)
	Administrative responsibility see KDZ-KH2 3269+
3249	Administrative inaction. Administrative silence (Table K11)
3250	Revocation of administrative acts (Table K11)
3252	Defective acts. Nullity. Annulment (Table K11)
3254	Enforcement of administrative acts. Execution (Table K11)
3256	Administrative sanctions (Table K11)
	Judicial functions. Remedies
3258	General (Table K11)

Administrative law

Judicial functions. Remedies -- Continued

3260   Administrative remedies (Table K11)
>Including exhaustion of administrative remedies

         Judicial review of administrative acts
>Including ordinary review by special administrative tribunals or
>by courts of general jurisdiction
>For judicial review by means of constitutional remedies
>see KDZ-KH2 2699+

3263   General (Table K11)

         Contentious-administrative jurisdiction and procedure.
Administrative courts

3265   General (Table K11)

         Council of State see KDZ-KH2 3154

3266.A-Z   Special topics, A-Z
>Subarrange each by Table K12
>Amparo in contentious-administrative proceedings see
>KDZ-KH2 2759.C64
>Annulment see KDZ-KH2 3252

3266.C66   Costs. Fees (Table K12)

3266.D54   Dilatory exceptions (Table K12)

         Enforcement see KDZ-KH2 3254

3266.E94   Evidence (Table K12)

         Fees see KDZ-KH2 3266.C66

3266.P73   Prescription (Table K12)

3266.R46   Res judicata in administrative proceedings (Table K12)

      Administrative responsibility. Indemnification for government
acts

3269   General (Table K11)

         Indemnification for unlawful acts

3270   General (Table K11)

         Contractual liability see KDZ-KH2 862+

         Expropriation see KDZ-KH2 3325

         Government tort liability see KDZ-KH2 1007

         Tort liability of public officials and government employees
see KDZ-KH2 998

         Criminal liability of public officials and government
employees see KDZ-KH2 5655+

      Public property. Public restraints on private property

3300   General (Table K11)

3302   Roads. Highway law (Table K11)

3303   Bridges (Table K11)

         Natural resources
>Including conservation, management, and environmental planning
>For environmental pollution see KDZ-KH2 3421+

3305   General (Table K11)

	Public property. Public restraints on private property
	Natural resources -- Continued
	Water resources
	Including watersheds, rivers, lakes, and watercourses
3310	General (Table K11)
	Conservation and management. Water resources development
	Including water power development
	For water power see KDZ-KH2 4145
3312	General (Table K11)
	Riparian rights see KDZ-KH2 613
	Water pollution see KDZ-KH2 3425
	Field irrigation see KDZ-KH2 3860
3314	River and harbor improvements (Table K11)
3316.A-Z	Particular inland waterways and channels, A-Z
	Subarrange each by Table K12
3318	Flood control. Levees. Dams (Table K11)
3320	Canals (Table K11)
3321.A-Z	Particular bodies of water, water districts, etc. A-Z
	Subarrange each by Table K12
	Shore protection. Coastal zone management see KDZ-KH2 3332
	Marine resources
3323	General (Table K11)
	Fishing industry see KDZ-KH2 3900+
3325	Expropriation. Eminent domain (Table K11)
	For expropriation or nationalization of special types of property, see such property, e.g. Church property, see KDZ-KH2 3817 ; agricultural land holdings, see KDZ-KH2 3831+ ; mines, see KDZ-KH2 3946 ; petroleum, oil and gas, see KDZ-KH2 3987 ; electric utilities, see KDZ-KH2 4139
	Public land law
3328	General (Table K11)
	Reclamation. Irrigation. Drainage
3330	General (Table K11)
3331.A-Z	Particular types of land, A-Z
	Subarrange each by Table K12
3332	Shore protection. Coastal zone management (Table K11)
	Including protection and use of publicly owned river banks
	National preserves
3334	Grazing lands (Table K11)
3335	Forest reserves (Table K11)
	National parks and forests. Wilderness preservation
3337	General (Table K11)

	Public property. Public restraints on private property
	Public land law
	National preserves
	National parks and forests. Wilderness preservation --
	Continued
	Wildlife protection. Game laws
	Including game, bird, and fish protection
	Cf. KDZ-KH2 3900+ Fishing industry
3338	General (Table K11)
3339.A-Z	Particular animals and birds, A-Z
3340.A-Z	Particular parks, monuments, etc., A-Z
	Agricultural use of public lands
3343	General (Table K11)
	Agrarian land policy legislation see KDZ-KH2 3825+
	Land reform see KDZ-KH2 3831+
	Colonization see KDZ-KH2 3826
	Architectural and historical monuments see KDZ-KH2 3632
	Indian lands see KDZ-KH2 3813+
	Feudal land grants see KDZ-KH2 3812
	Land grants under agrarian legislation see KDZ-KH2 3831+
	Environmental planning see KDZ-KH2 3302
	Regional and city planning. Zoning. Building
	Cf. KDZ-KH2 3305+ Environmental planning
3350	General (Table K11)
3352	Land use. Zoning. Land subdivision (Table K11)
	Building laws
3354	General (Table K11)
3355.A-Z	Particular types of buildings, A-Z
3356	Electric installations (Table K11)
3357	Plumbing. Sewers and drains. Pipe fitting (Table K11)
	Housing. Slum clearance. City redevelopment
	Cf. KDZ-KH2 4668.H67 Housing development tax
3360	General (Table K11)
	Housing for particular social classes
3362	Rural housing. Housing for small farmers and agricultural laborers (Table K11)
3363	Housing for industrial workers (Table K11)
	Government property
	Cf. KDZ-KH2 3637 Access to public records
	Administration. Powers and control
3367	General (Table K11)
3368	Real property (Table K11)
3369.A-Z	Personal property, A-Z
	Subarrange each by Table K12
3369.A96	Automobiles (Table K12)

KDZ-KH2

	Public property. Public restraints on private property --
	Continued
	Public works
	Cf. KDZ-KH2 898.P82 Public works contracts
3373	General (Table K11)
3375	Finance (Table K11)
	Public health. Sanitation
3400	General (Table K11)
3401	Public health services (Table K11)
3403.A-Z	Particular kinds of group hygiene, A-Z
	Subarrange each by Table K12
	Labor hygiene see KDZ-KH2 1954+
3403.M54	Military hygiene (Table K12)
3405	Disposal of the dead. Burial and cemetery laws (Table K12)
	Including regulating the transportation of dead bodies
	Cf. KDZ-KH2 4103.U53 Undertakers
	Contagious, infectious, and other diseases
3408	General (Table K11)
3409	Reporting (Table K11)
3411.A-Z	Particular diseases, A-Z
	Subarrange each by Table K12
3411.A53	AIDS (Table K12)
3411.M34	Malaria (Table K12)
3411.T82	Tuberculosis (Table K12)
3411.V44	Venereal diseases (Table K12)
	Particular measures
3413	Animal products inspection
	Meat inspection
	see 4030.3
3415	Immigration inspection. Quarantine
3416	Immunization. Vaccination (Table K11)
3418	Mosquito abatement (Table K11)
	Environmental pollution
	Including abatement of public nuisances
	For environmental planning see KDZ-KH2 3305+
3421	General (Table K11)
3425	Water pollution (Table K11)
3427	Air pollution (Table K11)
	Including control of smoke, noxious gases, etc.
	Criminal provisions see KDZ-KH2 5685
3428.A-Z	Other public health hazards and measures, A-Z
3428.N67	Noise (Table K12)
3428.R43	Refuse disposal (Table K12)
	Medical legislation
	For physicians and related professions see KDZ-KH2 4446+
3435	General (Table K11)

Medical legislation -- Continued

3436	Patients' rights (Table K11)
	Hospitals and other medical institutions
3437	Hospitals (Table K11)
	Cf. KDZ-KH2 3443 Psychiatric hospitals and mental health facilities
3439.A-Z	Other health services, A-Z
	Subarrange each by Table K12
	Ambulance service see KDZ-KH2 3439.E5
3439.B55	Blood banks (Table K12)
3439.E5	Emergency medical services. Ambulance service (Table K12)
	Pharmacies see KDZ-KH2 4095.D77
3440.A-Z	Special topics, A-Z
	Subarrange each by Table K12
3440.E96	Euthanasia. Right to die. Living wills (Table K12)
	Living wills see KDZ-KH2 3440.E96
	Right to die see KDZ-KH2 3440.E96
3443	The mentally ill
	Including psychiatric hospitals and mental health facilities
	For civil status of insane persons see KDZ-KH2 459+
	For mental incompetency proceedings see KDZ-KH2 460
	For criminal liability see KDZ-KH2 5457.I56
3445.A-Z	Disorders of character, behavior, and intelligence, A-Z
3445.A43	Alcoholism
	Including works on the treatment and rehabilitation of alcoholics in the criminal justice system
	Cf. KDZ-KH2 5479 Committal to an institution for alcoholics
	Drug addiction see KDZ-KH2 3445.N35
3445.N35	Narcotic addiction. Drug addiction
3446.A-Z	Special topics, A-Z
	Subarrange each by Table K12
3446.C45	Change of sex (Table K12)
3446.D64	Donation or sale and transplantation of human organs, tissues, etc. (Table K12)
	Cf. KDZ-KH2 3405 Disposal of the dead
3446.G45	Medical genetics (Table K12)
3446.I53	Informed consent (Table K12)
3446.P48	Physical therapy (Table K12)
3447	Eugenics. Sterilization (Table K11)
	Veterinary laws. Veterinary hygiene
	Cf. KDZ-KH2 4459.V46 Veterinarians. Practice of veterinary medicine
3450	General (Table K11)
3451	Reporting (Table K11)

KDZ-KH2

Veterinary laws. Veterinary hygiene -- Continued

3452.A-Z   Particular measures, A-Z
       Subarrange each by Table K12
       Quarantine see KDZ-KH2 3452.S74

3452.S74   Stock inspection. Quarantine (Table K12)

Animal diseases and causative agents
     Including prevention and control

3454   General (Table K11)

3455.A-Z   Particular diseases and causative agents, A-Z
       Subarrange each by Table K12

3455.C36   Cattle-tick (Table K12)

Prevention of cruelty to animals

3457   General (Table K11)

3458   Transportation (Table K11)
     Slaughtering and slaughterhouses see KDZ-KH2 4031

Food. Drugs. Cosmetics

3470   General (Table K11)

Food law
     Cf. KDZ-KH2 4020+ Regulation of food processing industry

3473   General (Table K11)

3475   Adulteration. Inspection (Table K11)

3477.A-Z   Particular food and food-related products, A-Z
       Subarrange each by Table K12

Drug laws
     Cf. KDZ-KH2 4004 Regulation of pharmaceutical industry
     Cf. KDZ-KH2 4095.D77 Pharmacies

3480   General (Table K11)

Narcotics
     Cf. KDZ-KH2 5703 Illicit possession, use of, and traffic in
       narcotics

3484   General (Table K11)

3485.A-Z   Particular narcotics, A-Z
       Subarrange each by Table K12

3485.O64   Opium (Table K12)

3487.A-Z   Other drugs, A-Z

Alcohol. Alcoholic beverages. Liquor laws
     Including production

3490   General (Table K11)

3492.A-Z   Particular products, A-Z
       Subarrange each by Table K12

3492.W54   Wine (Table K12)

Public safety

3500   Weapons. Firearms. Munitions (Table K11)

Hazardous articles and processes. Product safety
     Cf. KDZ-KH2 993 Products liability

3503   General (Table K11)

	Public safety
	Hazardous articles and processes. Product safety -- Continued
3505	Atomic power. Radiation (Table K11)
3507	Explosives (Table K11)
3508	Inflammable materials (Table K11)
	Poisons. Toxic substances
	Including economic and industrial poisons
3511	General (Table K11)
3512	Pesticides. Herbicides (Table K11)
3516	Accident control (Table K11)
	Fire prevention and control
3520	General (Table K11)
3521	Fire departments. Fire fighters (Table K11)
	Control of social activities. Recreation
3523	General (Table K11)
3525	Amusements (Table K11)
3527	Sports. Prizefighting. Horse racing. Bullfighting (Table K11)
	Cf. KDZ-KH2 4459.S65 Professional soccer players
	Cf. KDZ-KH2 5535 Criminal provisions
3528	Lotteries. Games of chance (Table K11)
	Cf. KDZ-KH2 931+ Aleatory contracts
	Cf. KDZ-KH2 5713 Criminal provisions
3530.A-Z	Other activities, A-Z
	Subarrange each by Table K12
	Cultural affairs
3532	General (Table K11)
3533	Cultural policy (Table K11)
3536	Language (Table K11)
	Including regulation of use, purity, etc.
	Education
	Education in general. Public education
3540	History
3541	General (Table K11)
3543	Organization. Administration. Offices and agencies (Table K11)
3545	Church and education. Denominational schools (Table K11)
	School government and finance
3547	General (Table K11)
3549	Finance. Federal aid to education (Table K11)
3550	Curricula. Courses of instruction (Table K11)
	Students. Compulsory education
3552	General (Table K11)
3553	Right to education (Table K11)
3554	Free textbooks (Table K11)

KDZ-KH2

Cultural affairs
Education
Education in general. Public education
Students. Compulsory education -- Continued

3556	Medical care and social assistance (Table K11)
3557	School discipline (Table K11)
	Teachers
3562	General (Table K11)
3564	Education and training. Examination (Table K11)
3568	Salaries, pensions (Table K11)
	Elementary and secondary education
3572	General (Table K11)
3574	Rural schools (Table K11)
3576	Secondary education (Table K11)
	Curricula. Courses of instruction
3577	General (Table K11)
3578	Moral and religious education. Civics (Table K11)
3579	Physical education (Table K11)
3581	Drawing (Table K11)
	Vocational education
	For vocational education in a specific field, see the subject, e.g. KDZ-KH2 3798 , Agricultural education and training
3583	General (Table K11)
3585	Business education (Table K11)
3587	Technical education. Manual training
	Cf. KDZ-KH2 1949 Apprentices. Learners
3589.A-Z	Particular teaching methods and media, A-Z
	Subarrange each by Table K12
3590	School libraries (Table K11)
3592	Private education. Private schools (Table K11)
	For denominational schools see KDZ-KH2 3545
3593	Adult education (Table K11)
3593.3	Distance education (Table K11)
	Higher education. Colleges and universities
3594	General (Table K11)
	Finance. Federal aid to higher education
3596	General (Table K11)
3598	Student aid. Scholarship (Table K11)
3601	Faculties. Legal status of academic teachers (Table K11)
3602	Academic freedom (Table K11)
3603	Academic degrees (Table K11)
3604.A-Z	Particular colleges and universities, A-Z
	Subarrange each by Table K12
	For state colleges and universities, see the state
	For law schools see KDZ-KH2 201.A+

	Cultural affairs
	Education
	Higher education. Colleges and universities -- Continued
3607	Cooperative education (Table K11)
	Science and the arts. Research
3610	General (Table K11)
3613.A-Z	Particular branches and subjects, A-Z
	Subarrange each by Table K12
3613.A35	Agriculture (Table K12)
3613.S7	Statistical service (General) (Table K12)
	For judicial statistics (census) see KDZ-KH2 112+
	For vital statistics see KDZ-KH2 464
	The arts
3615	Fine arts (Table K11)
	Performing arts
	Including cultural centers
3617	General (Table K11)
3621	Theater and theaters (Table K11)
	Motion pictures
3623	General (Table K11)
3624	Regulation of industry. Trade practices (Table K11)
3625	Censorship (Table K11)
3630	Museums and galleries (Table K11)
3632	Historical buildings and monuments. Archaeological excavations (Table K11)
	Including preservation and protection of cultural property
3635	Libraries (Table K11)
3637	Archives. Historical documents (Table K11)
	Including preservation of, microfilming of, and access to public records
3641	Educational, scientific and cultural exchanges
	Economic legislation
	Cf. KDZ-KH2 3729+ Regulation of industry, trade, and commerce
	Cf. KDZ-KH2 4950+ Economic emergency legislation
3700	General (Table K11)
	Economic constitution, policy, planning, and development
	Including plans for economic, social, and cultural development combined
3702	General (Table K11)
3704	Economic councils and other organs (Table K11)
	Economic assistance
3718	General (Table K11)

KDZ-KH2

	Economic legislation
	Economic assistance -- Continued
	Finance. Subsidies
	Including national (federal) subsidies to states, local government and private enterprises
	For economic assistance to a particular industry, trade, etc., see the subject, e.g., KDZ-KH2 3868+ , Economic assistance to agriculture; KDZ-KH2 4333 , Shipping bounties and subsidies
3721	General (Table K11)
	Public participation in private enterprise see KDZ-KH2 1378
3723.A-Z	Economic assistance to particular regions. By region, A-Z
	Subarrange each by Table K12
	Economic assistance to a particular state or municipality see the state or municipality
	Tax incentive legislation see KDZ-KH2 4612
3725	Foreign investments (Table K11)
	Cf. JZ1546.3 Drago doctrine
	Cf. KDZ-KH2 333.B86 Works for businesspeople and foreign investors
	Cf. KDZ-KH2 558 Alien property
	Cf. KDZ-KH2 1362 Foreign corporations
	Exclusive privileges. Concessions see KDZ-KH2 3757
	Economic controls
3727	General (Table K11)
	Trade regulations. Control of trade practices see KDZ-KH2 3731+
	Competition. Restraint of trade see Table KDZ-KH1 758+
	Export and import controls see KDZ-KH2 4066+
	Foreign exchange regulations see KDZ-KH2 4555+
	Economic emergency legislation see KDZ-KH2 4950+
	Regulation of industry, trade, and commerce. Occupational law
3729	General (Table K11)
	Boards of trade see KDZ-KH2 1081
	Trade regulations. Control of trade practices. Consumer protection
	For consumer credit see KDZ-KH2 1172.C64
	For foreign trade regulation see KDZ-KH2 4066+
	Cf. KDZ-KH2 1629+ Industrial property
3731-3739	General (Table K9b)
	Advertising
3742	General (Table K11)
	Legal advertising see KDZ-KH2 367.N66
3743.A-Z	By industry or product, A-Z
3744.A-Z	By medium, A-Z

	Regulation of industry, trade, and commerce. Occupational law
	Trade regulations. Control of trade practices. Consumer protection -- Continued
	Labeling
3746	General (Table K11)
3747.A-Z	By product, A-Z
	Competition. Restraint of trade
	Cf. KDZ-KH2 855 Contracts against public policy
	Cf. KDZ-KH2 5730 Offenses against the national economy
3750	General (Table K11)
	Monopolies and exclusive privileges
3753	General (Table K11)
3755	State monopolies (Table K11)
	Cf. KDZ-KH2 1377+ State enterprise
3757	Exclusive privileges. Concessions (Table K11)
	Cf. KDZ-KH2 4120+ Public utilities
	Cf. KDZ-KH2 4612 Tax-incentive legislation
	Cf. KDZ-KH2 4830+ Duty-free imports
3758	Monopolies (De facto). Antitrust laws (Table K11)
	Including antitrust aspects of cartels and other combinations
	Restrictive trade practices
3760	General (Table K11)
3761	Price discrimination. Price fixing (Table K11)
3763	Resale price maintenance (Table K11)
	Unfair competition see KDZ-KH2 1675+
	Protection against dumping see KDZ-KH2 4827
3766	Small business (Table K11)
3768	Trade associations (Table K11)
	Professional associations see KDZ-KH2 4442
3770	Weights and measures. Containers (Table K11)
	Primary production. Extractive industries
	Agriculture. Forestry. Rural law
3781-3789	General (Table K9b)
	Organization and administration
3792	Department of agriculture (Table K11)
3793	Other organs
	Including councils, boards, societies, etc.
	Agricultural courts and procedure
3795	General (Table K11)
3796.A-Z	Special topics, A-Z
	Agrarian amparo see KDZ-KH2 2759.A35
3798	Agricultural education and training
	Public land law see KDZ-KH2 3328+

KDZ-KH2

	Regulation of industry, trade, and commerce. Occupational law
	Primary production. Extractive industries
	Agriculture. Forestry. Rural law -- Continued
	Land tenure
	Cf. KDZ-KH2 881+ Lease of real property. Landlord and tenant
3810	History
3811	General (Table K11)
3812	Large estates. Haciendas. Feudal land grants (Table K11)
	Cf. KDZ-KH2 3831+ Land grants under agrarian legislation
	Common lands. Ejidos. Indian lands
3813	General (Table K11)
3814.A-Z	Particular communal lands. By tribe, reservation, territory, A-Z
	Church lands
3816	General (Table K11)
3817	Disentailment of mortmains. Nationalization of church lands (Table K11)
	Colonization see KDZ-KH2 3826
	Family property. Homestead law see KDZ-KH2 538
	Government-constituted homesteads see KDZ-KH2 3831+
3819	Squatters (Table K11)
	Cf. KDZ-KH2 584+ Acquisitive prescription
	Agrarian land policy legislation. Land reform
3825	General (Table K11)
3826	Colonization. Agrarian colonies (Table K11)
	Cf. KDZ-KH2 2983 Immigration
	Land reform. Transformation of the agricultural structure
	Including expropriation, nationalization, purchase of agricultural land holdings and their redistribution; land grants; government-constituted homesteads
3831-3839	General (Table K9b)
	Protection of tenants. Elimination of precarious tenancies see KDZ-KH2 3848+
3844.A-Z	Special topics, A-Z
	Subarrange each by Table K12
3844.I54	Inheritance of government-constituted homesteads
	Agricultural contracts
3846	General (Table K11)

	Regulation of industry, trade, and commerce. Occupational law
	Primary production. Extractive industries
	Agriculture. Forestry. Rural law
	Agricultural contracts -- Continued
	Farm tenancy. Rural partnerships
	Class here works on provisions of both civil law and other legislation ensuring stability for tenants and the land they cultivate
	Cf. KDZ-KH2 3825+ Agrarian land policy legislation. Land reform
3848	General (Table K11)
3850	Lease of pastures (Table K11)
3851	Sharecropping contracts. Metayer system (Table K11)
3852	Livestock share-partnership contracts (Table K11)
3854.A-Z	Special topics, A-Z
	Subarrange each by Table K12
3854.A72	Arbitration (Table K12)
3854.E45	Emergency legislation on rural leases (Table K12)
3854.E94	Eviction of rural tenants (Table K12)
3854.V34	Valuation (Table K12)
	Sale of cattle see KDZ-KH2 1115.C36
	Agricultural pledges and liens see KDZ-KH2 3873.5
	Collective bargaining. Collective labor agreements see KDZ-KH2 1832.A34
	Collective labor disputes see KDZ-KH2 1850.A33+
	Agricultural labor law in general see KDZ-KH2 1962.A34
	Social security for agricultural laborers see KDZ-KH2 2008.A34
	Rural police see KDZ-KH2 3228
	Rural housing see KDZ-KH2 3362
	Rural schools see KDZ-KH2 3574
	Rural economy see KDZ-KH2 3868+
	Rural electrification see KDZ-KH2 4138
3860	Conservation of agricultural and forestry lands (Table K12)
	Including soil conservation, field irrigation, erosion control
	Cf. KDZ-KH2 3330+ Land reclamation
	Control of agricultural pests, plant diseases, predatory animals
	Including weed control, plant import and quarantine
	Cf. KDZ-KH2 3450+ Veterinary laws
3862	General (Table K11)
3863.A-Z	Particular diseases, pests, etc., A-Z
	Pesticides. Herbicides see KDZ-KH2 3512
3865	Farm corporations (Table K11)
3866	Farm producers' and marketing cooperatives (Table K11)
3866.5	Farmers' associations (Table K11)

KDZ-KH2

	Regulation of industry, trade, and commerce. Occupational law
	Primary production. Extractive industries
	Agriculture. Forestry. Rural law -- Continued
	Economic legislation. Economic assistance
3868	General (Table K11)
3869	Distribution of seed grain, fertilizer, pesticides, etc. (Table K11)
	Price supports
3871	General (Table K11)
	By commoditiy
3872.A-Z	Field crops, A-Z
	Agricultural credit. Farm loans
3873	General (Table K11)
	Agricultural banks see KDZ-KH2 1154.A34
	Agricultural cooperative credit associations see KDZ-KH2 1154.A34
3873.5	Agricultural pledges and liens (Table K11)
	Agricultural production
	Including marketing, standards and grading
3875	General (Table K11)
3877	Seeds (Table K11)
	Cf. KDZ-KH2 3869 Distribution of seed grain
3879.A-Z	Field crops, A-Z
	Subarrange each by Table K12
3879.C63	Coffee (Table K12)
	Cf. KDZ-KH2 4073.C63 Export trade
3879.C65	Corn (Table K12)
3879.C66	Cotton (Table K12)
	Seeds see KDZ-KH2 3877
3879.S93	Sugar (Table K12)
	Livestock industry and trade. Cattle raising
	For meat industry see KDZ-KH2 4030+
3881	General (Table K11)
3882.A-Z	Special topics, A-Z
	Subarrange each by Table K12
3882.B7	Brands. Brand inspection (Table K12)
	Cattle sale see KDZ-KH2 1115.C36
	Cattle smuggling see KDZ-KH2 4825.4
	Product inspection see KDZ-KH2 3882.S24
3882.S24	Sanitation. Product inspection (Table K12)
	Cf. KDZ-KH2 4030+ Meat industry
3883.A-Z	Particular kinds of livestock, A-Z
	Dairy industry see KDZ-KH2 4035+
3886	Forestry. Timber law (Table K11)
3888	Viticulture (Table K11)
	For wine and wine making see KDZ-KH2 3492.W54

	Regulation of industry, trade, and commerce. Occupational law
	Primary production. Extractive industries
	Agriculture. Forestry. Rural law -- Continued
	Game laws see Table KDZ-KH1 649
	Fishing industry
3900	General (Table K11)
	Conservation and management
	For conservation and management of particular species see KDZ-KH2 3907.A+
3903	General (Table K11)
3905.A-Z	Coastal and inland fisheries. By area, A-Z
	For high seas fisheries, see K3898
	For particular species see KDZ-KH2 3907.A+
3907.A-Z	Particular fish and marine fauna, A-Z
	Subarrange each by Table K12
3907.S54	Shrimp (Table K12)
	Mining. Quarrying
3920	History
3921-3929	General (Table K9b)
3933	Administration. Procedure (Table K11)
3935	Conservation of mineral resources (Table K11)
3936	Mining registration (Table K11)
	Mining permits and concessions
3938	General (Table K11)
3939	Prospecting and exploration permits. Mining claims (Table K11)
3940	Concessions for exploitation (Table K11)
3941	Mining units (Table K11)
3943	Forfeiture of concessions (Table K11)
	Ownership of mines and mineral resources
	Cf. KDZ-KH2 594 Extent of land ownership above and below surface
3944	General (Table K11)
3945	Acquisitive prescription (Table K11)
3946	Expropriation. Nationalization. Government ownership (Table K11)
3948	Mine servitudes (Table K11)
	Mining corporations and partnerships
3949	General (Table K11)
3949.5.A-Z	Particular corporations, A-Z
	Mining contracts
3951	General (Table K11)
3952	Mining leases (Table K11)
	Mining banks see KDZ-KH2 1154.M54
3954	Coal (Table K11)
	Nonferrous metals

KDZ-KH2

	Regulation of industry, trade, and commerce. Occupational law
	Primary production. Extractive industries
	Mining. Quarrying
	Nonferrous metals -- Continued
3956	General (Table K11)
3957.A-Z	Particular metals, A-Z
	Subarrange each by Table K12
3957.C65	Copper (Table K12)
3957.G64	Gold (Table K12)
3957.T54	Tin (Table K12)
3957.U7	Uranium (Table K12)
	Petroleum. Oil and gas
3961-3969	General (Table K9b)
3972	Administration. Procedure (Table K11)
3974	Conservation (Table K11)
3975	Concessions (Table K11)
3977	Trade practices. Regulation of industry (Table K11)
3979	Oil and gas leases (Table K11)
3981.A-Z	Particular companies, A-Z
3983.A-Z	Particular oil fields, reserves, etc., A-Z
3985	Natural gas (Table K11)
3987	Expropriation. Nationalization. Government ownership (Table K11)
	Including state petroleum monopoly
3993.A-Z	Other nonmetallic minerals and gases, A-Z
	Subarrange each by Table K12
3993.S24	Saltpeter (Table K12)
	Manufacturing industries
4000	General (Table K11)
	Chemical industries
4001	General (Table K11)
4002.A-Z	Particular products, A-Z
	Subarrange each by Table K12
4002.F45	Fertilizers (Table K12)
4004	Drug and pharmaceutical industries (Table K11)
	Cf. KDZ-KH2 3480+ Drug laws
	Cf. KDZ-KH2 4095.D77 Retail trade
	Textile industries
4006	General (Table K11)
	Textile fabrics
4008	General (Table K12)
4009.A-Z	Particular products, A-Z
	Subarrange each by Table K12
4009.S56	Silks (Table K12)
4012.A-Z	Major and heavy industries, A-Z
	Subarrange each by Table K12

	Regulation of industry, trade, and commerce. Occupational law
	Manufacturing industries
	Major and heavy industries, A-Z -- Continued
4012.A95	Automobile industry (Table K12)
4012.E43	Electric industries (Table K12)
4012.I76	Iron and steel industries (Table K12)
4012.P34	Paper industry (Table K12)
4012.R83	Rubber industry (Table K12)
	Steel industry see KDZ-KH2 4012.I76
4014.A-Z	Consumer products. Light industries, A-Z
	Subarrange each by Table K12
4014.B56	Biotechnology industries (Table K12)
4014.B66	Book industries and trade (Table K12)
4014.L4	Leather industry (Table K12)
4014.T62	Tobacco products (Table K12)
	Food processing industries
4020	General (Table K11)
	Agricultural products
4022	Sugar refining (Table KDZ-KH18)
	Fruit and vegetables
4026	General (Table KDZ-KH18)
4027.A-Z	Particular products, A-Z
	Subarrange each by Table K12
4027.B34	Banana (Table K12)
	Wine and wine making see KDZ-KH2 3492.W54
	Meat industry
4030	General (Table KDZ-KH18)
4031	Slaughtering and slaughterhouses (Table K11)
	Dairy industry
	Including distribution
4035	General (Table KDZ-KH18)
4037.A-Z	Particular products, A-Z
4040	Fishery products. Seafood industry (Table KDZ-KH18)
4045	Beverages (Table K11)
	Cf. KDZ-KH2 3490+ Alcoholic beverages
4052	Construction and building industry. Contractors (Table K11)
	Cf. KDZ-KH2 898.B84 Building and construction contracts
	Cf. KDZ-KH2 3354+ Building laws
	Trade and commerce
	Cf. KDZ-KH2 1050+ Commercial law
	Cf. KDZ-KH2 3731+ Trade regulations
4060	General (Table K11)
4062.A-Z	Particular commodities, A-Z
	Subarrange each by Table K12
4062.C66	Cotton (Table K12)

KDZ-KH2

	Regulation of industry, trade, and commerce. Occupational law
	Trade and commerce
	Particular commodities, A-Z -- Continued
4062.G7	Grain (Table K12)
	Including grain elevators and boards of grain
4062.T62	Tobacco (Table K12)
	International trade. Export and import controls
4066	General (Table K11)
4068.A-Z	Particular commodities, A-Z
	Export trade
	Including export controls, regulations, and promotion
4071	General (Table K11)
4073.A-Z	Particular commodities, A-Z
	Subarrange each by Table K12
4073.B64	Books (Table K12)
4073.C63	Coffee (Table K12)
4073.C66	Cotton (Table K12)
4073.S93	Sugar (Table K12)
	Import trade
	Including import controls and regulations
	For tariff see KDZ-KH2 4801+
	For dumping see KDZ-KH2 4827
4075	General (Table K11)
4077.A-Z	Particular commodities, A-Z
4077.A96	Automobiles
4080	Wholesale trade (Table K11)
	Retail trade
4083	General (Table K11)
	Conditions of trading
4086	Sunday legislation (Table K11)
	Special modes of trading
4088	Franchises (Table K11)
4090	Markets. Fairs (Table K11)
4091	Peddling. Canvassing (Table K11)
4095.A-Z	Particular products, A-Z
	Subarrange each by Table K12
4095.A95	Automobile tires (Table K12)
4095.D77	Drugs. Pharmaceutical products (Table K12)
4095.G36	Gasoline (Table K12)
	Including regulation of gasoline stations
	Pharmaceutical products see KDZ-KH2 4095.D77
	Secondhand trade
4097	General (Table K11)
4098.A-Z	Particular types, A-Z
	Subarrange each by Table K12

Regulation of industry, trade, and commerce. Occupational law
Trade and commerce
Retail trade
Secondhand trade
Particular types, A-Z -- Continued
4098.A92   Auction houses (Table K12)
Cf. KDZ-KH2 1095 Auction sales
4098.P37   Pawnbrokers (Table K12)
Including charitable pawnshops
Service trades
Including licensing
4101   General (Table K11)
4103.A-Z   Particular service trades, A-Z
Subarrange each by Table K12
Auctioneers see KDZ-KH2 1095
4103.E46   Employment agencies (Table K12)
4103.H66   Hotels. Restaurants (Table K12)
Cf. KDZ-KH2 904 Innkeeper and guest
Insurance agents and brokers see KDZ-KH2 1222
4103.L4   Lease and rental services (Table K12)
4103.R4   Real estate agents. Real estate business (Table K12)
Rental services see KDZ-KH2 4103.L4
Restaurants see KDZ-KH2 4103.H66
Stockbrokers see KDZ-KH2 1084
4103.T67   Tourist trade (Table K12)
4103.U53   Undertakers (Table K12)
Cf. KDZ-KH2 3405 Disposal of the dead
4110   Warehouses. Storage (Table K11)
For warehouse contracts see KDZ-KH2 1121+
For grain-elevators see KDZ-KH2 4062.G7
Public utilities
Including private, publicly owned, and public-private (mixed) utility
companies
Regulated industries in general
4120   General (Table K11)
4122   Public service commissions (Table K11)
4123   National (Federal), state, and local jurisdiction (Table K11)
4125   Concessions (Table K11)
4127   Valuation (Table K11)
4128   Finance (Table K11)
4130   Ratemaking (Table K11)
4132   Expropriation or nationalization of public utilities (General)
(Table K11)
For expropriation or nationalization or a particular type of
utility, see the utility, e.g. KDZ-KH2 4139 , Electric utilities
Particular utilities

KDZ-KH2

	Regulation of industry, trade, and commerce. Occupational law
	Public utilities
	Particular utilities -- Continued
	Power supply
	Including energy policy, and energy resources and development in general
4134	General (Table K11)
	Electricity
4136	General (Table K11)
4137	Concessions (Table K11)
	For particular concessions see KDZ-KH2 4140.A+
4138	Rural electrification (Table K11)
4139	Expropriation. Nationalization. Purchase by the public (Table K11)
	Including national, state, and municipal utilities
4140.A-Z	Particular companies, A-Z
	Including concessions, litigation, decisions, awards, rulings, etc.
4142	Gas (Table K11)
4145	Water (Table K11)
	Including water supply
	For water power development see KDZ-KH2 3310+
	Atomic power
4148	General (Table K11)
4149	Atomic energy commissions (Table K11)
4150	Liability (Table K11)
4151.A-Z	Other sources of power, A-Z
	Transportation and communication see KDZ-KH2 4160+
	Transportation and communication
4160	General (Table K11)
4162	Transportation commissions, directorates, etc. (Table K11)
	Offenses against means of transportation and communication see KDZ-KH2 5686
	Road traffic. Automotive transportation
4170	General (Table K11)
4175	Safety responsibility laws. Financial responsibility laws. Compulsory insurance (Table K11)
4180.A-Z	Particular vehicles, A-Z
	Traffic regulation and enforcement
4183	General (Table K11)
4184	Criminal provisions. Traffic violations. Drunk driving (Table K11)
	Carriage of passengers and goods
4187	General motor carrier regulation (Table K11)
	Passenger carriers
4190	General (Table K11)

	Regulation of industry, trade, and commerce. Occupational law
	Transportation and communication
	Road traffic. Automotive transportation
	Carriage of passengers and goods
	Passenger carriers -- Continued
4191.A-Z	Particular types of passenger carriers, A-Z
	Subarrange each by Table K12
4191.B86	Bus lines (Table K12)
4191.T37	Taxicabs (Table K12)
4193	Carriers of goods. Truck lines (Table K11)
	Railroads
	Including corporate structure and regulation of industry
4200	General (Table K11)
4202	Railroad commissions (Table K11)
	Including practice and procedure
4204	National and state jurisdiction (Table K11)
4206	Concessions for railroad construction and operation (Table K11)
	Including public works contracts for railroad construction
	For particular concessions see KDZ-KH2 4235.A+
4208	Consolidation and merger (Table K11)
4210	Government ownership (Table K11)
4212	Finance (Table K11)
	Operation of railroads
4214	General (Table K11)
	Rates and ratemaking
4217	General (Table K11)
	Freight. Freight classification
4218	General (Table K11)
4221	Dumurrage (Table K11)
4222.A-Z	Particular commodities, A-Z
4225	Passenger fares
	Liability
	Including damage to property
4230	General (Table K11)
4231	Freight claims
4233	Personal injuries
4235.A-Z	Special railroads and railroad companies, A-Z
	Including concessions, litigation, decisions, awards, rulings, etc.
4240	Local transit
4243	Pipe lines
	Aviation
4250	General (Table K11)

	Regulation of industry, trade, and commerce. Occupational law
	Transportation and communication
	Aviation -- Continued
4253	Air safety (Table K11)
	Including air traffic rules and airworthiness; aeronautical telecommunication and radio aids to air navigation
	Aircraft
4255	General (Table K11)
4256	Nationality. Registration. Transfer (Table K11)
	Aircraft mortgages see KDZ-KH2 1200.M65
	Particular types of aircraft
4258	Helicopters
4259	Airports (Table K11)
4261	Pilots. Crews. Ground personnel (Table K11)
	Commercial aviation. Airlines
4265	General (Table K11)
4266	Regulatory agencies (Table K11)
4268	Finance. Accounting. Auditing (Table K11)
4270	Rates (Table K11)
	Including ratemaking, rate agreements, and passenger fares
4272	Air charters (Table K11)
4274	Cargo. Air freight (Table K11)
	Liability
	For general tort liability for aviation accidents see KDZ-KH2 988.A96
4276	General (Table K11)
4277	Limited liability clause (Table K11)
4278	Damage to property (Table K11)
4279	Personal injuries (Table K11)
4281.A-Z	Particular airlines, A-Z
4285	Space law (Table K11)
	Cf. KZD1002+ , International law
	Water transportation. Navigation and shipping
4300	General (Table K11)
	Merchant mariners see KDZ-KH2 1434+
	Ships
4303	General (Table K11)
4304	Registration (Table K11)
	Safety regulations
4306	General (Table K11)
4307	Inspection (Table K11)
4308	Manning requirements (Table K11)
4310.A-Z	Particular types of vessels, A-Z
4312.A-Z	Particular types of cargo, A-Z
	Ship mortgages see KDZ-KH2 1417+

	Regulation of industry, trade, and commerce. Occupational law
	Transportation and communication
	Water transportation. Navigation and shipping
	Ships -- Continued
	Navigation and pilotage
	Including coastwise navigation
	Cf. K4184 , International rules of the road
4314	General (Table K11)
4316.A-Z	Particular waterways, A-Z
	Subarrange each by Table K12
	Harbors and ports
	Including port charges and tonnage feees
	For harbor improvement see KDZ-KH2 3314
	For free ports and zones see KDZ-KH2 4832+
4319	General (Table K11)
4320.A-Z	Particular ports, A-Z
	Subarrange each by Table K12
4322	Lighthouses (Table K12)
	Shipping laws. The merchant marine
4326	General (Table K11)
4328	Regulation of the shipping industry (Table K11)
	Merchant marine
4330	General (Table K11)
	Finance
4332	General (Table K11)
4333	Shipping bounties and subsidies (Table K11)
4335	Officers (Table K11)
	Including examinations, qualification, promotion, etc.
	For the rights and responsibilities of merchant
	marine officers as established by commercial
	law see KDZ-KH2 1410
	Merchant mariners
	Legal status see KDZ-KH2 1410
	Maritime labor law see KDZ-KH2 1434+
	Social insurance see KDZ-KH2 1441+
4337	Domestic shipping. Coastwise shipping
	Including inland water carriers
4339	Ocean freight forwarders
	Customhouse brokers see KDZ-KH2 4821.5
	Communication. Mass media
4350	General (Table K11)
	Postal service
	Including works on postal service, telegraph, and telephone
	combined
4352	General (Table K11)
	Organization and administration

Regulation of industry, trade, and commerce. Occupational law
Transportation and communication
Communication. Mass media
Postal service
Organization and administration -- Continued
4354   General (Table K11)
4356   Officers and personnel (Table K11)
Including salaries, wages, and pension
Classification of mails. Rates
4360   General (Table K11)
4362.A-Z   Special classes, A-Z
4366   Postal money orders. Postal notes (Table K11)
Crimes committed through the mail see KDZ-KH2 5741+
Violation of the privacy of letters (Torts) see KDZ-KH2
972.L46
Violation of the privacy of letters (Criminal law) see KDZ-
KH2 5582
4368   Forwarding agents. Freight forwarders (Table K11)
For ocean freight forwarders see KDZ-KH2 4339
Press law
Including legal status of journalists
For works on freedom of the press see KDZ-KH2
3015+
4370   General (Table K11)
Press censorship see KDZ-KH2 3016
4372   Criminal provisions (Table K11)
Including procedural aspects
Cf. KDZ-KH2 5593 Libel and slander committed
through the press
Telecommunication
4380   General (Table K11)
Particular companies see KDZ-KH2 4417.A+
Telegraph. Teletype
Including telegraph and telephone combined
4385   General (Table K11)
4387   Ratemaking (Table K11)
Particular companies see KDZ-KH2 4417.A+
Telephone
Including radio telephone
4390   General (Table K11)
Particular companies see KDZ-KH2 4417.A+
Radio and television communication
4400   General (Table K11)
4403   Radio and televisions stations. Concessions.
Licensing (Table K11)
Including frequency allocations

	Regulation of industry, trade, and commerce. Occupational law
	Transportation and communication
	Communication. Mass media
	Telecommunication
	Radio and television communication -- Continued
	Radio broadcasting
4406	General (Table K11)
	Radio aids to air navigation see KDZ-KH2 4253
4410	Television broadcasting (Table K11)
4417.A-Z	Particular companies, A-Z
	Professions and occupations
4440	General (Table K11)
4442	Professional associations (General) (Table K11)
4444	Fees. Professional economics (Table K11)
4445.A-Z	Special topics, A-Z
4445.L5	Licensing. Certification
	Including licensing of foreign graduates
	Particular professions
	Including licensing, certification, professional ethics, and liability
	The health professions
	For medical legislation see KDZ-KH2 3435+
	General see KDZ-KH2 4446
	Physicians
	Including the health professions in general
4446	General (Table K11)
4447.A-Z	Special topics, A-Z
	Subarrange each by Table K12
	Economics see KDZ-KH2 4447.F43
4447.E37	Education and training (Table K12)
4447.F43	Fees. Medical economics (Table K12)
4447.M34	Malpractice liability (Table K12)
	Medical economics see KDZ-KH2 4447.F43
	Privileged communications see KDZ-KH2 2653.5.A86
	Retirement pensions see KDZ-KH2 2008.P48
	Violation of professional secrets (Criminal law) see KDZ-KH2 5584
4448.A-Z	Particular branches of medicine, A-Z
	Subarrange each by Table K12
4448.D44	Dentists and dental specialists (Table K12)
4448.P75	Psychiatrists. Psychotherapists. Psychologists. Counselors (Table K12)
4449.A-Z	Other health practitioners, A-Z
4450.A-Z	Auxiliary professions, A-Z
	Subarrange each by Table K12
4450.M53	Midwives (Table K12)
4450.N85	Nurses (Table K12)

KDZ-KH2

	Regulation of industry, trade, and commerce. Occupational law
	Professions and occupations
	Particular professions
	The health professions
	Physicians
	Auxiliary professions, A-Z -- Continued
4450.P48	Pharmacists (Table K12)
	Lawyers see Table KDZ-KH1 206
	Notaries see KDZ-KH2 250+
4453	Accountants. Auditors (Table K11)
	Engineering and construction
4456	Architects (Table K11)
4457	Engineers (Table K11)
4458	Mining engineers (Table K11)
4459.A-Z	Other professions and occupations, A-Z
	Subarrange each by Table K12
4459.A25	Actors (Table K12)
4459.B76	Broadcasters (Table K12)
4459.C48	Chemists (Table K12)
4459.C65	Consultants (Table K12)
4459.E43	Electricians (Table K12)
	Journalists see KDZ-KH2 4370+
4459.P47	Performing artists (Table K12)
4459.P82	Public relations consultants and officers (Table K12)
4459.S65	Soccer players, Professional (Table K12)
	Teachers see KDZ-KH2 3562+
4459.V46	Veterinarians (Table K12)
	Cf. KDZ-KH2 3450+ Veterinary laws
	Public finance
4550	General (Table K11)
	Money. Currency. Coinage
4552	General (Table K11)
4553.A-Z	Special topics, A-Z
	Subarrange each by Table K12
4553.C85	Currency stabilization (Table K12)
4553.I53	Indexation (Table K12)
	Foreign exchange and regulations
4555	General (Table K11)
4556	Criminal provisions (Table K11)
4560	Budget. Government expenditures (Table K11)
	Expenditure control. Public auditing and accounting
4565	General (Table K11)
4566	General accounting office. Comptroller general (Table K11)
	Public debts. Loans. Bond issues
	Including compulsory loans
4570	General (Table K11)

	Public finance
	Public debts. Loans. Bond issues -- Continued
4572	Development banks (Table K11)
	National revenue
4574	History
4575	General (Table K11)
4576	Fees. Fines (Table K11)
	Including user charges
	Taxation
4578	History
4578.5	War and emergency legislation (Table K11)
4581-4589	General (Table K9b modified)
4590	Tables
4591	Taxing power and its limitations (Table K11)
4592	Interpretation and construction of tax laws (Table K11)
4594	Tax saving. Tax planning (Table K11)
	Including income tax planning
	Tax administration and procedure
	Including administration and procedure relating to federal taxes in general and to federal income tax. General works and works on special aspects and topics relating to other taxes are classed with those taxes
	Cf. KDZ-KH2 4861+ State taxation
	Cf. KDZ-KH2 4905+ Local taxation
4597	General (Table K11)
4598	National revenue service (Table K11)
	National, state, and local jurisdiction see KDZ-KH2 4854
4600	Double taxation (Table K11)
	Tax collection. Procedure. Practice
4603	General (Table K11)
4605	Remedies. Tax courts. Appeals (Table K11)
4607.A-Z	Special topics, A-Z
4607.A25	Accounting, Tax (Table K12)
4607.C64	Compromise, Tax (Table K12)
4607.E53	Enforcement. Execution. Tax sales (Table K12)
	Execution see KDZ-KH2 4607.E53
4607.J64	Joint tax obligations. Solidarity (Table K12)
4607.L53	Liens, Tax (Table K12)
4607.L55	Limitation of actions (Table K12)
4607.N66	Notice (Table K12)
4607.R43	Refund (Table K12)
4607.R45	Remission (Table K12)
4607.R47	Res judicata (Table K12)
	Solidarity see KDZ-KH2 4607.J64
	Tax sales see KDZ-KH2 4607.E53
4609.A-Z	Tax treatment of special activities, A-Z

KDZ-KH2

	Public finance
	National revenue
	Taxation
	Tax treatment of special activities, A-Z -- Continued
4609.B36	Bankruptcy (Table K12)
	Exemptions. Tax reductions and other tax benefits
	For exemptions from a special tax, see the tax
4611	General (Table K11)
4612	Tax incentive legislation (Table K11)
4613	Criminal law. Tax evasion (Table K11)
	Particular taxes
4619	Direct taxes (General) (Table K11)
	Income tax
4621-4629	General (Table K9b modified)
4629.6.A-Z	Works for particular groups of individual users, A-Z
	For particular lines of corporate business see
	KDZ-KH2 4700.A+
4630	Income tax tables
	Tax planning see KDZ-KH2 4594
	Tax administration and procedure see KDZ-KH2 4597+
	Tax accounting see KDZ-KH2 4607.A25
	Income
4632	General (Table K11)
	Exclusion from income. Exempt income
4634	General (Table K11)
4635	Tax-exempt securities. Government bonds (Table K11)
	Particular sources of income
	Foreign source income see KDZ-KH2 4648
	Income from personal services
4637	General (Table K11)
	Income from office and employment. Salaries and wages
	Including fringe benefits
	For social security tax see KDZ-KH2 2004
4638	General (Table K11)
4639.A-Z	Particular payments and benefits, A-Z
	Subarrange each by Table K12
4639.P74	Profit sharing (Table K12)
4641	Income from occupation and profession (Table K11)
4642	Income from real property (Table K11)
4644	Business income (Table K11)
	Including income from industry, trade, and commerce
	For income of particular lines of corporate business see KDZ-KH2 4700.A+

Public finance
National revenue
Taxation
Particular taxes
Income tax
Income -- Continued
Income from capital investment

4646   Securities. Dividends. Interest (Table K11)
     Cf. KDZ-KH2 4635 Tax-exempt securities
     Cf. KDZ-KH2 4674 Taxation of dividends and
      interest paid to nonresidents
4648   Foreign source income. Foreign investments
     (Table K11)
4649   Capital gains tax (Table K11)
     Class here works on capital gains tax levied either
      under the income tax law or under other special
      laws
4650.A-Z   Other sources, A-Z
     Subarrange each by Table K12
4650.G35   Gambling gains (Table K12)
4650.I53   Industrial property (Table K12)
Deductions. Allowances. Personal exemptions
4652   General (Table K11)
4654   Amortization. Depreciation allowances (Table K11)
4659   Tax returns (Table K11)
Surtaxes
     Including complementary and additional taxes
4662   General
4663   Unjust enrichment tax (Table K11)
4665   Emergency tax (Table K11)
4666   Excess profits tax (Table K11)
    Surtax on income from foreign investment and on
     other foreign source income see KDZ-KH2 4648
    Surtax on income earned by non-residents see KDZ-
     KH2 4674
4668.A-Z   Special purpose surtaxes, complementary, and
     additional taxes. By purpose, A-Z
     Subarrange each by Table K12
4668.E44   Electrification (Table K12)
4668.H67   Housing development (Table K12)
Particular methods of assessment and collection
Payment at source
4672   Payroll deduction. Withholding tax (Table K11)
    Social security tax see KDZ-KH2 2004
    Withholding taxes on dividends, interest, etc. see
     KDZ-KH2 4646

KDZ-KH2

Public finance
National revenue
Taxation
Particular taxes
Income tax -- Continued
Particular classes of taxpayers
Business organizations see KDZ-KH2 4680+
Corporations see KDZ-KH2 4685+

4674	Nonresident taxpayers (Table K11)
	Including both nationals and alien residents abroad, and foreign companies not operating in the taxing country
4676	Trusts (Table K11)
	Tax exempt entities see KDZ-KH2 4678
4678	Income of nonprofit organizations (Table K11)
	Including nonprofit corporations, foundations, endowments, pension funds, etc.
	Income of business organizations
	Including both business associations and individual merchants
4680	General (Table K11)
4681	Partnerships and joint ventures (Table K11)
	Juristic persons. Corporations
	For foreign companies not operating in the taxing country see KDZ-KH2 4674
	For nonprofit corporations see KDZ-KH2 4678
4684	General (Table K11)
	Corporation income tax
4685	General (Table K11)
	Surtaxes. Complementary and additional taxes
4688	General (Table K11)
4689	Excess profits tax (Table K11)
4691	Undistributed profits (Table K11)
	Substitute inheritance tax on corporate capital see KDZ-KH2 4740+
4693	Family corporations (Table K11)
4694	Cooperatives (Table K11)
4700.A-Z	Particular lines of corporate business, A-Z
	Subarrange each by Table K12
4700.A34	Agriculture (Table K12)
4700.B35	Banks (Table K12)
4700.I56	Insurance companies (Table K12)
4700.M54	Mining (Table K12)
	Oil and gas see KDZ-KH2 4700.P4
4700.P4	Petroleum. Oil and gas (Table K12)
4700.S45	Service trades (Table K12)

Public finance
National revenue
Taxation
Particular taxes
Income tax
Income of business organizations
Juristic persons. Corporations
Particular lines of corporate business, A-Z --
Continued

4700.S46	Shipping (Table K12)
	Tax incentive legislation see KDZ-KH2 4612

Property taxes. Taxation of capital

4710	General (Table K11)
4712	Tax valuation (Table K11)
	Cf. KDZ-KH2 4654 Amortization. Depreciation allowances

National taxes affecting real property
Including income tax, estate, inheritance, and gift taxes, and others; and works on national and state taxes combined

4717	General (Table K11)
4717.5	Cadasters (Table K11)
4719	Special assessments (Table K11)
4722	Real estate transactions (Table K11)
4723	Personal property taxes (Table K11)
4725	Wealth tax (Table K11)

Other taxes on capital and income
Capital gains tax see KDZ-KH2 4649

4732	Presumed minimum income tax (Table K11)

Estate, inheritance, and gift taxes

4736	General (Table K11)
4737	Estate tax. Inheritance tax (Table K11)
4739	Gift taxes (Table K11)

Substitute inheritance tax

4740	General (Table K11)
4740.3	Substitute inheritance tax on individuals (Table K11)
4740.6	Substitute inheritance tax on corporate capital (Table K11)

Taxes on transactions. Taxes on production and consumption

4750	General (Table K11)
4752	Retail sales taxes (Table K11)
4754	Excise taxes (Table K11)
4756	Turnover tax. Gross receipts-tax (Table K11)
4758	Value-added tax (Table K11)
4760	Use tax (Table K11)

KDZ-KH2

	Public finance
	National revenue
	Taxation
	Particular taxes
	Taxes on transactions. Taxes on production and consumption -- Continued
	Stamp duties see KDZ-KH2 4796
	Customs duties see KDZ-KH2 4801+
4763.A-Z	Particular commodities, services, and transactions, A-Z
	Subarrange each by Table K12
4763.A43	Alcohol. Alcoholic beverages. Liquor taxes (Table K12)
	Alcoholic beverages see KDZ-KH2 4763.A43
	Automobiles see KDZ-KH2 4763.M66
4763.A96	Automotive transportation
4763.C65	Computers (Table K12)
4763.E43	Electricity (Table K12)
4763.E44	Electronic commerce. Internet sales (Table K12)
	Gasoline see KDZ-KH2 4763.M65
	Internet sales see KDZ-KH2 4763.E44
	Liquor taxes see KDZ-KH2 4763.A43
4763.L87	Luxury articles (Table K12)
4763.M65	Motor fuels (Table K12)
4763.M66	Motor vehicles (Table K12)
	Real estate transactions see KDZ-KH2 4722
4763.S42	Securities. Stock exchange transactions (Table K12)
	Stock exchange transactions see KDZ-KH2 4763.S42
4763.S93	Sugar (Table K12)
4763.T62	Tobacco and tobacco products (Table K12)
4763.T7	Transportation (Table K12)
4770.A-Z	Other taxes, A-Z
	Subarrange each by Table K12
4770.D44	Departure tax on residents (Table K12)
	Import and export taxes see KDZ-KH2 4801+
4770.R43	Registration fees. Transfer taxes (Table K12)
	Social security taxes see KDZ-KH2 2004
4770.S64	Special assessments (Table K12)
	Stamp duties see KDZ-KH2 4796
	Transfer taxes see KDZ-KH2 4770.R43
	Taxation of natural resources
4780	General (Table K11)
	Particular resources and resource industries
	Cf. KDZ-KH2 4700.A+ Income tax on particular lines of corporate business
	Mining
4782	General (Table K11)

               Public finance
                National revenue
                  Taxation of natural resources
                    Particular resources and resource industries
                      Mining -- Continued

4783	Petroleum. Oil and gas (Table K11)
4785	Copper (Table K11)
4788.A-Z	Other, A-Z

                  Particular methods of assessment and collection
                    For assessment and collection of particular taxes, see those
                      taxes

4796	Stamp duties (Table K11)

                Tariff. Customs
                  For regional multilateral trade agreements and related bilateral
                    trade agreements, see the appropriate region
                  For trade agreements not limited to a region, see K4600+
                  For trade agreements of the United States, see KF6665+
                  For foreign trade regulation see KDZ-KH2 4066+

4801-4809	General (Table K9b)
4812	Tariff commission (Table K11)

                Particular tariffs

4815	General (Table K11)
4817.A-Z	Particular commodities, A-Z

                    Subarrange each by Table K12

4817.C36	Cattle (Table K12)
4817.C64	Coffee (Table K12)
4817.M32	Machinery (Table K12)

                Customs administration

4820	General (Table K11)

                  Customs service

4821	General (Table K11)
4821.5	Customhouse brokers (Table K11)
4823	Procedure. Remedies. Customs courts (Table K11)

                Enforcement. Criminal law. Smuggling

4825	General (Table K11)
4825.4	Cattle smuggling (Table K11)
4827	Dumping. Antidumping duties (Table K11)
4828	Drawbacks (Table K11)

                Exemptions. Duty-free imports

4830	General (Table K11)
	Particular commodities see KDZ-KH2 4817.A+

                Free ports and zones

4832	General (Table K11)
4833.A-Z	Particular free ports and zones, A-Z

                    Subarrange each by Table K12

4834.A-Z	Other, A-Z

KDZ-KH2

Public finance
National revenue
Tariff. Customs
Other, A-Z -- Continued
4834.A67   Appraisal of goods (Table K11)
Nomenclature see KDZ-KH2 4834.T48
4834.T48   Terminology and classification. Nomenclature (Table
K11)
State (Provincial, etc.) and local finance
4840   General (Table K11)
4842   Budget. Expenditure control. Auditing and accounting
(Table K11)
4843   Public debts. Securities. Bonds (Table K11)
4847   State and local taxation (Table K11)
4850   Federal grants-in-aid. Revenue sharing. Intergovernmental
tax relations (Table K11)
State (Provincial, etc.) finance
4852   General (Table K11)
4854   Jurisdiction. Limitations on state taxing power (Table K11)
Cf. KDZ-KH2 4850 Intergovernmental tax relations
4856   Budget. Expenditure control. Auditing and accounting
(Table K11)
4858   Public debts. Securities. Bonds (Table K11)
Taxation
4861   General (Table K11)
Particular taxes
Income tax
4863   General (Table K11)
4865   Corporation income tax (Table K11)
Property taxes. Taxation of capital
4870   General (Table K11)
4872   Real property taxes (Table K11)
For cadasters see KDZ-KH2 4717.5
4875   Personal property taxes (Table K11)
4878   Estate, inheritance, and gift taxes (Table K11)
4879   Business taxes. Business property taxes. Licenses
(Table K11)
Taxes on transactions. Taxes on production and
consumption
4881   General (Table K11)
4882   Retail sales taxes (Table K11)
4884   Excise taxes (Table K11)
4886   Use tax (Table K11)
4888.A-Z   Particular commodities, services, and transactions, A-
Z
4890   Stamp duties (Table K11)

	Public finance
	State (Provincial, etc.) and local finance
	State (Provincial, etc.) finance
	Taxation
	Particular taxes -- Continued
4891.A-Z	Other taxes, A-Z
4895.A-Z	Other sources of revenue, A-Z
	Subarrange each by Table K12
4895.F43	Federal grants-in-aid (Table K12)
	Revenue sharing see KDZ-KH2 4850
	Local finance
4900	General (Table K11)
4902	Budget. Expenditure control. Auditing and accounting (Table K11)
4903	Municipal debts. Loans. Municipal bonds (Table K11)
	Revenue sharing. Intergovernmental tax relations see KDZ-KH2 4850
	Taxation
	Including municipal taxing power
4905	General (Table K11)
4906	Income tax (Table K11)
	Real property taxes
4908	General (Table K11)
4910	Real property assessment. Land valuation (Table K11)
	For special assessments see KDZ-KH2 4915.S66
4911	Exempted property (Table K11)
4913.A-Z	Particular kinds of real property, A-Z
	Subarrange each by Table K12
4913.R85	Rural property (Table K12)
4913.U72	Urban property (Table K12)
4915.A-Z	Special topics, A-Z
	Subarrange each by Table K12
	Assessment for public improvements see KDZ-KH2 4915.S66
4915.R4	Real property transfer tax (Table K12)
4915.S66	Special assessments (Table K12)
4915.U52	Unearned increment (Table K12)
4917	Personal property taxes (Table K11)
4919	Business taxes. License fees (Table K11)
	Including taxes on occupations and professions
	Taxes on transactions. Taxes on production and consumption
4921	General (Table K11)
4922	Sales taxes (Table K11)
4924	Excise taxes (Table K11)

KDZ-KH2

	Public finance
	State (Provincial, etc.) and local finance
	Local finance
	Taxation
	Taxes on transactions. Taxes on production and consumption -- Continued
4925.A-Z	Particular commodities, services, and transactions, A-Z
	Subarrange each by Table K12
4925.S47	Service industries (Table K12)
4927.A-Z	Other taxes, A-Z
4929.A-Z	Other sources of revenue, A-Z
	Subarrange each by Table K12
4929.G7	Grants-in-aid (Table K12)
4929.L52	License fees (Table K12)
	Government measures in time of war, national emergency, or economic crisis. Emergency economic legislation
4950	General (Table K11)
4960.A-Z	Special topics, A-Z
	Subarrange each by Table K12
	Alien property see KDZ-KH2 558
4960.D42	Debtors' relief. General moratorium (Table K12)
	Cf. KDZ-KH2 3854.E45 Emergency legislation on rural leases
	Moratorium see KDZ-KH2 4960.D42
4960.P74	Price control. Profiteering (Table K12)
	For offenses against the national economy see KDZ-KH2 5730
4960.R36	Rationing (Table K12)
	Rent control see KDZ-KH2 887
	Taxation see KDZ-KH2 4578.5
	National defense. Military law
5100	General (Table K11)
5103	Wartime and emergency legislation (Table K11)
	For economic controls see KDZ-KH2 4950+
	The military establishment. Armed forces
5110	General (Table K11)
5112	Organization and administration. Department of defense (Table K11)
	Armed forces
	General see KDZ-KH2 5110
	Conscription. Draft
5116	General (Table K11)
5118.A-Z	Special topics, A-Z
	Subarrange each by Table K12
5118.A44	Aliens (Table K12)
	Personnel. Services

	National defense. Military law
	The military establishment. Armed forces
	Armed forces
	Personnel. Services -- Continued
5121	General (Table K11)
5122	Enlistment. Recruiting. Discharge (Table K11)
	Education. Training
5123	General (Table K11)
	Academies. Schools. Courses of instruction
5123.3	General (Table K11)
5123.6.A-Z	Special topics, A-Z
	Subarrange each by Table K12
5123.6.S34	Scholarships (Table K12)
5123.7.A-Z	Particular schools, A-Z
	Pay, allowances, benefits
	Including retirement benefits
5125	General (Table K11)
5125.3	Retirement pensions (Table K11)
5125.5	Disability pensions (Table K11)
5125.6	Social security benefits for members of the armed forces (Table K11)
5125.7.A-Z	Other, A-Z
5127	Uniform regulations. Wearing of decorations and medals
	Cf. KDZ-KH2 3165+ Decorations of honor. Awards
5129	Officers
	Including appointments, promotions, retirement
5130	Enlisted personnel
	Militia. National guard see KDZ-KH2 5152
5134.A-Z	Special services, A-Z
5135	Equipment. Weapons. Munitions. Supplies and stores
5136	Hospitals (Table K11)
	Military hygiene see KDZ-KH2 3403.M54
	Particular branches of service
	Army
5140	Organization. Administration (Table K11)
	Personnel. Services. Equipment. Plants. Hospitals
5141	General (Table K11)
5142	Enlistment. Recruiting. Discharge (Table K11)
	Education. Training
5143	General (Table K11)
	Academies. Schools. Courses of instruction
5143.3	General (Table K11)
5143.6.A-Z	Special topics, A-Z
	Subarrange each by Table K12
5143.6.S34	Scholarships (Table K12)
5143.7.A-Z	Particular schools, A-Z

KDZ-KH2

National defense. Military law
The military establishment. Armed forces
Armed forces
Particular branches of service
Army
Personnel. Services. Equipment. Plants. Hospitals --
Continued
Pay, allowances, benefits
Including retirement benefits

5145	General (Table K11)
5145.3	Retirement pensions (Table K11)
5145.5	Disability pensions (Table K11)
5145.6	Social security benefits for members of the armed forces (Table K11)
5145.7.A-Z	Other, A-Z
5147	Uniform regulations. Wearing of decorations and medals
5149	Officers
	Including appointments, promotions, retirement
5150	Enlisted personnel
5152	Militia. National guard
5154.A-Z	Special services, A-Z
5154.A76	Artillery
5154.C48	Army chaplains
5155	Equipment. Weapons. Munitions. Supplies and stores
5156	Hospitals (Table K11)
	Navy
5160	Organization. Administration (Table K11)
	Personnel. Services. Equipment. Plants. Hospitals
5161	General (Table K11)
5162	Enlistment. Recruiting. Discharge (Table K11)
	Education. Training
5163	General (Table K11)
	Academies. Schools. Courses of instruction
5163.3	General (Table K11)
5163.6.A-Z	Special topics, A-Z
	Subarrange each by Table K12
5163.6.S34	Scholarships (Table K12)
5163.7.A-Z	Particular schools, A-Z
	Pay, allowances, benefits
	Including retirement benefits
5165	General (Table K11)
5165.3	Retirement pensions (Table K11)
5165.5	Disability pensions (Table K11)
5165.6	Social security benefits for members of the armed forces (Table K11)

National defense. Military law
The military establishment. Armed forces
Armed forces
Particular branches of service
Navy
Personnel. Services. Equipment. Plants. Hospitals
Pay, allowances, benefits

5165.7.A-Z	Other, A-Z
5167	Uniform regulations. Wearing of decorations and medals
5169	Officers
	Including appointments, promotions, retirement
5170	Enlisted personnel
5174.A-Z	Special services, A-Z
5174.C48	Navy chaplains
5175	Equipment. Weapons. Munitions. Supplies and stores
5176	Hospitals (Table K11)

Air Force

5180	Organization. Administration (Table K11)
	Personnel. Services. Equipment. Plants. Hospitals
5181	General (Table K11)
5182	Enlistment. Recruiting. Discharge (Table K11)
	Education. Training
5183	General (Table K11)
	Academies. Schools. Courses of instruction
5183.3	General (Table K11)
5183.6.A-Z	Special topics, A-Z
	Subarrange each by Table K12
5183.6.S34	Scholarships (Table K12)
5183.7.A-Z	Particular schools, A-Z
	Pay, allowances, benefits
	Including retirement benefits
5185	General (Table K11)
5185.3	Retirement pensions (Table K11)
5185.5	Disability pensions (Table K11)
5185.6	Social security benefits for members of the armed forces (Table K11)
5185.7.A-Z	Other, A-Z
5187	Uniform regulations. Wearing of decorations and medals
5189	Officers
	Including appointments, promotions, retirement
5190	Enlisted personnel
5194.A-Z	Special services, A-Z
5194.C48	Air Force chaplains
5195	Equipment. Weapons. Munitions. Supplies and stores

	National defense. Military law
	The military establishment. Armed forces
	Armed forces
	Particular branches of service
	Air Force -- Continued
5196	Hospitals (Table K11)
5240	Military discipline (Table K11)
5242	Law enforcement. Criminal investigation (Table K11)
	Military criminal law and procedure
5246	General (Table K11)
	Criminal law
5248	General (Table K11)
5250	Naval criminal law (Table K11)
5252	Scope and applicability. Criminal jurisdiction (Table K11)
	Justification of an otherwise illegal act
5258	General (Table K11)
5259.A-Z	Particular grounds, A-Z
	Subarrange each by Table K12
5259.D85	Duress and threats. Fear
	Fear see KDZ-KH2 5259.D85
5259.S44	Self-defense
	Penalties and punishment see KDZ-KH2 5308+
	Sentencing. Determining the measure of punishment
5265	General (Table K11)
5267.A-Z	Special topics, A-Z
	Subarrange each by Table K12
5267.E95	Extenuating circumstances
	Probation see KDZ-KH2 5310.P74
5270.A-Z	Particular offenses, A-Z
	Subarrange each by Table K12
	Absence without leave see KDZ-KH2 5270.D45
5270.D45	Desertion. Absence without leave (Table K12)
5270.D56	Disobedience (Table K12)
	Criminal procedure. Military justice
5280	General (Table K11)
	Courts-martial
5282	General (Table K11)
5284	Evidence (Table K11)
	Particular branches of service
	Army
	General see KDZ-KH2 5282
	Trials
5288	Collected works
5289.A-Z	Particular trials. By defendant, A-Z
	Navy
5292	General (Table K11)

	National defense. Military law
	The military establishment. Armed forces
	Military criminal law and procedure
	Criminal procedure. Military justice
	Courts-martial
	Particular branches of service
	Navy -- Continued
	Trials
5294	Collected works
5295.A-Z	Particular trials. By defendant, A-Z
	Appellate procedure. Remedies
5303	General (Table K11)
5305.A-Z	Particular remedies, A-Z
	Subarrange each by Table K12
5305.A47	Amparo (Table K12)
	Execution of sentence. Penalties. Punishment
5308	General (Table K11)
5310.A-Z	Special topics, A-Z
	Subarrange each by Table K12
	Parole see KDZ-KH2 5310.P74
5310.P74	Probation. Parole (Table K12)
5313	Civil defense (Table K11)
	Criminal law and procedure
	Cf. KDZ-KH2 5246+ Military criminal law and procedure
	Cf. KDZ-KH2 5936+ Juvenile criminal law and procedure
5400	History
5402	General (Table K11)
5404	Administration of criminal justice (Table K11)
	Including reform of criminal law, enforcement, and procedure
	Criminal courts. Criminal procedure see KDZ-KH2 5801+
	Criminal law
	Cf. HV6001+ , Criminology
	Cf. K5018+ , Philosophy and theory of criminal law
	History see KDZ-KH2 5400
	For handbooks and manuals on criminal law and procedure for police magistrates and justices of the peace see KDZ-KH2 5805
	For judicial police see KDZ-KH2 5840
5411-5419	General (Table K9b)
	General principles and provisions
5422	General (Table K11)
	Scope and applicability
5424	General (Table K11)
5426	Territorial applicability (Table K11)

KDZ-KH2

	Criminal law
	General principles and provisions
	Scope and applicability -- Continued
5427	Temporal applicability (Table K11)
	Including retroactive and intertemporal law, and ex post facto laws
	Personal applicability
5428	General (Table K11)
5429	Privileges and immunities (Table K11)
	Cf. KDZ-KH2 3093 Parliamentary immunity
	Extradition see KDZ-KH2 5862+
	Right of asylum see KDZ-KH2 5863
5431	Interpretation and construction of criminal law. Analogy (Table K11)
	The criminal offense
5434	General (Table K11)
	Elements of crime. Statutory statement of facts
5435	General (Table K11)
	Commission or omission of an act
5436	General (Table K11)
5437	Causality. Proximate cause (Table K11)
5439	Attempt. Preparatory act (Table K11)
5441	Perpetrators. Principals and accessories (Table K11)
	Cf. KDZ-KH2 5451 Criminal liability of juristic persons
5443	Compound offenses (Table K11)
	Including multiplicity of offenses and continuous crimes
	Public and private offenses see KDZ-KH2 5836+
	Criminal liability
5445	General (Table K11)
	Culpability. Guilt
5446	General (Table K11)
5447	Intent. Premeditation (Table K11)
	Violent emotion in the commitment of homicide see KDZ-KH2 5519
5449	Criminal negligence (Table K11)
5451	Criminal liability of juristic persons (Table K11)
5453	Criminal liability of deaf or blind persons (Table K11)
	Cf. KDZ-KH2 5480 Committal of deaf or blind defenders to institutions
5454	Criminal liability of epileptics (Table K11)
	Criminal liability of Indians see KDZ-KH2 2210.C74
	Circumstances excluding liability. Justification. Defenses
	Cf. KDZ-KH2 5594 Justification in actions for libel and slander
5456	General (Table K11)

KDZ-KH2

	Criminal law
	General principles and provisions
	Criminal liability
	Punishment and penalties. Measures of rehabilitation
	Measures of rehabilitation and safety -- Continued
5479	Committal to an institution for alcoholics and drug addicts (Table K11)
	Cf. KDZ-KH2 3445.A43 Alcoholism
5480	Committal to an institution for deaf or blind offenders (Table K11)
	Juvenile criminal law and procedure see KDZ-KH2 5936+
	Other consequences of conviction or committal
	Sterilization of criminals see KDZ-KH2 3447
	Criminal registration see KDZ-KH2 5934
5482	Reparation of damages. Payment of civil claims through criminal sentence (Table K11)
	Cf. KDZ-KH2 1011 Compensation of victims of crimes through civil sentence
	Compensation of judicial error see KDZ-KH2 5933
	Extinction of punishment see KDZ-KH2 5490+
	Exercise of prosecution functions. Public and private offenses see KDZ-KH2 5837+
	Extinction of criminal actions and criminal sentences
5490	General (Table K11)
5491	Amnesty (Table K11)
	Lack of private complaint see KDZ-KH2 5872
5492	Pardon (Table K11)
5493	Prescription (Table K11)
	Marriage with victim of sex crimes see KDZ-KH2 5547
	Particular offenses
	Including comparative state law
	For the criminal law of a particular state, see the state
5510	General (Table K11)
	Offenses against the person
5513	General (Table K11)
	Homicide
5514	General (Table K11)
5515	Murder (Table K11)
5517	Manslaughter (Table K11)
	Homicide produced in an affray see KDZ-KH2 5531
5518	Parricide. Vericide. Uxoricide (Table K11)
5519	Killing while subject to violent emotion (Table K11)
	Cf. KDZ-KH2 5465 Extenuating circumstances
5521	Infanticide (Table K11)
	Euthanasia. Right to die see KDZ-KH2 3440.E96

Criminal law
Particular offenses
Offenses against the person
Homicide -- Continued

5524	Suicide (Table K11)
	Including aiding and abetting suicide
5526	Abortion. Procuring miscarriage (Table K11)
	Offenses against physical integrity and health. Bodily injuries
5528	General (Table K11)
5531	Homicide and injuries produced in an affray (Table K11)
	Including affray as an autonomous crime
5532	Torture (Table K11)
5533	Communication of venereal or other diseases (Table K11)
5535	Offenses committed while engaged in sports (Table K11)
5537	Abandonment of persons (Table K11)
5540	Failure to assist in emergencies (Table K11)
5542	Duel (Table K11)
	Sexual offenses see KDZ-KH2 5546+
	Offenses against chastity, public morality, and the integrity of the family
5544	General (Table K11)
	Sexual offenses
	Including works on the legal implications of sexual behavior in general
5546	General (Table K11)
5547	Exemption from punishment by marriage with victim (Table K11)
5548	Rape (Table K11)
5549	Seduction. Corruption of children (Table K11)
5551	Abduction (Table K11)
	Communicating venereal diseases see KDZ-KH2 5533
	Prostitution. Procuring. Pimps
5553	General (Table K11)
5555	White slave traffic (Table K11)
5556	Obscenity (Table K11)
	Offenses against the integrity of the family
5560	General (Table K11)
5562	Adultery (Table K11)
	Bigamy. Illegal marriage see KDZ-KH2 5567
5564	Incest (Table K11)
	Abduction see KDZ-KH2 5551
	Abandonment of spouse, children, and invalid ascendants see KDZ-KH2 5537
	Offenses against the civil status of persons

KDZ-KH2

	Criminal law
	Particular offenses
	Offenses against the civil status of persons -- Continued
5566	General (Table K11)
5567	Bigamy. Illegal marriage (Table K11)
	Offenses against personal liberty, security, and tranquility
5570	General (Table K11)
	Abduction see KDZ-KH2 5551
5572	Kidnapping (Table K11)
	Peonage. Slavery see KDZ-KH2 2920.P44
5575	False imprisonment. Illegal detention (Table K11)
	Threats see KDZ-KH2 5607
5578	Violation of the integrity of the home. Unlawful entry. Criminal trespass (Table K11)
	Criminal violation of privacy and the right of secrecy
	Cf. KDZ-KH2 971+ Tort liability for invasion of privacy
5580	General (Table K11)
5582	Violation of privacy of correspondence and telecommunication (Table K11)
5584	Violation of professional and official secrecy (Table K11)
	Cf. KDZ-KH2 1166.S42 Bank secrecy
	Cf. KDZ-KH2 2653+ Privileged communications (Evidence)
	Cf. KDZ-KH2 5655+ Misconduct in office
5586	Criminal violation of civil rights and other constitutional guarantees (Table K11)
	Including violation of the right to trade, work, etc.
	Offenses against honor
	Libel, slander, defamation
	For tort liability see KDZ-KH2 974+
5591	General (Table K11)
5593	Libel, slander, or defamation committed through the press (Table K11)
5594	Exclusion of criminal liability. Justification (Table K11)
5596	Malicious prosecution (Table K11)
	Offenses against property
	For crimes against the national economy, industry, and commerce see KDZ-KH2 5730
5600	General (Table K11)
	Larceny
5602	General (Table K11)
5604	Cattle stealing (Table K11)
5606	Robbery (Table K11)

Criminal law
Particular offenses
Offenses against property -- Continued
5607   Threats. Extortion. Blackmail (Table K11)
      Cf. KDZ-KH2 5572 Kidnapping
      Cf. KDZ-KH2 5659 Extortion and blackmail by a public
        officer
5609   Theft of use (Table K11)
5610   Malicious mischief (Table K11)
    Embezzlement see KDZ-KH2 5620
5612   Usurpation. Criminal detainer of real property (Table K11)
      Cf. KDZ-KH2 5578 Unlawful entry. Criminal trespass
    Fraud. False pretenses
5613   General (Table K11)
5615   Insurance fraud (Table K11)
5616   Fraud by forgery. Bad checks (Table K11)
      Cf. KDZ-KH2 5726 Forgery
5617   Credit card fraud (Table K11)
      Cf. KDZ-KH2 1172.C64 Credit cards
5618   Fraudulent bankruptcy (Table K11)
      Including other fraudulent acts of debtors detrimental to
        creditors
5620   Embezzlement (Table K11)
      Cf. KDZ-KH2 5660 Misappropriation by public officers
5622   Commercial, industrial, and economic crimes (Table K11)
    Receiving stolen goods see KDZ-KH2 5676
    Arson see KDZ-KH2 5684
    Forgery see KDZ-KH2 5726
5624   Usury (Table K11)
      Cf. KDZ-KH2 787 Obligations
    Offenses against particular types of property
    Offenses against copyright see KDZ-KH2 1614+
Offenses against the security of the state and against the
    government. Political offenses
      Cf. KDZ-KH2 5804 Special courts for the trial of offenses
        against the security of the state
      Cf. KDZ-KH2 5912 Proceedings for political offenses
5630   General (Table K11)
5631   Treason (Table K11)
5632   Espionage (Table K11)
5634   Sabotage (Table K11)
5636   Sedition. Subversive activities (Table K11)
5638   Terrorism (Table K11)
5640   Conspiracy to commit offenses against the security of the
      state and against the government (Table K11)
    International offenses

	Criminal law
	Particular offenses
	International offenses -- Continued
5645	General (Table K11)
5646	Piracy (Table K11)
(5648)	Torture
	see KDZ-KH2 5532
	Offenses against the public administration and administration of justice
5651	General (Table K11)
	Offenses against the public administration
5653	General (Table K11)
	Misconduct in office
	Cf. KDZ-KH2 998 Tort liability of public officials
	Cf. KDZ-KH2 3269+ Administrative responsibility
5655	General (Table K11)
5657	Corruption and bribery (Table K11)
	For corrupt election practices see KDZ-KH2 3068
5659	Illegal exactions (Table K11)
	Illegal detention see KDZ-KH2 5575
5660	Misappropriation of public funds and other property (Table K11)
	Including private funds and property in public custody
5662	Violation of conflict-of-interest laws (Table K11)
5664	Force against, resistance to, or disrespect for public authorities or officers (Table K11)
5665	Usurpation of authority, titles, or names (Table K11)
	Offenses against the administration of justice
5668	General (Table K11)
5670	Contempt of court (Table K11)
	Cf. KDZ-KH2 2589 Disciplinary power of courts
5672	Judicial corruption (Table K11)
	Cf. KDZ-KH2 2560.6 Discipline. Judicial ethics
5673	Perjury. Subornation of perjury (Table K11)
5674	Prevarication (Table K11)
	Malicious prosecution see KDZ-KH2 977
5676	Receiving stolen goods (Table K11)
5678	Escape of prisoners (Table K11)
	Offenses against public safety and public order
5682	General (Table K11)
5684	Arson and other devastations (Table K11)
	Including explosions or floods
5685	Offenses against the environment (Table K11)
5686	Offenses against means of transportation and communication (Table K11)

Criminal law

  Particular offenses

    Offenses against public safety and public order -- Continued

5688	Crimes on the high seas (Table K11)
	Cf. KDZ-KH2 5646 Piracy
5689	Crimes aboard aircraft and against aeronautics (Table K11)
5691	Riot (Table K11)
	Affray see KDZ-KH2 5531
5693	Illegal organizations. Gangs (Table K11)
	Sabotage see KDZ-KH2 5634
	Traffic violations. Drunk driving see KDZ-KH2 4184

    Offenses against public health

5700	General (Table K11)
	Communication of venereal and other diseases see KDZ-KH2 5533
5703	Illicit possession of, use of, and traffic in narcotics (Table K11)

    Offenses against public convenience and decency

5710	General (Table K11)
	Adultery see KDZ-KH2 5562
	Bigamy see KDZ-KH2 5567
5713	Violation of lottery regulations. Unlawful gambling (Table K11)
	Obscenity see KDZ-KH2 5556
	Prostitution. Procuring see KDZ-KH2 5553+
5714	Drunkenness (Table K11)
5715	Disorderly conduct (Table K11)
5716	Vagrancy. Begging (Table K11)

    Offenses against public faith

      Including offenses against public property, public finance, and currency

5721	General (Table K11)
5723	Counterfeiting (Table K11)
5724	Forgery of seals, stamped paper, postage stamps, etc. (Table K11)
5726	Forgery of documents (Table K11)
	Including both public and private documents
	Cf. KDZ-KH2 5616 Fraud by forgery
	Malicious prosecution see KDZ-KH2 977
	Tax crimes see KDZ-KH2 4613
	Customs crimes. Smuggling see KDZ-KH2 4825+
	Perjury. Subornation of perjury see KDZ-KH2 5673
5730	Offenses against the national economy, industry, and commerce (Table K11)
	Including penal aspects of monopolies, trusts, speculation, etc.
	Offenses committed through the mail

KDZ-KH2

	Criminal law
	Particular offenses
	Offenses committed through the mail -- Continued
5741	General (Table K11)
	Blackmail see KDZ-KH2 5607
	Extortion see KDZ-KH2 5607
	Gambling see KDZ-KH2 5713
	Lotteries see KDZ-KH2 5713
	Obscenity see KDZ-KH2 5556
	Threats see KDZ-KH2 5607
	Contraventions
5750	General (Table K11)
5753.A-Z	Particular contraventions, A-Z
	Subarrange each by Table K12
	Criminal courts. Criminal procedure
	Cf. KDZ-KH2 5404 Administration of criminal justice
5800	General (Table K11)
	Criminal courts
5801	General (Table K11)
	Particular courts and procedure (General) before such courts
5804	Courts for the trial of offenses against the security of the state (Table K11)
	Cf. KDZ-KH2 5630+ Offenses against the security of the state
	Cf. KDZ-KH2 5912 Proceedings for political offenses
5805	Police magistrates' courts. Justices of the peace (Table K11)
	Class here handbooks and manuals on criminal law and procedure for police magistrates and justices of the peace
	Criminal procedure
5806	History
	For magistrate courts see KDZ-KH2 5805
	For handbooks and manuals for judicial police see KDZ-KH2 5840
5811-5819	General (Table K9b)
	Special principles of criminal procedure
5822	General (Table K11)
	Orality and publicity of trial see KDZ-KH2 5875
	Protection of human rights in criminal proceedings see KDZ-KH2 5866+
	Judicial assistance in criminal matters see KDZ-KH2 5862+
5824	Jurisdiction. Venue (Table K11)
	Challenges and disqualification of judges see KDZ-KH2 2590
5828	Prejudicial actions. Penal effects of civil judgments (Table K11)

Criminal courts. Criminal procedure
Criminal procedure -- Continued
Powers of the judge see KDZ-KH2 2589
Parties see KDZ-KH2 5833+
Judicial decisions see KDZ-KH2 5896+
Preliminary proceedings. The "sumario"
5831   General (Table K11)
Parties. Prosecution and defense
5833   General (Table K11)
Prosecution
5835   General (Table K11)
Public and private offenses and their prosecution
5836   General (Table K11)
Public crimes. Public prosecution. Indictment
Including initiation of criminal proceedings ex officio
and penal actions requiring the complaint of the
victim but publicly prosecuted
Class here denunciation of public crimes
5837   General (Table K11)
5838   Public prosecutors. District attorneys. Fiscals
(Table K11)
5840   Judicial police (Table K11)
Including auxiliaries
Class here police handbooks and manuals on
criminal law and procedure
Cf. KDZ-KH2 3228 Police
5842   Private crimes. Private prosecution (Table K11)
Including complainant, private prosecutor, information
Abandonment of criminal action see KDZ-KH2 5872
5844   Defense. Public defenders (Table K11)
Investigation
Including investigation by judicial police, judges of examination
and police magistrates
5848   General (Table K11)
5850   Corpus delicti (Table K11)
Evidence see KDZ-KH2 5880+
Compulsory and precautionary measures against the
suspect
5852   General (Table K11)
Arrest
5853   General (Table K11)
5855   Flagrant crimes (Table K11)
5857   Provisional liberty. Bail (Table K11)
Amparo see KDZ-KH2 2701+
Habeas corpus see KDZ-KH2 2772+
5859   Searches and seizures (Table K11)

Criminal courts. Criminal procedure
  Criminal procedure
    Preliminary proceedings. The "sumario"
      Compulsory and precautionary measures against the
        suspect
      Extradition. Interstate rendition
        Including judicial assistance in criminal matters in general

5862	General (Table K11)
5863	Right of asylum. Refusal of extradition (Table K11)
	Rights of suspects
	Including protection of human rights in criminal proceedings
5866	General (Table K11)
5868	Right to counsel. Public defenders. In forma pauperis (Table K11)
5870	Due process of law in criminal proceedings (Table K11)
	Bail see KDZ-KH2 5857
	Self-incrimination see KDZ-KH2 5882
	Amparo see KDZ-KH2 2701+
	Habeas corpus see KDZ-KH2 2772+
5872	Conclusion of sumario. Dismissal of criminal action
	Including dismissal for lack of private complaint
	Plenary proceedings. Trial
5874	General (Table K11)
5875	Orality and publicity of trial (Table K11)
	Powers of the judge see KDZ-KH2 2589
	Contempt of court see KDZ-KH2 5670
	Trial practice. Trial tactics
5876	General (Table K11)
	Confrontation see KDZ-KH2 5889
5877	Forensic psychology (Table K11)
	Preliminary exceptions
5878	General (Table K11)
	Res judicata see KDZ-KH2 5898
	Evidence
5880	General (Table K11)
5881	Confession (Table K11)
5882	Self-incrimination (Table K11)
5884	Documentary evidence (Table K11)
5885	Witnesses (Table K11)
	Expert evidence. Expert witnesses
5887	General (Table K11)
5888	Medical evidence. Medical witnesses (Table K11)
5889	Confrontation. Cross-examination (Table K11)
5890	Circumstantial evidence (Table K11)
5891	Presumptions (Table K11)

KDZ-KH2

	Criminal courts. Criminal procedure
	Criminal procedure
	Execution of sentence
	Imprisonment -- Continued
5926	Reformatories (Table K11)
	Juvenile detention homes see KDZ-KH2 5946
5928	Political prisoners (Table K11)
5930	Conditional liberty. Probation. Parole (Table K11)
5931	Indeterminate sentence (Table K11)
5933	Compensation for judicial error (Table K11)
5934	Criminal registration and registers (Table K11)
	Judicial assistance in criminal matters see KDZ-KH2 5862+
	Victims of crimes
	Including participation of victims in criminal procedure
5935	General (Table K11)
	Compensation to victims of crimes. Reparation see KDZ-KH2 1011
	Military criminal law and procedure see KDZ-KH2 5246+
	Juvenile criminal law and procedure. Administration of juvenile justice
5936	General (Table K11)
5937	Juvenile courts (Table K11)
	Criminal law
5939	General (Table K11)
5940.A-Z	Special topics, A-Z
5940.C75	Criminal liability
	Criminal procedure
5942	General (Table K11)
	Execution of sentence
5944	General (Table K11)
	Imprisonment
5945	General (Table K11)
5946	Juvenile detention homes (Table K11)
5947	Probation (Table K11)
	Church and state. Secular ecclesiastical law see KDZ-KH2 3034+
	Individual political and administrative subdivisions
	States, provinces, etc.
	Subarrange each by Table KDZ-KH4
	For listing and number assignments, see KG+
	Cities
	Subarrange each by Table KDZ-KH5 or Table KDZ-KH6 , as applicable
	For listing and number assignments, see KG+
	Counties, parishes and other units of local self-government see KDZ-KH4 97

Bibliography
    For manuals on legal bibliography, legal research, and the
        use of law books see KDZ-KH3 20

1	General bibliography
1.2	Library catalogs
1.3	Sales catalogs
1.4	Indexes to periodical literature, society publications, and collections

    For indexes to particular publications, see the publication

<2>	Periodicals

    For periodicals consisting predominantly of legal articles, regardless
        of subject matter and jurisdiction, see K1+
    For periodicals consisting primarily of informative material
        (Newsletters, bulletins, etc.) relating to a special subject, see
        the subject and form division for periodicals
    For law reports, official bulletins or circulars intended chiefly for the
        publication of laws and regulations, see appropriate entries in
        the text or form division tables

3	Monographic series
4	Official gazettes
	Legislative documents
	see J
7	Other materials relating to legislative history
	Including recommended legislation; legislation passed and vetoed
	Legislation

    For legislation on a particular subject, see the subject
    Treaties
        General
            see KZ

KDZ-KH3

        Treaties on international uniform law not limited to a region
            see K
        Treaties on international uniform law of American regions
            see KDZ, KG, KGJ and KH
    Statutes
        Including decree laws (Decreto-leyes), and works containing
            statutes and administrative regulations, or federal and
            comparative state legislation combined
        Sessional volumes. Annual volumes
            Serials

8.A2-.A29	Official editions
	Arranged chronologically
8.A3-Z	Unofficial editions. By publisher or editor, A-Z
8.2	Monographs. By date of initial session
	Compilations. Collections. Revisions
	Official editions
9	Serials

	Legislation
	Statutes
	Compilations. Collections. Revisions
	Official editions -- Continued
9.2	Monographs. By date
	Unofficial editions
10	Serials
10.2	Monographs. By date
	Private, local and personal acts
10.3	Serials
10.35	Monographs. By date
10.4	Abridgments and digests of statutes
10.5	Indexes to statutes
	Class indexes to a particular publication with the publication
10.6	Other bibliographical aids
10.7.A-Z	Collected codes. By editor, A-Z
	Class here works consisting of both private and public law codes
	For codes on a particular branch of law, see the subject
	Administrative and executive publications
	Including statutory rules, orders and regulations; orders in council; proclamations, etc.
	For regulations on a particular subject, see the subject
	Serials
11.A2-.A29	Official editions
	Arranged chronologically
11.A3-Z	Unofficial editions. By publisher or editor, A-Z
11.2	Monographs. By date
	Royal, gubernatorial or presidential messages to the legislature see J
	Attorneys General's opinions see KDZ-KH3 307
	Law reports and related materials
	Subarrange courts represented by a whole number by Table KDZ-KH9 , as indicated
	Do not further subarrange courts represented by a Cutter or decimal number
	Including federal reports and reports of two or more states, and federal and state reports combined
	Reports of particular states are classed with the law of the respective jurisdiction
	For reports relating to a particular subject, see the subject
	Cf. KDZ-KH3 31.5.A+ Collected opinions
11.7	Privy Council Judicial Committee
12	Highest court of appeals. Supreme Court (Table KDZ-KH9)
	Lower courts
	Including highest court and lower courts combined

	Law reports and related materials
	Lower courts -- Continued
13	Collective (Table KDZ-KH9)
	Courts of appeal, or appeal divisions
14	Collective (Table KDZ-KH9)
14.7.A-Z	Particular courts of appeal or appeal divisions, A-Z
	Trial courts, or trial divisions
	Including magistrates' courts
15	Collective (Table KDZ-KH9)
15.7.A-Z	Particular courts, etc., A-Z
16	Encyclopedias
16.2	Dictionaries. Words and phrases
	For bilingual and multilingual dictionaries, see K52+
	For dictionaries on a particular subject, see the subject
16.3	Form books
	Class here general works only
	For form books on a particular subject, see the subject
(16.4)	Yearbooks
	For publications issued annually, containing information, statistics, etc. relating to a special subject, see the subject and form division for periodicals. For other publications appearing yearly, see K1+
	Judicial statistics
17	General
	Criminal statistics
17.3	General
17.4	Juvenile crime
18	Directories
	Trials
19	General collections
	Criminal trials
19.2	Collected works
19.4.A-Z	Particular trials. By defendant or best known name, A-Z
	Including records, briefs, commentaries, and stories on particular trials
	Civil trials
19.5	Collected works
19.7.A-Z	Particular trials. By plaintiff, A-Z
	Including records, briefs, commentaries, and stories on particular trials
20	Legal research. Legal bibliography
	Including methods of bibliographic research and how to find the law
	Legal education
21	General
21.5.A-Z	Particular law schools. By name, A-Z

KDZ-KH3

22.A-Z	Law societies and institutes
	Each society or institute is subarranged by Table KDZ-KH11
	Class here works on individual societies and institutes and their activities, e.g. administrative reports, minutes, etc.
	For works issued by individual law societies and institutes on particular subjects, see the subject
	The legal profession
	Including law as a career
23	General (Table K11)
	Directories see KDZ-KH3 18
23.2	Admission to the bar. Bar examinations (Table K11)
23.3	Legal ethics and etiquette
	Cf. KDZ-KH3 219 Judicial ethics
23.4	Attorney and client (Table K11)
	Economics of law practice
23.6	General (Table K11)
23.65	Fees (Table K11)
23.7	Law office management. Secretaries' handbooks, manuals, etc.
	Bar associations
	Including law societies organized to regulate the profession
	For publications of bar associations on special subjects, see the subject
	For membership directories see KDZ-KH3 18
24	General
24.5.A-Z	Particular bar associations, A-Z
	Each association is subarranged by Table KDZ-KH12
	For biography see KDZ-KH3 28.4+
	Law and lawyers in literature
	see PB+
	Legal anecdotes, wit and humor
	see K184.7
	For purely fictitious works, see PN6231.L4 , and PN6268.L4
25	Community legal services. Legal aid. Legal services to the poor (Table K11)
	Notarial law. Public instruments
26	General (Table K11)
26.3	The notarial profession
26.4	Public instruments (Table K11)
	Including protocolization, certification, authentication, legalization and recording of documents
26.7	Consular functions
	Public registers. Registration
26.8	General (Table K11)
	Civil registry see KDZ-KH3 41
	Land registry see KDZ-KH3 49

	Public registers. Registration -- Continued
	Ship registration see KDZ-KH3 393.3+
	History
	For works on the history of a particular subject, see the subject
28	General
	Biography
28.4	Collective
28.5.A-Z	Individual, A-Z
	Subarranged by Table KDZ-KH13
28.7	Influence of foreign law
	Relationship of law to other disciplines, subjects, or phenomena
	see K486+
29	Criticism. Legal reform
	Cf. KDZ-KH3 209.2+ Judiciary
	Cf. KDZ-KH3 443.5 Administration of criminal justice
30	Congresses. By date of congress
	For intergovermental congresses and conferences, see subclass K
	and regional subclasses
	Collected works (nonserial)
	For monographic series see KDZ-KH3 3
31	Several authors
31.5.A-Z	Individual authors, A-Z
	Subarranged by Table KDZ-KH14
	Including collected opinions
31.7	Casebooks. Readings
	Class here general works only
	For casebooks on particular subjects, see the subject
32	General works. Treatises
32.2	Compends. Outlines, syllabi, etc.
32.3	Examination aids
32.4	Addresses, essays, lectures
	Including single essays, collected essays of several authors, etc.
	Festschriften, etc.
32.6.A-Z	Works for particular users, A-Z
32.6.B87	Businesspeople. Foreign investors
	Foreign investors see KDZ-KH3 32.6.B87
32.7.A-Z	Works on diverse aspects of particular subjects and falling within
	several branches of the law. By subject, A-Z
	Subarrange each by Table K12
	Conflict of laws
34	History
34.2	General (Table K11)
34.4.A-Z	Special topics, A-Z
	Subarrange each by Table K12
	Regional unification of conflicts rules
	see KDZ-KH1 110+ in Table KDZ-KH1

KDZ-KH3

	Conflict of laws -- Continued
	Conflict of laws with the United States of America
	see KF416
34.6.A-Z	Particular branches and subjects of the law, A-Z
	Subarrange each by Table K12
34.6.A45	Aliens (Table K12)
	Cf. KDZ-KH3 275+ Status of aliens in public law
	Extradition see KDZ-KH3 456+
	Foreign corporations see KDZ-KH3 106.2
34.6.F65	Foreign judgments and arbitral awards (Table K12)
	Including recognition and execution
36.A-Z	Concepts applying to several branches of law, A-Z
	Civil law
38	General (Table K11)
39	Juristic facts. Juristic acts (Table K11)
	Persons
	Natural persons
40	General (Table K11)
	Status. Capacity and disability. Personality
40.3	General (Table K11)
40.6.A-Z	Particular groups of persons, A-Z
	Subarrange each by Table K12
	Aliens see KDZ-KH3 34.6.A45
	Indians see KDZ-KH3 198+
40.6.M55	Minors
40.6.S58	Slaves (Table K12)
	Cf. KDZ-KH3 269.5 Peonage. Slavery
	(Constitutional law)
40.6.W62	Women (Table K12)
	Including works on civil and public law status combined
	For works on women in relation to particular subjects, see
	the subject, e.g. KDZ-KH3 43.4 , Civil status of
	married women; KDZ-KH3 274.5.W64 , Nationality of
	women
41	Civil registry. Registration of civil status (Table K11)
	Including registers of births, marriages, deaths; birth and
	death certificates; census; vital statistics, etc.
	Juristic persons
42	General (Table K11)
42.3	Endowments. Foundations. Charitable trusts (Table K11)
	Nonprofit associations see KDZ-KH3 63
	Business associations. Commercial companies see KDZ-KH3 101+
	Domestic relations. Family law
43	General (Table K11)
43.2	Domestic relations courts and procedure (Table K11)

KDZ-KH3

	Civil law
	Property. Real rights -- Continued
	Personal property
50	General (Table K11)
	Intellectual property see KDZ-KH3 130+
51	Trusts and trustees (Table K11)
	Succession upon death
	Class here works on succession upon death and gifts combined
53	General (Table K11)
53.3	Testamentary succession. Wills (Table K11)
53.5	Intestate succession (Table K11)
53.6	Probate courts and procedure (Table K11)
53.7	Administration of decedents' estates. Execution of wills (Table K11)
	Including executors and administrators
	Obligations
55	General (Table K11)
	Class here works on debtor and creditor in general
55.5.A-Z	Special topics, A-Z
	Subarrange each by Table K12
55.5.I55	Interest. Usury (Table K12)
	Including legal interest
	Usury see KDZ-KH3 55.5.I55
	Contracts
56	General (Table K11)
	Particular types of contracts
	Sale
57	General (Table K11)
	Conditional sale. Installment sale. Lease purchase see KDZ-KH3 77.5.C64
	Lease and hire
58	General (Table K11)
	Lease of things
58.2	General (Table K11)
58.3	Lease of real property. Landlord and tenant (Table K11)
	Cf. KDZ-KH3 367.4+ Land tenure
	Contract of service. Labor contract. Master and servant
59	Individual labor contract (Table K11)
	Collective labor agreements see KDZ-KH3 159+
59.5	Contract for work and labor. Independent contractor (Table K11)
	Contracts involving bailments
61	General (Table K11)
61.2	Deposit (Table K11)

	Civil law
	Obligations
	Contracts
	Particular types of contracts
	Contracts involving bailments -- Continued
61.3	Innkeeper and guest. Innkeepers' liens (Table K11)
61.4	Loans for use (Commodatum) (Table K11)
	Loans for consumption (Mutuum)
	Including loan of money
	For bank loans see KDZ-KH3 88.B34
	For commercial loans and credit see KDZ-KH3 90+
61.5	General (Table K11)
	Interest. Usury see KDZ-KH3 55.5.I55
63	Associations (Table K11)
	Including nonprofit associations, civil partnerships and civil companies
	For business associations see KDZ-KH3 101+
	Cf. KDZ-KH3 42+ Juristic persons
65.A-Z	Other contracts, A-Z
	Torts. Obligations from wrongful acts (Delicts and quasi delicts)
67	General (Table K11)
69.A-Z	Particular torts, A-Z
	Subarrange each by Table K12
69.A27	Abuse of legal process. Malicious prosecution. Chicanery (Table K12)
	Chicanery see KDZ-KH3 69.A27
	Malicious prosecution see KDZ-KH3 69.A27
69.N43	Negligence (Table K12)
70	Employers' liability (Table K11)
71	Government torts (Table K11)
	Commercial law
73	General (Table K11)
	Commercial courts and procedure see KDZ-KH3 125
73.5	Merchants (Table K11)
74	Auxiliaries and intermediaries of commerce (Table K11)
	Including boards of trade, stock exchanges, independent commercial agents and middlemen, and commercial employees
	Commercial contracts
	General see KDZ-KH3 73
76	Commercial mandate and consignment
	Commercial sale
77	General (Table K11)
77.5.A-Z	Particular types of sale, A-Z
	Subarrange each by Table K12

KDZ-KH3

Commercial law
  Commercial contracts
    Commercial sale
      Particular types of sale, A-Z -- Continued

77.5.C64	Conditional sale. Installment sale. Lease purchase (Table K12)
	Installment sale see KDZ-KH3 77.5.C64
	Lease purchase see KDZ-KH3 77.5.C64
78	Commercial leases (Table K11)
79	Deposit of goods. Warehouses (Table K11)
	Negotiable instruments. Titles of credit
	Including commercial instruments and documents
82	General (Table K11)
82.5.A-Z	Special topics, A-Z
	Subarrange each by Table K12
82.5.P74	Protest. Waiver of protest (Table K12)
	Waiver of protest see KDZ-KH3 82.5.P74
	Particular kinds of negotiable instruments
83	Bills of exchange (Table K11)
83.5	Checks (Table K11)
	For criminal provisions see KDZ-KH3 445.F7
83.6	Other (Table K11)
	Banking
86	General (Table K11)
87.A-Z	Particular types of banks and credit institutions, A-Z
	Subarrange each by Table K12
87.C64	Cooperative banks. Credit unions (Table K12)
	Credit unions see KDZ-KH3 87.C64
88.A-Z	Particular banking transactions, A-Z
	Subarrange each by Table K12
	Bank credit see KDZ-KH3 88.B34
88.B34	Bank loans (Table K12)
	Commercial loans and credit
	Cf. KDZ-KH3 82+ Negotiable instruments. Titles of credit
90	General (Table K11)
	Interest. Usury see KDZ-KH3 55.5.I55
	Bank loans. Bank credit see KDZ-KH3 88.B34
92	Investments (Table K11)
	For foreign investments see KDZ-KH3 360
	Carriers. Carriage of goods and passengers
94	General (Table K11)
	Automotive transportation see KDZ-KH3 388.3+
	Railroads see KDZ-KH3 389
	Carriage by air see KDZ-KH3 391+
	Carriage by sea see KDZ-KH3 110+

	Commercial law
	Commercial contracts -- Continued
	Insurance
	Including regulation of insurance business
97	General (Table K11)
97.5.A-Z	Special topics, A-Z
	Subarrange each by Table K12
97.5.A34	Admission of foreign insurance companies (Table K12)
98.A-Z	Particular types of insurance, A-Z
	Business associations. Commercial companies
	Including partnerships and incorporated companies
101	General (Table K11)
102	Partnerships (Table K11)
103	Limited liability companies. Private companies (Table K11)
	Business corporations
104	General (Table K11)
	Corporate finance
105	General (Table K11)
105.3	Accounting. Auditing. Financial statements (Table K11)
105.5	Shares and shareholders' rights. Stock transfers (Table K11)
	Particular types of corporations
106	Cooperative societies (Table K11)
106.2	Foreign corporations (Table K11)
	Private companies see KDZ-KH3 103
	Maritime law
	Including carriage by sea, marine insurance and maritime social legislation
	For administrative regulations see KDZ-KH3 393+
109	General (Table K11)
	Carriage by sea. Maritime commercial law. Admiralty
110	General (Table K11)
111	Admiralty courts and proceedings (Table K11)
112	Ocean bills of lading (Table K11)
112.5	Charter parties (Table K11)
	Maritime loans, credits and security
113	General (Table K11)
113.2.A-Z	Special topics, A-Z
	Risk and damages in maritime commerce
114	General (Table K11)
114.2	Maritime torts. Collision at sea (Table K11)
116	Marine insurance (Table K11)
	Including inland marine insurance
	Maritime social legislation
118	General (Table K11)

KDZ-KH3

271

	Commercial law
	Maritime law
	Maritime social legislation -- Continued
	Maritime labor law. Merchant mariners
119	General (Table K11)
120.A-Z	Special topics, A-Z
	Maritime social insurance
122	General (Table K11)
122.5.A-Z	Special topics, A-Z
	Insolvency and bankruptcy. Creditors' rights
	General see KDZ-KH3 125
	Bankruptcy
124	General (Table K11)
124.3.A-Z	Special topics, A-Z
124.3.R42	Receivers
124.6	Debtors' relief (Table K11)
125	Commercial courts and procedure
	Cf. KDZ-KH3 249 Commercial arbitration
	Intellectual property
130	General (Table K11)
131	Copyright (Table K11)
	Industrial property
134	General (Table K11)
135	Patent law (Table K11)
138	Trademarks (Table K11)
140	Unfair competition (Table K11)
	Social legislation
150	General (Table K11)
	Labor law
151	General (Table K11)
152	Administration. Department of labor (Table K11)
	Management-labor relations
154	General (Table K11)
	Labor unions
156	General (Table K11)
158	Collective bargaining. Collective labor agreements (Table K11)
	Collective labor disputes
159	General (Table K11)
160	Arbitration. Conciliation (Table K11)
161	Labor courts and procedure (Table K11)
162	Strikes. Boycotts. Lockouts (Table K11)
162.5.A-Z	By industry, occupation, or group of employees, A-Z
	Subarrange each by Table K12
162.5.P82	Public employees (Table K12)
	Labor standards. Labor conditions

	Courts. Procedure
	Civil procedure
	Hearings. Trial
	Evidence -- Continued
235	General (Table K11)
235.5	Letters rogatory (Table K11)
	Including international letters rogatory
236.A-Z	Particular kinds of evidence, A-Z
237	Jury and jurors (Table K11)
	Special proceedings see KDZ-KH3 249+
	Judgment
239	General (Table K11)
240	Costs. Fees (Table K11)
	Cf. KDZ-KH3 25 Legal aid
	Remedies
242	General (Table K11)
243	Injunctions. Provisional remedies (Table K11)
245	Execution of judgment. Attachment and garnishment (Table K11)
	Constitutional remedies against arbitrary official action. Judicial review
246	General (Table K11)
	Amparo
247	General (Table K11)
247.4.A-Z	Application of amparo in relation to particular subjects, A-Z
	Subarrange each by Table K12
247.4.A34	Agrarian amparo (Table K12)
247.4.C64	Contentious-administrative proceedings, Amparo in (Table K12)
247.7	Habeas corpus (Table K11)
248	Appellate procedure (Table K11)
	Special proceedings
249	Arbitration and award. Commercial arbitration (Table K11)
	Probate see KDZ-KH3 53.6
	Admiralty see KDZ-KH3 111
	Bankruptcy see KDZ-KH3 124+
249.5	Summary suits and procedure. Interdictal actions (Table K11)
	Workers' compensation see KDZ-KH3 184+
250	Noncontentious (ex parte) jurisdiction (Table K11)
	Cf. KDZ-KH3 26+ Notarial practice and procedure
	Constitutional law
	Sources
260	Collected works
	Sources other than constitutions

Constitutional law
  Sources
    Sources other than constitutions -- Continued
261   Collected works. By date
261.5   Individual documents
        By date of adoption or proclamation
    Constitutions
      Class works containing federal constitutions and constitutions of
        a particular state with the state
      Collected works
265   Texts. By date
265.5   Digests. Indexes. By date
266   Particular constitutions. By date of constitution
        Subarrange each by Table K17
    Constitutional history
268   General (Table K11)
269.5   Peonage. Slavery (Table K12)
        Including emancipation, prohibition, and criminal provisions
270   Constitutional law in general (Table K11)
    Separation of powers. Delegation of powers
271   General (Table K11)
271.4   Conflict of interests (Table K11)
        Including incompatibility of offices and ethics in government
272   Structure of government (Table K11)
        Including federal and state relations, relations between the states,
        and jurisdiction
  Individual and state
    Nationals. Aliens
273   General (Table K11)
      Nationals. Citizenship
274   General (Table K11)
        Naturalization see KDZ-KH3 275.3
274.5.A-Z   Particular groups, A-Z
        Subarrange each by Table K12
274.5.W64   Women (Table K12)
      Aliens
275   General (Table K11)
275.3   Immigration and naturalization (Table K11)
275.6   Control of individuals (Table K11)
        Including internal security and control of subversive activities
        Cf. KDZ-KH3 445.P64 Political offenses
    Civil and political rights and liberties
      Including protection of human rights
      For protection of human rights in criminal proceedings
        see KDZ-KH3 457
278   General (Table K11)

Constitutional law
Individual and state
Nationals. Aliens
Civil and political rights and liberties -- Continued
278.2   Freedom of speech (Table K11)
Prohibition of peonage and slavery see KDZ-KH3 269.5
278.8   Political parties (Table K11)
279   Church and state. Secular ecclesiastical law (Table K11)
Organs of government
The people
Election law
280   General (Table K11)
280.5   Election districts (Table K11)
The legislature. Legislative power
The Congress (Parliament, Legislative Council, etc.)
Including general works on the legislature, if unicameral, or
on the body that exercises legislative power if other than
a congress, e.g. the Council of Ministers in Cuba
281   General (Table K11)
281.2   Rules and procedure (Table K11)
281.3   The legislative process (Table K11)
281.4   Impeachment power and procedure (Table K11)
281.5   Legal status of legislators (Table K11)
282   Upper house (Senate, etc.) (Table K11)
282.5   Lower house (Chamber of deputies, House of
representatives, etc.) (Table K11)
The executive branch. Executive power
284   General (Table K11)
The President. Governor. Governor-General
285   General (Table K11)
Powers and duties
286   General (Table K11)
287   War and emergency powers. Martial law (Table K11)
288   The Prime Minister and the Cabinet (Table K11)
Executive departments and non-departmental
organizations
288.5   General (Table K11)
288.7   Department of justice. Attorney general (Table K11)
Including the solicitor general and other chief law officers of
the government

Constitutional law
Organs of government -- Continued
290   The Judiciary. Judicial power (Table K11)
Class here constitutional status only
For courts, administration of justice, and organization of
the Judiciary see KDZ-KH3 209.2+
Cf. KDZ-KH3 246+ Constitutional remedies against
arbitrary official action
Cf. KDZ-KH3 443.5 Administration of criminal justice
Local government
293   General (Table K11)
Municipal government. Municipal corporations. Municipal
services
294   General (Table K11)
295   Municipal officials. Organs of local government (Table K11)
Municipal civil service see KDZ-KH3 299
Civil service. Government officials and employees
298   General (Table K11)
299   Local civil service. Municipal civil service (Table K11)
301   Police and power of the police (Table K11)
Including comparative works on state, local, and rural police
Administrative law
For the administrative law of a particular subject, see the subject,
e.g., 406.2+, Tax administration and procedure
304   General (Table K11)
Administrative organization
305   General (Table K11)
Executive departments and non-departmental organizations
see KDZ-KH3 288.5+
307   Attorneys General's opinions
Administrative acts
308   General (Table K11)
308.5.A-Z   Special topics, A-Z
Judicial functions. Remedies
310   General (Table K11)
311   Administrative remedies (Table K11)
312   Judicial review of administrative acts (Table K11)
314   Contentious-administrative jurisdiction and procedure.
Administrative courts (Table K11)
For amparo in contentious-administrative proceedings
see KDZ-KH3 247.4.C64
314.7.A-Z   Special topics, A-Z
Subarrange each by Table K12
314.7.C65   Costs. Fees (Table K12)
Fees see KDZ-KH3 314.7.C65

Administrative law -- Continued
315   Administrative responsibility. Indemnification for government
     acts (Table K11)
      Cf. KDZ-KH3 71 Government tort liability
   Public property. Public restraints on private property
317   General (Table K11)
318   Conservation and management of natural resources.
     Environmental planning (Table K11)
      Cf. KDZ-KH3 340+ Environmental pollution
319   Roads. Highway law (Table K11)
320   Water resources. Rivers. Lakes. Watercourses (Table K11)
      Including water power development
      For water power see KDZ-KH3 386.7
321   Marine resources (Table K11)
      For fishing industry see KDZ-KH3 370+
     Mineral resources see KDZ-KH3 371+
322   Expropriation. Eminent domain (Table K11)
     Public land law
323   General (Table K11)
     Reclamation. Irrigation. Drainage
324   General (Table K11)
324.3.A-Z   Particular types of land, A-Z
324.5   Shore protection. Coastal zone management (Table K11)
      Including protection and use of publicly owned river banks
     National parks and forests. Wilderness preservation
325   General (Table K11)
325.5   Wildlife protection. Game laws (Table K11)
      Including game, bird, and fish protection
      Cf. KDZ-KH3 370+ Fishing industry
     Agrarian land policy legislation. Land reform see KDZ-KH3
     368+
     Colonization see KDZ-KH3 368.3
     Regional and city planning. Zoning. Building
      Cf. KDZ-KH3 318 Environmental planning
328   General (Table K11)
328.3   Land use. Zoning. Land subdivision (Table K11)
328.5   Building laws (Table K11)
329   Housing. Slum clearance. City redevelopment (Table K11)
     Government property
331   General (Table K11)
331.3   Real property (Table K11)
331.5.A-Z   Personal property, A-Z
331.5.A96   Automobiles (Table K12)
333   Public works (Table K11)
   Public health. Sanitation
336   General (Table K11)

	Cultural affairs -- Continued
351.6	Language (Table K11)
	Including regulation of use, purity, etc.
	Education
352	General (Table K11)
353	Elementary and secondary education (Table K11)
	Higher education. Colleges and universities
354	General (Table K11)
354.5.A-Z	Particular colleges and universities, A-Z
	Subarrange each by Table K12
	For state colleges and universities, see the state
355	Science and the arts. Research (Table K11)
	Economic legislation
	Cf. KDZ-KH3 364+ Regulation of industry, trade, and commerce
	Cf. KDZ-KH3 440+ Economic emergency legislaton
357	General (Table K11)
358	Economic constitution, policy, planning, and development (Table K11)
359	Economic assistance (Table K11)
360	Foreign investments (Table K11)
	Cf. JZ1546.3 Drago doctrine
	Cf. KDZ-KH3 106.2 Foreign corporations
	Cf. KDZ-KH3 406.6 Tax incentive legislation
	Economic controls
361	General (Table K11)
	Trade regulations. Control of trade practices see KDZ-KH3 365+
	Export and import controls see KDZ-KH3 379+
	Foreign exchange regulations see KDZ-KH3 405.3
	Regulation of industry, trade, and commerce. Occupational law
364	General (Table K11)
364.5	Industrial courts and procedure (Table K11)
	Trade regulations. Control of trade practices. Consumer protection
365	General (Table K11)
365.3	Advertising (Table K11)
365.4	Labeling (Table K11)
365.6	Competition. Restraint of trade (Table K11)
	Cf. KDZ-KH3 140 Unfair competition
365.8	Weights and measures. Containers (Table K11)
	Primary production. Extractive industries
	Agriculture. Forestry. Rural law
367	General (Table K11)
	Public land law see KDZ-KH3 323+

KDZ-KH3

Regulation of industry, trade, and commerce. Occupational law
Primary production. Extractive industries
Agriculture. Forestry. Rural law -- Continued
Land tenure
Cf. KDZ-KH3 58.3 Lease of real property. Landlord
and tenant

367.4	General (Table K11)
367.5	Common lands. Ejidos. Indian lands (Table K11)
	Agrarian land policy legislation. Land reform
368	General (Table K11)
368.3	Colonization. Agrarian colonies (Table K11)
	Cf. KDZ-KH3 275.3 Immigration
368.4	Land reform. Transformation of the agricultural structure (Table K11)

Including expropriation, nationalization, purchase of
agricultural land holdings and their redistribution; land
grants; government-constituted homesteads
Agricultural contracts

368.5	General (Table K11)
368.6	Farm tenancy. Rural partnerships (Table K11)

Class here works on provisions of both civil law and other
legislation ensuring stability for tenants and the land
they cultivate
Cf. KDZ-KH3 368+ Agrarian land policy legislation.
Land reform

368.7	Control of agricultural pests, plant diseases, predatory animals
368.8	Economic legislation. Economic assistance (Table K11)
	Agricultural production

Including marketing, standards and grading

369	General (Table K11)
369.3.A-Z	Field crops, A-Z
369.5	Livestock industry and trade. Cattle raising (Table K11)

For meat industry see KDZ-KH3 376.6
Dairy industry see KDZ-KH3 376.6

369.7	Forestry. Timber law
	Game laws see KDZ-KH3 325.5
	Fishing industry
370	General (Table K11)
370.5.A-Z	Particular fish and marine fauna, A-Z

Subarrange each by Table K12
Mining. Quarrying
Including preservation and management of mining resources

371	General (Table K11)
371.5.A-Z	Nonferrous metals
	Petroleum. Oil and gas

Regulation of industry, trade, and commerce. Occupational law

Primary production. Extractive industries

Mining. Quarrying

Petroleum. Oil and gas -- Continued

372	General (Table K11)
372.3	Oil and gas leases (Table K11)
	Manufacturing industries
374	General (Table K11)
374.5.A-Z	Particular industries and products, A-Z
	Subarrange each by Table K12
374.5.T62	Tobacco products (Table K12)
	Food processing industries
376	General (Table K11)
	Particular industries and products
	Agricultural products
376.3	Sugar refining (Table K11)
376.4	Fruits and vegetables (Table K11)
376.6	Meat industry (Table K11)
376.7	Dairy industry (Table K11)
376.8	Beverages (Table K11)
	Cf. KDZ-KH3 345+ Alcoholic beverages
	Trade and commerce
	Cf. KDZ-KH3 73+ Commercial law
	Cf. KDZ-KH3 365+ Trade regulation
378	General (Table K11)
378.5.A-Z	Particular commodities, A-Z
	Subarrange each by Table K12
378.5.T62	Tobacco (Table K12)
	International trade. Export and import controls
379	General (Table K11)
379.5.A-Z	Particular commodities, A-Z
	Export trade
	Including export controls, regulations, and promotion
380	General (Table K11)
380.5.A-Z	Particular commodities, A-Z
	Import trade
	Including import controls and regulations
381	General (Table K11)
381.5.A-Z	Particular commodities, A-Z
	Retail trade
382	General (Table K11)
382.5.A-Z	Particular products, A-Z
	Subarrange each by Table K12
382.5.D77	Drugs. Pharmaceutical products (Table K12)
	Pharmaceutical products see KDZ-KH3 382.5.D77
	Service trades

	Regulation of industry, trade, and commerce. Occupational law
	Trade and commerce
	Service trades -- Continued
383	General (Table K11)
383.3.A-Z	Particular service trades, A-Z
383.6	Warehouses. Storage (Table K11)
	For warehouse contracts see KDZ-KH3 79
	Public utilities
	Including private, publicly owned, and public-private (mixed) utility companies
386	General (Table K11)
	Particular utilities
	Power supply
	Including energy policy. and energy resources development, in general
386.3	General (Table K11)
386.5	Electricity (Table K11)
386.7	Water (Table K11)
	Including water supply
	For water power development see KDZ-KH3 320
	Transportation and communication
388	General (Table K11)
	Road traffic. Automotive transportation
388.3	General (Table K11)
388.4	Traffic regulation and enforcement (Table K11)
388.5	Carriage of passengers and goods (Table K11)
389	Railroads (Table K11)
389.5	Local transit (Table K11)
	Aviation
390	General (Table K11)
390.2	Air safety (Table K11)
390.4	Aircraft (Table K11)
390.6	Airports (Table K11)
390.7	Pilots. Crews. Ground personnel (Table K11)
	Commercial aviation. Airlines
391	General (Table K11)
391.5.A-Z	Special topics, A-Z
	Water transportation. Navigation and shipping
393	General (Table K11)
	Merchant mariners see KDZ-KH3 119+
	Ships
	Including registration and safety regulations
393.3	General (Table K11)
393.5	Navigation and pilotage (Table K11)
	Including coastwise navigation
	Cf. K4184, International rules of the road at sea

	Regulation of industry, trade, and commerce. Occupational law
	Transportation and communication
	Water transportation. Navigation and shipping -- Continued
	Harbors and ports
	Including port charges and tonnage fees
394	General (Table K11)
394.3.A-Z	Particular ports, A-Z
394.5	Shipping laws. The merchant marine (Table K11)
	Communication. Mass media
396	General (Table K11)
	Postal service
	Including works on postal service, telegraph, and telephone combined
397	General (Table K11)
	Classification of mails. Rates
397.4	General (Table K11)
397.5.A-Z	Special classes, A-Z
397.8	Press law (Table K11)
	Telecommunication
399	General (Table K11)
399.3	Telegraph. Teletype (Table K11)
	Including telegraph and telephone combined
399.5	Telephone (Table K11)
	Including radio telephone
	Radio and television communication
400	General (Table K11)
400.3	Radio and television stations. Concessions. Licensing (Table K11)
	Including frequency allocations
400.4	Radio broadcasting (Table K11)
400.5	Television broadcasting (Table K11)
	Professions and occupations
402	General (Table K11)
	Particular professions and occupations
	Including licensing, certification, professional ethics, and liability
	The health professions
	For medical legislation see KDZ-KH3 342+
	General see KDZ-KH3 402.2
	Physicians
	Including the health professions in general
402.2	General (Table K11)
402.4.A-Z	Special topics, A-Z
	Subarrange each by Table K12
402.5.A-Z	Auxiliary professions, A-Z
	Lawyers see KDZ-KH3 23+
	Notaries see KDZ-KH3 26.3

Public finance
National revenue
Taxation
Income tax
Particular classes of taxpayers -- Continued
413   Nonresident taxpayers (Table K11)
Including both nationals and alien residents abroad, and
foreign companies not operating in the taxing country
Income of business organizations
Including both business associations and individual
merchants
415   General (Table K11)
416   Partnerships and joint ventures (Table K11)
Juristic persons. Corporations
For foreign corporations not operating in the taxing
country see KDZ-KH3 413
417   General (Table K11)
418   Surtaxes. Complementary and additional taxes
(Table K11)
420.A-Z   Particular lines of business, A-Z
Subarrange each by Table K12
420.S45   Service trades (Table K12)
Tax incentive legislation see KDZ-KH3 406.6
Property taxes. Taxation of capital
422   General (Table K11)
National taxes affecting real property
Including income tax, estate, inheritance, and gift taxes,
and others; and works on national and state taxes
combined
422.3   General (Table K11)
422.5.A-Z   Special topics, A-Z
422.5.C33   Cadasters (Table K11)
422.8   Personal property taxes (Table K11)
423   Estate, inheritance, and gift taxes (Table K11)
Taxes on transactions. Taxes on production and
consumption
425   General (Table K11)
425.2   Retail sales taxes (Table K11)
425.3   Excise taxes (Table K11)
425.5   Turnover tax. Gross receipts-tax. Value-added tax. Use
tax (Table K11)
Stamp duties see KDZ-KH3 428
Customs duties see KDZ-KH3 429+
425.7.A-Z   Particular commodities, services, and transactions, A-Z
Subarrange each by Table K12
425.7.T62   Tobacco and tobacco products (Table K12)

KDZ-KH3

	Public finance
	National revenue
	Taxation -- Continued
	Taxation of natural resources
427	General (Table K11)
427.5.A-Z	Particular resources and resource industries, A-Z
	Particular methods of assessment and collection
	For assessment and collection of particular taxes, see those taxes
428	Stamp duties (Table K11)
	Tariff. Customs
	For regional multilateral trade agreements and related bilateral trade agreements, see the appropriate region
	For trade agreements not limited to a region, see K4600+
	For trade agreements of the United States, see KF6665+
	For foreign trade regulations see KDZ-KH3 379+
429	General (Table K11)
	Particular tariffs
430	General (Table K11)
430.5.A-Z	Particular commodities, A-Z
	Customs administration. Customs service
431	General (Table K11)
431.3	Enforcement. Criminal law. Smuggling (Table K11)
	Exemptions. Duty-free imports
431.5	General (Table K11)
	Particular commodities see KDZ-KH3 430.5.A+
431.8	Free ports and zones (Table K11)
	State (provincial, etc.) finance
432	General (Table K11)
	Taxation
433	General (Table K11)
434	Income tax (Table K11)
435	Real property tax (Table K11)
	Local finance
437	General (Table K11)
	Taxation
	Including municipal taxing power
437.3	General (Table K11)
437.4	Income tax (Table K11)
437.5	Real property taxes (Table K11)
437.6	Business taxes. License fees (Table K11)
	Including taxes on occupations and professions
438	Excise and sales taxes. Taxes on transactions (Table K11)
438.5.A-Z	Other taxes, A-Z
	Government measures in time of war, national emergency, or economic crisis. Emergency economic legislation

	Government measures in time of war, national emergency, or economic crisis. Emergency economic legislation -- Continued
440	General (Table K11)
440.5.A-Z	Special topics, A-Z
	Subarrange each by Table K12
440.5.P74	Price control. Profiteering (Table K12)
	Profiteering see KDZ-KH3 440.5.P74
	Military law
441	General (Table K11)
441.5	Military criminal law and procedure (Table K11)
	Criminal law and procedure
	Cf. KDZ-KH3 441.5 Military criminal law and procedure
	Cf. KDZ-KH3 466+ Juvenile criminal law and procedure
443	General (Table K11)
443.5	Administration of criminal justice (Table K11)
	Including reform of criminal law, enforcement, and procedure
	Criminal law
	Cf. HV60001+ , Criminology
	Cf. K5018+ , Philosophy and theory of criminal law
444	General (Table K11)
	General principles and provisions
444.3	Criminal liability (Table K11)
444.4.A-Z	Other, A-Z
444.5	Punishment and penalties. Measures of rehabilitation (Table K11)
444.7	Extinction of criminal actions and criminal sentences (Table K11)
445.A-Z	Particular offenses, A-Z
	Subarrange each by Table K12
	Bad checks see KDZ-KH3 445.F7
445.C64	Contempt of court (Table K12)
	Customs crimes see KDZ-KH3 431.3
445.F36	Family violence (Table K12)
445.F7	Fraud. Fraud by forgery. Bad checks (Table K12)
445.O36	Obscenity (Table K12)
445.P64	Political offenses (Table K12)
	Smuggling see KDZ-KH3 431.3
445.V34	Vagrancy (Table K12)
	Criminal courts. Criminal procedure
	Cf. KDZ-KH3 443.5 Administration of criminal justice
447	General (Table K11)
448	Police and magistrates' courts. Justices of the peace (Table K11)
	Criminal procedure
450	General (Table K11)

KDZ-KH3

	Criminal courts. Criminal procedure
	Criminal procedure -- Continued
	Judicial assistance in criminal matters see KDZ-KH3 456+
452	Jurisdiction. Venue (Table K11)
454	Prosecution and defense (Table K11)
455	Compulsory and precautionary measures against the suspect (Table K11)
	Extradition. Interstate rendition
	Including judicial assistance in criminal matters in general
456	General (Table K11)
456.5	Right of asylum. Refusal of extradition (Table K11)
457	Rights of suspects
	Including protection of human rights in criminal proceedings
	Plenary proceedings. Trials
458	General (Table K11)
459	Jury. Jurors (Table K11)
	Including instructions to jury
	Remedies
460	General (Table K11)
461	Appeals. Appellate procedures (Table K11)
	Amparo see KDZ-KH3 247+
	Habeas corpus see KDZ-KH3 247.7
	Execution of sentence. Corrections
463	General (Table K11)
463.3	Imprisonment (Table K11)
	Juvenile criminal law and procedure. Administration of juvenile justice
466	General (Table K11)
466.3	Juvenile courts (Table K11)
466.5.A-Z	Special topics, A-Z
	Military criminal law and procedure see KDZ-KH3 441.5
	Church and state. Secular ecclesiastical law see KDZ-KH3 279
	Individual political and administrative subdivisions
480.A-Z	Cities, A-Z
	Subarrange each by Table KDZ-KH6
482.A-Z	Counties, parishes, and other units of local self-government, A-Z
	Subarrange each by Table KDZ-KH6

See the list of jurisdictions in KG+ for the names of the states, provinces, etc., and the numbers assigned to them. To determine a subject subdivision for a given state, etc., add the number or numbers in the table for the subject to the basic number for the state, etc. For example, for election law in Tierra del Fuego, Argentina, add 38.8 from this table to the basic number for Tierra del Fuego, KHA8500, to make KHA8538.8

Including departments, Federal districts, and other first order political and administrative subdivisions

1	Bibliography
<1.2>	Periodicals

For periodicals consisting predominantly of legal articles, regardless of subject matter and jurisdiction, see K1+

For periodicals consisting primarily of informative material (Newsletters, bulletins, etc.) relating to a special subject, see the subject and form division for periodicals

For law reports, official bulletins or circulars intended chiefly for the publication of laws and regulations, see appropriate entries in the text or form division tables

1.5	Monographic series
1.7	Official gazettes
	Legislative documents
	see J
	Legislation

For legislation on a particular subject, see the subject

	Statutes
	Sessional volumes. Annual volumes
	Serials
3.A2-.A29	Official editions
	Arranged chronologically
3.A3-Z	Unofficial editions. By publisher or editor, A-Z
3.2	Monographs. By date of initial session
	Collections. Compilations
3.25	Serials
3.3	Monographs. By date
3.4	Abridgements and digests of statutes
3.5	Indexes to statutes
	Class indexes to a particular publication with the publication
	Administrative and executive publications
3.6	Serials
3.65	Monographs. By date
3.7	Digests
3.8	Indexes
3.9	Customary law

Law reports and related materials
> Subarrange courts represented by a whole number by Table KDZ-KH9 , as indicated
> Do not further subarrange courts represented by a decimal or Cutter number
> For reports relating to a particular subject, see the subject

4	Highest court of appeals. Supreme Court (Table KDZ-KH9)
	Lower courts
4.7	Various courts (Table KDZ-KH9)

> Including highest court and lower courts, and state cases decided by federal courts, combined

Intermediate appellate courts. Courts of appeal
> Including reports of the only intermediate appellate court of a state and reports of federal court of appeals in Federal Districts

5	General (Table KDZ-KH9)
5.7.A-.Z	Particular courts, A-Z
	Trial courts

> Including reports of federal district courts in Federal Districts

6	General (Table KDZ-KH9)
6.7.A-Z	Particular courts. By city, country, district, etc., A-Z
	Local courts

> Including justices of the peace courts, magistrates' courts

6.8	General (Table KDZ-KH9)
6.9.A-Z	Particular courts. By city, etc., A-Z
7.3	Encyclopedias
7.33	Dictionaries. Words and phrases
7.34	Form books
(7.35)	Yearbooks

> For publications issued annually, containing information, statistics, etc. relating to a special subject, see the subject and form division for periodicals. For other publications appearing yearly, see K1+

	Judicial statistics
7.4	General
	Criminal statistics
7.42	General
7.43	Juvenile crime
	Directories (6000 number countries)

> see the numbers provided for directories at the national level

The legal profession. Practice of law
General
> see the numbers provided for the legal profession at the national level

7.5	Admission to the bar. Bar examinations (Table K11)

	The legal profession -- Continued
7.55	Law office management. Attorneys' and legal secretaries handbooks, manuals, etc. of state law (Table K11)
7.6.A-Z	Special topics, A-Z
	Subarrange each by Table K12
7.6.F44	Fees (Table K12)
	Including fee schedules for attorneys, procurators, and notaries combined
	Notarial law. Public instruments
7.65	General (Table K11)
7.67	Public instruments (Table K11)
	History
	For biography, see the numbers provided at the national level
7.7	General
7.8.A-Z	Special topics, A-Z
7.9	Criticism. Legal reform
7.93	Congresses
7.95	Collected works (nonserial)
	For monographic series see KDZ-KH4 1.5
8	General works. Treatises
8.2	Compends. Outlines, syllabi, etc.
8.3	Addresses, essays, lectures
	Including single essays, collected essays of several authors, Festschriften, etc.
8.4.A-Z	Works for particular users, A-Z
8.45.A-Z	Works on diverse aspects of particular subjects and falling within several branches of the law. By subject, A-Z
	Conflict of laws
9	General (Table K11)
9.2.A-Z	Special topics, A-Z
9.4	Retroactive law. Intertemporal law (Table K11)
9.5	Usage and custom (Table K11)
9.6	Codification (Table K11)
	Civil law
11	General (Table K11)
	Persons
	Natural persons
11.2	General (Table K11)
11.3	Civil status. Name (Table K11)
	Capacity and disability
11.4	General (Table K11)
11.6.A-Z	Particular groups of persons, A-Z
11.6.A34	Aged. Older people (Table K12)
11.6.M57	Minors (Table K12)
	Older people see KDZ-KH4 11.6.A34

KDZ-KH4

KDZ-KH4

	Civil law
	Obligations
	Torts. Obligations from wrongful acts (Delicts and quasi delicts)
	Other torts, A-Z -- Continued
20.6.A27	Abuse of legal process. Chicanery. Malicious prosecution (Table K12)
	Chicanery see KDZ-KH4 20.6.A27
	Malicious prosecution see KDZ-KH4 20.6.A27
20.7.A-Z	Parties to actions in torts, A-Z
20.8.A-Z	Special topics, A-Z
	Subarrange each by Table K12
20.8.G67	Government liability (Table K12)
20.8.P35	Parents' liability for torts of minor children (Table K12)
20.85	Compensation to victims of crimes. Reparation (Table K11)
	Commercial law
21	General (Table K11)
	Commercial courts and procedure see KDZ-KH4 25.8
21.5.A-Z	Special topics, A-Z
21.5.A93	Auctioneers. Auctions (Table K12)
21.5.B6	Boards of trade (Table K12)
21.5.B74	Brokers (Table K12)
	Commercial contracts
	General works see KDZ-KH4 21
22	Commercial sale (Table K11)
	Including conditional and installment sale
22.5	Negotiable instruments. Titles of credit (Table K11)
	Banking
23	General (Table K11)
23.5.A-Z	Particular types of banks and credit institutions, A-Z
	Subarrange each by Table K12
23.5.C64	Cooperative banks. Credit unions (Table K12)
	Credit unions see KDZ-KH4 23.5.C64
23.7.A-Z	Particular banking transactions, A-Z
	Insurance
	Including regulation of insurance business
24	General (Table K11)
24.5.A-Z	Particular types of insurance, A-Z
	Subarrange each by Table K12
24.5.H34	Hail insurance (Table K12)
	Business associations. Commercial companies
25	General (Table K11)
25.2	Partnerships (Table K11)
25.3	Limited liability companies. Private companies (Table K11)
	Business corporations

	Commercial law
	Commercial contracts
	Business associations. Commercial companies
	Business corporations -- Continued
25.5	General (Table K11)
25.6.A-Z	Special topics, A-Z
	Subarrange each by Table K12
25.6.A25	Accounting. Auditing. Financial statements (Table K12)
	Auditing see KDZ-KH4 25.6.A25
	Financial statements see KDZ-KH4 25.6.A25
25.65.A-Z	Particular types of business corporations, A-Z
	Subarrange each by Table K12
25.65.C64	Cooperative societies (Table K12)
25.65.F65	Foreign corporations (Table K12)
	Private companies see KDZ-KH4 25.3
25.7	Insolvency and bankruptcy. Creditors' rights (Table K11)
25.8	Commercial courts and procedure (Table K11)
	Social legislation
27	General (Table K11)
	Labor law
27.2	General (Table K11)
	Management-labor relations. Labor unions. Collective labor agreements
27.3	General (Table K11)
	Collective labor disputes. Strikes and lockouts
27.4	General (Table K11)
27.43	Arbitration. Conciliation (Table K11)
27.45	Labor courts and procedure (Table K11)
	Including fact finding boards
27.47.A-Z	Particular industries, A-Z
	Labor standards. Labor conditions
27.6	General (Table K11)
27.63.A-Z	Special topics, A-Z
	Subarrange each by Table K12
27.63.D56	Dismissal (Table K12)
27.63.H67	Hours of labor. Night work (Table K12)
	Minimum wage see KDZ-KH4 27.63.W33
	Night work see KDZ-KH4 27.63.H67
27.63.W33	Wages. Minimum wage (Table K12)
	Protection of labor. Labor hygiene and safety
27.7	General (Table K11)
27.73	Women (Table K11)
27.74	Children (Table K11)
27.76.A-Z	Particular industries and types of labor, A-Z

	Social legislation
	Labor law -- Continued
27.8.A-Z	Labor law of particular industries, occupations, or types of employment, A-Z
	Subarrange each by Table K12
27.8.S45	Servants (Table K12)
	Social insurance
28	General (Table K11)
28.3.A-Z	Particular branches, A-Z
	Subarrange each by Table K12
28.3.W67	Workers' compensation (Table K12)
	Public welfare. Public assistance. Private charities
28.5	General (Table K11)
28.6.A-Z	Special topics and groups, A-Z
	Subarrange each by Table K12
	Almshouses see KDZ-KH4 28.6.P64
	Charity laws see KDZ-KH4 28.6.P64
	Child welfare see KDZ-KH4 28.6.C48
28.6.C48	Children. Child welfare. Youth services (Table K12)
	Including protection of children in general
28.6.P64	The poor. Charity laws. Almshouses (Table K12)
	Cf. KDZ-KH4 70.3.P37 Charitable pawnshops
	Youth services see KDZ-KH4 28.6.C48
29	Indians (Table K11)
	Courts. Procedure
	Administration of justice. Organization of the judiciary
	Judicial statistics see KDZ-KH4 7.4+
30	General (Table K11)
30.12	Judicial councils. Judicial conferences (Table K11)
	Administration and management
30.13	General (Table K11)
30.15	Records management (Table K11)
	Court organization and procedure
30.2	General (Table K11)
	Particular courts
30.3	Highest court of appeals. Supreme Court (Table K11)
	Intermediate appellate courts
30.4	General (Table K11)
30.45.A-Z	Particular courts, A-Z
	Trial courts
30.5	General (Table K11)
30.55.A-Z	Particular courts. By city, county, etc. A-Z
	Subarrange each by Table K12
	Minor courts. Local courts
30.6	General (Table K11)

Courts. Procedure
  Court organization and procedure
    Particular courts
      Minor courts. Local courts -- Continued

30.65	Justices of the peace. Magistrates' courts (Table K11)

        For criminal jurisdiction see KDZ-KH4 93
     Judicial officers. Court employees
      Judges
        Including judicial ethics

31	General (Table K11)
31.3.A-Z	Special topics, A-Z

        Subarrange each by Table K12
        Impeachment see KDZ-KH4 31.3.R44
        Justices of the peace see KDZ-KH4 30.65
        Pensions see KDZ-KH4 31.3.S24

31.3.R44	Procedure for removal. Impeachment (Table K12)

        Including individual cases

31.3.S24	Salaries. Pensions (Table K12)
31.5.A-Z	Other, A-Z

        Subarrange each by Table K12

31.5.M37	Court marshals and auxiliaries (Table K12)

  Civil procedure
    Including works on civil and commercial procedure combined

32	General (Table K11)
32.2	Procedural deadlines. Preclusions (Table K11)
32.3	In forma pauperis (Table K11)

    Pleading and motions

32.4	General (Table K11)
32.5	Defenses and objections. Exceptions (Table K11)
32.6	Joinder of issue (Table K11)

    Trial. Trial practice. Trial tactics

33	General (Table K11)

     Evidence

33.3	General (Table K11)
33.4	Presumptions (Table K11)
33.5	Witnesses (Table K11)
33.56	Expert evidence. Expert witnesses (Table K11)

     Judgment

33.6	General (Table K11)
33.7	Costs. Fees (Table K11)
33.75	Res judicata (Table K11)
33.8	Dismissal and nonsuit (Table K11)

    Remedies

34	General (Table K11)
34.3	Injunctions (Table K11)

KDZ-KH4

	Courts. Procedure
	Civil procedure
	Remedies -- Continued
34.4-.6	Constitutional remedies against arbitrary official action. Judicial review (Table K11)
34.4	General (Table K11)
34.5	Amparo (Table K11)
34.6	Habeas corpus (Table K11)
34.7	Appellate procedure (Table K11)
	Special proceedings
34.75	Summary suits and procedure. Interdictal actions (Table K11)
34.8	Noncontentious (ex-parte) jurisdiction (Table K11)
	Cf. KDZ-KH4 7.65+ Notarial practice and procedure
35	Public law (Table K11)
	Constitutional law
	Sources
36	Collections. By date
	Sources other than constitutions
36.2	Collections. By date
36.3	Individual documents. By date of adoption or proclamation
	Constitutions
37	Collections. By date
37.2	Particular constitutions. By date of constitution
	Subarrange each by Table K17
	Constitutional history
37.3	General (Table K11)
37.4.A-Z	Special topics, A-Z
	Subarrange each by Table K12
37.4.S55	Slavery (Table K12)
37.5	Constitutional law in general
	Separation of powers. Delegation of powers
37.7	General (Table K11)
37.75	Conflict of interests (Table K11)
	Judicial review see KDZ-KH4 34.4+
	Structure of government. Jurisdiction
38	General (Table K11)
38.3	Federal intervention (Table K11)
	State territory. Administrative and political divisions see KDZ-KH4 43.4
	Individual and state
38.4	Aliens. Immigration (Table K11)
	Civil and political rights and liberties
38.5	General (Table K11)

	Constitutional law
	Individual and state
	Civil and political rights and liberties -- Continued
38.6.A-Z	Particular rights and freedoms, A-Z
	Subarrange each by Table K12
38.6.S65	Freedom of speech (Table K12)
38.7	Polticial parties (Table K11)
	Organs of government
	The people
	Election law
38.8	General (Table K11)
38.83.A-Z	Special topics, A-Z
	Subarrange each by Table K12
38.83.E43	Election districts (Table K12)
	The legislature. Congress
39	General (Table K11)
39.3	Upper house (Senate, etc.) (Table K11)
39.4	Lower house (Chamber of deputies, House of representatives, etc.) (Table K11)
39.6.A-Z	Special topics, A-Z
	Subarrange each by Table K12
	Including topics relating to both or either chamber of the legislature
39.6.L43	Legal status of legislators. Parliamentary immunity (Table K12)
39.6.L45	The legislative process (Table K12)
	Parliamentary immunity see KDZ-KH4 39.6.L43
39.6.R84	Rules and procedure (Table K12)
	The executive branch. Executive power
40	General (Table K11)
	The Governor. Vice-Governor
40.2	General (Table K11)
	Impeachment
40.3	General (Table K11)
40.35.A-Z	Particular cases. By governor or vice-governor, A-Z
	Including proposed impeachments
	Executive departments. Ministries
40.4	General (Table K11)
40.6.A-Z	Particular departments, A-Z
	Subarrange each by Table K12
40.6.J86	Department of justice. Attorney general (Table K12)
40.7	The judiciary. Judicial power (Table K11)
40.8	State emblem. Flag. Seal (Table K11)
40.9	Decorations of honor. Awards. Dignities (Table K11)
	Local government

KDZ-KH4

	Local government -- Continued
41	General (Table K11)
	Municipal government. Municipal corporations. Municipal services
41.2	General (Table K11)
41.4.A-Z	Special topics, A-Z
41.7	Other units of local authority (Table K11)
	Including counties, districts, townships, villages, etc.
	State civil service. State officials
42	General (Table K11)
42.3	Tenure and remuneration. Salaries. Pensions (Table K11)
42.4.A-Z	Particular offices, positions, types of employment, A-Z
	Subarrange each by Table K12
42.4.R34	Railway employees (Table K12)
42.5	Municipal and county civil service. City and county officials (Table K11)
42.8	Police and power of police (Table K11)
	Including local and rural police in general
	Administrative law
43	General (Table K11)
	Administrative organization
43.2	General (Table K11)
	Executive departments. Ministries see KDZ-KH4 40.4+
	State civil service see KDZ-KH4 42+
43.4	State territory. Administrative and political divisions (Table K11)
	Local government see KDZ-KH4 41+
43.5	Attorneys General's opinions (Table K11)
	Administrative acts
43.6	General (Table K11)
43.65.A-Z	Special topics, A-Z
	Contentious-administrative jurisdiction and procedure. Administrative courts
43.7	General (Table K11)
43.72.A-Z	Special topics, A-Z
	Public property. Public restraints on private property
45	General (Table K11)
45.2	Roads. Highway law (Table K11)
	Natural resources
	Including conservation, management, and environmental planning
	For environmental pollution see KDZ-KH4 52
45.3	General (Table K11)
	Water resources
	Including watersheds, rivers, lakes, and watercourses
45.4	General (Table K11)

	Public property. Public restraints on private property
	Natural resources
	Water resources -- Continued
	Conservation. Water resources development
	Including water power development
	For water power see KDZ-KH4 71.5.W36
45.5	General (Table K11)
45.55.A-Z	Special topics, A-Z
	Irrigation law see KDZ-KH4 46.3
	Water supply see KDZ-KH4 71.5.W36
	Waterways. Canals
45.6	General (Table K11)
45.65.A-Z	Particular waterways or canals, A-Z
45.7	Marine resources (Table K11)
	For fish protection see KDZ-KH4 46.3
	For fishing industry see KDZ-KH4 66
	Mineral resources see KDZ-KH4 67+
45.75	Expropriation. Eminent domain (Table K11)
	Public land law
46	General (Table K11)
46.3	Reclamation. Irrigation. Drainage (Table K11)
	State or provincial parks and forests. Wilderness preservation
46.5	General (Table K11)
46.6	Wildlife protection. Game laws (Table K11)
	Including game, bird, and fish protection
	Cf. KDZ-KH4 66 Fishing industry
	Agrarian land policy legislation. Land reform see KDZ-KH4 63.6+
	Colonization see KDZ-KH4 63.63
	Regional and city planning. Zoning. Building laws
48	General (Table K11)
48.2	Land use. Zoning. Land subdivision (Table K11)
	Building laws
48.3	General (Table K11)
48.4.A-Z	Particular types of buildings, A-Z
	Subarrange each by Table K12
48.4.S34	School buildings (Table K12)
48.6	Housing. Slum clearance. City redevelopment (Table K11)
	Government property
49	General (Table K11)
49.3.A-Z	Particular types of government property, A-Z
	Subarrange each by Table K12
49.3.A96	Automobiles (Table K12)
49.6	Public works (Table K11)

KDZ-KH4

	Public health. Sanitation
51	General (Table K11)
	Labor hygiene see KDZ-KH4 27.7+
51.5	Disposal of the dead. Burial and cemetery laws (Table K11)
	Contagious and infectious diseases
51.6	General (Table K11)
51.63.A-Z	Particular diseases, A-Z
51.65.A-Z	Particular measures, A-Z
	Subarrange each by Table K12
51.65.Q35	Quarantine (Table K12)
52	Environmental pollution (Table K11)
	Including abatement of public nuisances
	For environmental planning see KDZ-KH4 45.3+
	Medical legislation
53	General (Table K11)
53.3	Hospitals and other medical institutions (Table K11)
	Veterinary laws. Veterinary hygiene
54.2	General (Table K11)
54.4.A-Z	Particular measures, A-Z
	Subarrange each by Table K12
54.4.Q35	Quarantine (Table K12)
54.6.A-Z	Particular animals diseases and causative agents, A-Z
	Food. Drugs. Cosmestics
55	General (Table K11)
55.2	Food law (Table K11)
	Drug laws
55.3	General (Table K11)
55.4	Narcotics (Table K11)
55.7	Alcohol. Alcoholic beverages. Liquor laws (Table K11)
	Public safety
56	General (Table K11)
56.3-.8	Weapons. Firearms. Munitions (Table K11)
	Hazardous articles and processes. Product safety
56.4	General (Table K11)
56.5.A-Z	Particular articles and processes, A-Z
	Subarrange each by Table K12
56.5.E97	Explosives (Table K12)
	Accident control
56.55	General (Table K11)
56.6	Steam boilers (Table K11)
56.8	Fire prevention and control (Table K11)
	Control of social activities. Recreation
56.9	General (Table K11)
57	Sports. Prizefighting. Bullfighting (Table K11)
57.3	Lotteries. Games of chance (Table K11)

	Cultural affairs
57.5	General (Table K11)
57.6	Cultural policy (Table K11)
57.8	Language (Table K11)
	Including regulation of use, purity, etc.
	Education
58	General (Table K11)
58.2	School government and finance (Table K11)
58.25	Curricula. Courses of instruction (Table K11)
58.3	Students. Compulsory education (Table K11)
	Teachers
58.4	General (Table K11)
58.5.A-Z	Special topics, A-Z
	Subarrange each by Table K12
58.5.E37	Education and training. Teachers' colleges (Table K12)
58.5.S24	Salaries and pensions (Table K12)
	Teachers' colleges see KDZ-KH4 58.5.E37
	Elementary and secondary education
58.6	General (Table K11)
58.65	Vocational education (Table K11)
	Higher education. Colleges and universities
58.7	General (Table K11)
58.8.A-Z	Special topics, A-Z
	Subarrange each by Table K12
	Scholarships see KDZ-KH4 58.8.S77
58.8.S77	Student aid. Scholarships (Table K12)
58.87.A-Z	Particular colleges and universities, A-Z
	Subarrange each by Table K12
	Science and the arts. Research
59	General (Table K11)
59.3	Statistical services (General) (Table K11)
	For judicial statistics see KDZ-KH4 7.4+
	For vital statistics see KDZ-KH4 11.7
	Performing arts
59.5	General (Table K11)
59.6	Theaters. Motion pictures (Table K11)
	Including censorship
59.7	Historical buildings and monuments. Archaeological excavations (Table K11)
	Including preservation and protection of cultural property
59.8	Libraries. Archives (Table K11)
	Economic legislation
	Cf. KDZ-KH4 61.6+ Regulation of industry, trade, and commerce
	Cf. KDZ-KH4 87+ Economic emergency legislation

KDZ-KH4

	Regulation of industry, trade, and commerce. Occupational law
	Trade and commerce
	Service trades
	Particular service trades, A-Z -- Continued
70.5.H66	Hotels. Restaurants (Table K12)
	Restaurants see KDZ-KH4 70.5.H66
70.5.T67	Tourist trade (Table K12)
70.7	Warehouses. Storage (Table K11)
	Public utilities
71	General (Table K11)
	Power supply
	Including energy policy, and energy resources and
	development in general
71.3	General (Table K11)
71.5.A-Z	Particular sources of power, A-Z
	Subarrange each by Table K12
71.5.E44	Electricity (Table K12)
	Including rural electrification
71.5.W36	Water (Table K12)
	Including water supply
	For waterpower development see KDZ-KH4 45.5+
	Transportation and communication
72	General (Table K11)
	Road traffic. Automotive transportation
72.15	General (Table K11)
	Motor vehicle laws
72.2	General (Table K11)
72.25.A-Z	Special topics, A-Z
	Subarrange each by Table K12
72.25.T7	Traffic regulations (Table K12)
	Including enforcement and traffic violations
72.3	Motor carriers (Table K11)
	Railroads
72.4	General (Table K11)
72.45.A-Z	Particular railroad companies, A-Z
72.5	Aviation (Table K11)
	Water transportation. Navigation and shipping
72.6	General (Table K11)
72.62.A-Z	Special topics, A-Z
	Subarrange each by Table K12
72.62.H35	Harbors and ports (Table K12)
	Ports see KDZ-KH4 72.62.H35
	Communication. Mass media
72.7	Press law (Table K11)
	Telecommunication

Regulation of industry, trade, and commerce. Occupational law
Transportation and communication
Communication. Mass media
Telecommunication -- Continued
73   General (Table K11)
73.2   Telephone (Table K11)
73.8.A-Z   Particular companies, A-Z
Professions and occupations
74   General (Table K11)
74.3.A-Z   Particular professions and occupations, A-Z
Subarrange each by Table K12
74.3.A25   Accountants. Auditors (Table K12)
Auditors see KDZ-KH4 74.3.A25
74.3.D44   Dentists and dental specialists (Table K12)
74.3.E54   Engineers (Table K12)
Health professions (General) see KDZ-KH4 74.3.P48
74.3.M53   Midwives (Table K12)
74.3.P45   Pharmacists (Table K12)
74.3.P48   Physicians (Table K12)
Including the health professions in general
74.5.A-Z   Special topics, A-Z
Subarrange each by Table K12
74.5.F44   Fees (Table K12)
74.5.L52   Licensing (Table K12)
Public finance
76   General (Table K11)
76.2   Budget. Expenditure control. Public auditing (Table K11)
76.3   Public debts. Loans. Bond issues (Table K11)
State (Provincial, etc.) revenue
76.5   General (Table K11)
Taxation
Including works on both state and local taxation
77   General (Table K11)
77.2   Intergovernmental tax relations (Table K11)
Tax administration and procedure
77.3   General (Table K11)
77.4.A-Z   Special topics, A-Z
Subarrange each by Table K12
77.4.C64   Collection. Enforcement (Table K12)
77.4.D67   Double taxation (Table K12)
Enforcement see KDZ-KH4 77.4.C64
77.4.P74   Procedure. Remedies. Tax courts (Table K12)
Remedies see KDZ-KH4 77.4.P74
Tax courts see KDZ-KH4 77.4.P74
77.4.T37   Tax sales (Table K12)

KDZ-KH4

	Public finance
	State (Provincial, etc.) revenue
	Taxation -- Continued
77.6	Exemptions. Deductions. Tax credits (Table K11)
	Including tax incentive legislation
	Particular taxes
	Income tax
78	General (Table K11)
	Income of business organizations
78.4	General (Table K11)
78.5	Corporate income tax (Table K11)
78.6.A-Z	Particular lines of business, A-Z
	Property taxes. Taxation of capital
80	General (Table K11)
	Real property taxes
80.2	General (Table K11)
80.3	Cadasters (Table K11)
80.4	Special assessments (Table K11)
80.5	Real estate transactions (Table K11)
80.6.A-Z	Special topics, A-Z
80.7	Personal property taxes (Table K11)
80.8	Estate, inheritance, and gift taxes (Table K11)
	Business taxes. Licenses
81	General (Table K11)
81.5.A-Z	Particular lines of business, A-Z
	Excise and sales taxes. Taxes on transactions
83	General (Table K11)
83.2	Retail sales tax (Table K11)
83.25	Value-added tax (Table K11)
83.3.A-Z	Particular commodities, services, and transactions, A-Z
	Subarrange each by Table K12
83.3.A43	Alcoholic beverages. Liquor taxes (Table K12)
	Liquor taxes see KDZ-KH4 83.3.A43
83.3.L66	Lotteries (Table K12)
	Real estate transactions see KDZ-KH4 80.5
83.4	Registration fees. Transfer taxes (Table K11)
83.5	Stamp duties (Table K11)
83.6.A-Z	Other taxes, A-Z
	Other sources of revenue
83.8	Federal grants-in-aid (Table K11)
	Local finance
	For works on both state and local finance see KDZ-KH4 77+
85	General (Table K11)
85.15	Municipal debts. Loans. Municipal bonds (Table K11)

	Public finance
	Local finance -- Continued
	Particular sources of revenue
	Taxation
85.2	General (Table K11)
85.3	Income tax (Table K11)
85.4	Real property taxes (Table K11)
85.45	Business taxes. License fees (Table K11)
	Including taxes on occupations and professions
85.5	Excise and sales taxes. Taxes on transactions (Table K11)
85.55.A-Z	Other taxes, A-Z
	Government measures in time of war, national emergency, or economic crisis. Emergency economic legislation
87	General (Table K11)
87.5.A-Z	Special topics, A-Z
	Subarrange each by Table K12
87.5.M65	Moratorium (Table K12)
	Rent control see KDZ-KH4 18.7
	Military law
88	General (Table K11)
88.5.A-Z	Special topics, A-Z
	Subarrange each by Table K12
88.5.M54	Military police (Table K12)
88.5.S7	State militia (Table K12)
	Criminal law
	Cf. KDZ-KH4 95+ Juvenile criminal law and procedure
90	General (Table K11)
90.2	Administration of criminal justice (Table K11)
90.4.A-Z	Particular offenses, A-Z
	Subarrange each by Table K12
90.4.C36	Cattle stealing (Table K12)
90.4.C64	Communication of venereal or other disease (Table K12)
90.4.C65	Contempt of court (Table K12)
90.4.D45	Desertion and non-support (Table K12)
90.4.F34	Family violence (Table K12)
90.4.L35	Larceny (Table K12)
90.4.O26	Obscenity (Table K12)
90.4.P64	Political crimes (Table K12)
90.4.S47	Sex crimes (Table K12)
90.6	Contraventions (Table K11)
90.7.A-Z	Special topics, A-Z
	Subarrange each by Table K12
90.7.A45	Amnesty (Table K12)

	Criminal law
	Special topics, A-Z -- Continued
90.7.C74	Criminal liability (Table K12)
	Including exemption from criminal liability
90.7.P84	Punishment (Table K12)
	Criminal procedure
91	General (Table K11)
91.2	Jurisdiction. Venue (Table K11)
	Arrest and pre-trial detention. Rights of suspects. Criminal investigation
	Including investigation by judicial police, judges of examination, or police magistrates
91.4	General (Table K11)
	Habeas corpus see KDZ-KH4 34.6
91.6	Bail (Table K11)
92	Indictment. Information. Public prosecutors (Table K11)
92.2	Defense. Public defenders (Table K11)
92.4	Pretrial proceedings. Sumario (Table K11)
	Trial
92.6	General (Table K11)
92.7	Jury. Jurors (Table K11)
92.8	Judgment. Sentence (Table K11)
93	Proceedings before magistrates' courts and justices of the peace (Table K11)
93.4	Appeals. Appellate procedure (Table K11)
93.6	Pardon (Table K11)
	Execution of sentence. Corrections
94	General (Table K11)
94.2	Imprisonment (Table K11)
94.5	Probation (Table K11)
	Juvenile criminal law and procedure. Administration of juvenile justice
95	General (Table K11)
95.5	Juvenile courts (Table K11)
	Cities
	Subarrange each by Table KDZ-KH5 or Table KDZ-KH6 , as applicable
	For listing and number assignments, see KG+
97.A-Z	Counties, parishes, and other units of local self-government (except cities and other municipal corporations). By county, etc., A-Z
	Subarrange each by Table KDZ-KH6

1	Bibliography
1.2	Periodicals
	For periodicals consisting predominantly of legal articles, regardless of subject matter and jurisdiction, see K1+
	For periodicals consisting primarily of informative material (Newsletters, bulletins, etc.) relating to a special subject, see the subject and form division for periodicals
	For law reports, official bulletins or circulars intended chiefly for the publication of laws and regulations, see appropriate entries in the text or form division tables
1.3.A2-.A29	Official gazettes
	Arranged chronologically
	Legislative documents
	For documents relating to a particular subject, see the subject
1.4	Serials
1.45	Monographs. By agency and date
1.5	Statutes (federal, national and/or state) affecting cities, etc. By date
	Ordinances and local laws. Charters
2	Serials
2.2	Collections. By date
2.3	Charters. Acts of incorporation. By date
	Local law reports. Collections of decisions and rulings affecting a particular city, etc.
	For decisions and rulings relative to a particular subject, see the subject
2.5	Serials
2.6	Monographs. By date
	Yearbooks. Judicial statistics. Surveys of local administration of justice
2.8	Serials
2.82	Monographs. By date
	Directories
	see see the numbers provided for directories at the national level
	Legal profession, local practice of law in general
	see the numbers provided for the legal profession at the national level
	Local bar associations, lawyers' clubs, etc.
	see the numbers provided for local bar associations at the national level
	Community legal services. Legal aid, etc.
	see the numbers provided for local agencies and legal aid societies at the national level
3	General works. Local legal history
	Particular subjects

	Particular subjects -- Continued
	Private law
	Including civil and/or commercial law
4	General (Table KDZ-KH15)
4.5.A-Z	Special topics, A-Z
	Subarrange each by Table KDZ-KH16
4.5.B34	Banks and banking (Table KDZ-KH16)
4.5.G68	Government contracts. Public contracts (Table KDZ-KH16)
4.5.H67	Housing condominium (Table KDZ-KH16)
	Land tenure see KDZ-KH5 4.5.R4
4.5.L34	Landlord and tenant (Table KDZ-KH16)
4.5.P47	Persons (Table KDZ-KH16)
	Public contracts see KDZ-KH5 4.5.G68
4.5.R4	Real property. Land tenure (Table KDZ-KH16)
	Social legislation. Labor relations. Public welfare
5	General (Table KDZ-KH15)
5.5.A-Z	Special topics, A-Z
	Subarrange each by Table KDZ-KH16
5.5.O74	Orphanages (Table KDZ-KH16)
	Courts and procedure
6	General (Table KDZ-KH15)
6.2.A-Z	Particular courts, A-Z
	Subarrange each by Table KDZ-KH16
6.2.P64	Police courts (Table KDZ-KH16)
	Government
	For charters and acts of incorporation see KDZ-KH5 2.3
7	General (Table KDZ-KH15)
7.2	Elections (Table KDZ-KH15)
7.3	Legislative functions. City council (Table KDZ-KH15)
7.4	Executive functions. Mayor. Administrative departments and commissions (Table KDZ-KH15)
	Judicial functions see KDZ-KH5 6+
7.6	Municipal civil service (Table KDZ-KH15)
7.7	Police (Table KDZ-KH15)
	Public property. Public restraints on private property
8	General (Table KDZ-KH15)
8.2	Expropriation. Eminent domain (Table KDZ-KH15)
8.3	Roads. Streets. Parks. Public buildings (Table KDZ-KH15)
	City planning and redevelopment. Zoning. Building. Housing
8.5	General (Table KDZ-KH15)
8.55.A-Z	Special topics, A-Z
	Subarrange each by Table KDZ-KH16
	Sewers see KDZ-KH5 13.75.W36
8.7	Public works (Table KDZ-KH15)
	Public health. Sanitation. Environmental law

	Particular subjects
	Public health. Sanitation. Environmental law -- Continued
9	General (Table KDZ-KH15)
9.3.A-Z	Special topics, A-Z
	Subarrange each by Table KDZ-KH16
9.3.S58	Slaughterhouses (Table KDZ-KH16)
	Medical legislation. The health professions
9.5	General (Table KDZ-KH15)
9.6	Hospitals (Table KDZ-KH15)
	Including psychiatric hospitals
9.7	Food. Drugs. Cosmetics (Table KDZ-KH15)
9.8	Alcohol. Alcoholic beverages. Liquor laws (Table KDZ-KH15)
	Public safety
10	General (Table KDZ-KH15)
10.2.A-Z	Special topics, A-Z
	Subarrange each by Table KDZ-KH16
10.2.E97	Explosives (Table KDZ-KH16)
10.2.F55	Fire prevention and control (Table KDZ-KH16)
10.5.A-Z	Control of social activities, A-Z
	Subarrange each by Table KDZ-KH16
10.5.A47	Amusements (Table KDZ-KH16)
10.5.B84	Bullfights (Table KDZ-KH16)
10.5.S65	Sports (Table KDZ-KH16)
11	Education. Teachers. Schools (Table KDZ-KH15)
	Cultural affairs
11.6	General (Table KDZ-KH15)
11.7.A-Z	Special topics, A-Z
	Subarrange each by Table KDZ-KH16
11.7.H56	Historical buildings and monuments (Table KDZ-KH16)
11.7.M66	Motion pictures. Theaters (Table KDZ-KH16)
	Including censorship
	Theaters see KDZ-KH5 11.7.M66
	Regulation of industry, trade, and commerce. Occupational law
	Including municipal licenses and franchises
12	General (Table KDZ-KH15)
	Trade regulations. Control of trade practices
12.3	General (Table KDZ-KH15)
12.4.A-Z	Special topics, A-Z
	Subarrange each by Table KDZ-KH16
12.4.W44	Weights and measures (Table KDZ-KH16)
	Trade and commerce
13	General (Table KDZ-KH15)
	Retail trade
	Including secondhand trade
13.3	General (Table KDZ-KH15)

	Particular subjects
	Regulation of industry, trade, and commerce. Occupational law
	Trade and commerce
	Retail trade -- Continued
13.4.A-Z	By product or mode of trading, A-Z
	Subarrange each by Table KDZ-KH16
13.4.P37	Pawnbrokers (Table KDZ-KH16)
	Including charitable pawnbrokers
	Service trades
13.5	General (Table KDZ-KH15)
13.6.A-Z	Particular trades, A-Z
	Subarrange each by Table KDZ-KH16
	Public utilities
13.7	General (Table KDZ-KH15)
13.75.A-Z	Particular utilities, A-Z
	Subarrange each by Table KDZ-KH16
13.75.E43	Electricity (Table KDZ-KH16)
13.75.W36	Water and sewers (Table KDZ-KH16)
	Transportation. Local and metropolitan transit
	Including motor bus lines, taxicabs, street-railroads, subways, etc.
13.8	General (Table KDZ-KH15)
13.85	Traffic regulations (Table KDZ-KH15)
	Professions and occupations
14	General (Table KDZ-KH15)
14.5.A-Z	Particular professions and occupations, A-Z
	Subarrange each by Table KDZ-KH16
14.5.A72	Architects (Table KDZ-KH16)
14.5.A75	Artisans (Table KDZ-KH16)
	Health professions see KDZ-KH5 9.5+
	Teachers see KDZ-KH5 11
	Public finance
16	General (Table KDZ-KH15)
16.5	Budget. Accounting and auditing. Public debts (Table KDZ-KH15)
	Taxation. Fees
	Including criminal provisions
17	General (Table KDZ-KH15)
17.5.A-Z	Particular taxes, fees, etc., A-Z
	Subarrange each by Table KDZ-KH16
17.5.L52	Licenses and permits (Table KDZ-KH16)
17.5.R4	Real property tax (Table KDZ-KH16)
17.5.S24	Sales tax (Table KDZ-KH16)
17.7.A-Z	Taxation of particular lines of business activites, A-Z
	Subarrange each by Table KDZ-KH16

	Particular subjects
	Public finance
	Taxation. Fees
	Taxation of particular lines of business activites, A-Z -- Continued
17.7.S45	Service industries (Table KDZ-KH16)
	Criminal offenses (Violation of local laws) and local administration of criminal justice
18	General (Table KDZ-KH15)
18.5.A-Z	Particular offenses, A-Z
	Subarrange each by Table KDZ-KH16
18.5.P74	Prostitution (Table KDZ-KH16)
18.7	Correctional and penal institutions (Table KDZ-KH15)
19.A-Z	Particular districts, wards, etc., A-Z

.xA15-.xA159	Bibliography
<.xA2-.xA25>	Periodicals
	For periodicals consisting predominantly of legal articles, regardless of subject matter and jurisdiction, see K1+
	For periodicals consisting primarily of informative material (Newsletters, bulletins, etc.) relating to a special subject, see the subject and form division for periodicals
	For law reports, official bulletins or circulars intended chiefly for the publication of laws and regulations, see appropriate entries in the text or form division tables
	Legislative documents
	For documents relating to a particular subject, see the subject
.xA3-.xA34	Serials
.xA35-.xA39	Monographs. By agency and date
.xA4	Statutes (federal, national and/or state) affecting cities, etc. By date
	Ordinances and local laws. Charters
.xA44-.xA49	Serials
.xA5	Collections. By date
.xA55	Charters. Acts of incorporation. By date
	Local law reports. Collections of decisions and rulings affecting a particular city, etc.
	For decisions and rulings relative to a particular subject, see the subject
.xA7-.xA74	Serials
.xA75	Monographs. By date
.xA8-.xZ	General works. Local legal history
.x2A-.x2Z	Particular subjects, A-Z
.x2A42	Alcohol. Alcoholic beverages. Liquor laws
.x2A72	Architects
.x2A76	Artisans
	Budget see KDZ-KH6 .x2F54
	Building see KDZ-KH6 .x2Z64
	Bullfights see KDZ-KH6 .x2S67
	City government see KDZ-KH6 .x2G67
	City planning and redevelopment see KDZ-KH6 .x2Z64
	Condominium see KDZ-KH6 .x2P74
.x2C65	Correctional and penal institutions
.x2C67	Courts and procedure
.x2C74	Criminal offenses (Violation of local law) and local administration of criminal justice
	For particular offenses, see the offense
	Drugs see KDZ-KH6 .x2F64
.x2E37	Education. Teachers. Schools
.x2E43	Elections
.x2E45	Electricity

	Particular subjects, A-Z -- Continued
	Eminent domain see KDZ-KH6 .x2P82
	Explosives see KDZ-KH6 .x2P83
	Expropriation see KDZ-KH6 .x2P82
	Fees see KDZ-KH6 .x2T38
.x2F54	Finance
	Including budget, accounting and auditing, public debts
	For taxation see KDZ-KH6 .x2T38
	Fire prevention and control see KDZ-KH6 .x2P83
.x2F64	Food. Drugs. Cosmetics
.x2G67	Government
	For municipal civil service see KDZ-KH6 .x2M84
.x2H4	Health regulations. Sanitation
	Hospitals see KDZ-KH6 .x2M43
	Housing see KDZ-KH6 .x2Z64
	Housing condominium see KDZ-KH6 .x2P74
	Labor relations see KDZ-KH6 .x2S65
	Land tenure see KDZ-KH6 .x2P74
	Landlord and tenant see KDZ-KH6 .x2P74
	Liquor laws see KDZ-KH6 .x2A42
	Local transit see KDZ-KH6 .x2T72
.x2M43	Medical legislation. Hospitals
	Including psychiatric hospitals
.x2M66	Motion pictures
	Including censorship
.x2M84	Municipal civil service
	Orphanages see KDZ-KH6 .x2S65
.x2P37	Pawnbrokers
	Including charitable pawnbrokers
	Penal institutions see KDZ-KH6 .x2C65
.x2P64	Police
	Prisons see KDZ-KH6 .x2C65
.x2P74	Property. Real property
	Including land tenure, housing condominium, landlord and tenant
.x2P76	Prostitution
	Psychiatric hospitals see KDZ-KH6 .x2M43
	Public debts see KDZ-KH6 .x2F54
	Public finance see KDZ-KH6 .x2F54
	Public health see KDZ-KH6 .x2H4
.x2P82	Public property. Public restraints on private property. Expropriation. Eminent domain
	Including roads, parks, public buildings
	Public restraints on private property see KDZ-KH6 .x2P82
.x2P83	Public safety. Explosives. Fire prevention and control
	Public service commission see KDZ-KH6 .x2G67
	Public welfare see KDZ-KH6 .x2S65

	Particular subjects, A-Z -- Continued
.x2P84	Public works
	Real property see KDZ-KH6 .x2P74
	Roads see KDZ-KH6 .x2P82
	Sanitation see KDZ-KH6 .x2H4
	Sewers see KDZ-KH6 .x2W36
.x2S58	Slaughterhouses
.x2S65	Social legislation. Labor relations. Public welfare
	Including orphanages
.x2S67	Sports. Bullfights
.x2T38	Taxation. Fees
	Including criminal provisions
	Theaters see KDZ-KH6 .x2M66
.x2T68	Tourist trade
.x2T7	Traffic regulations
.x2T72	Transportation. Local and metropolitan transit
	Violation of local laws see KDZ-KH6 .x2C74
.x2W36	Water and sewers
.x2W44	Weights and measures
.x2Z64	Zoning. Building. City planning and redevelopment. Housing
	Including slum clearance and city redevelopment
.x4A-.x4Z	Particular districts, A-Z

> For indexes and other finding aids relating to a particular
> publication, see the publication

KDZ-KH7—
KDZ-KH18

.xA2-.xA29	Journals
	Class here journals restricted to society activities
	For journals devoted to legal subjects, wholly or in part, see K1+
.xA3-.xA39	Proceedings. Annual reports
.xA4	Constitution. Bylaws. Organization handbooks. By date
.xA43	Regulations. Rules. By date
.xA45-.xA459	Other documents. Special meetings, etc.
.xA7-.xZ	General works
	For collective biography, see KDZ-KH1 81 ; for individual biography see the subclass for the country of the biographee

	Reports
0.A2<date>	Serials
	Arrange chronologically by appending the year the publication began (or best estimate) to this number and deleting any trailing zeros
0.A3	Monographs. By date
0.2	Digests
0.3	Citators. Tables of cases
0.5	Indexes
	For indexes and other finding aids relating to a particular publication, see the publication
0.6	Records

**KDZ-KH7—
KDZ-KH18**

.xA2-.xA29	Charters. Legislation. Regulations
	Including both national and state enactments
	Catalogs, bulletins
	see KDZ-KH2 180
.xA3-.xA39	Outlines of study, teachers' manuals, etc.
	Administration
	Including organization and policy
.x3A5-.x3A59	General works
.x4A5-.x4Z49	Special topics, A-Z
.x4C85	Curricula
	For study and teaching of special subjects, see KDZ-KH2 187
	History. General works
.x5A5-.x5Z6	Treatises
.x5Z7-.x5Z79	Addresses, essays, lectures
.x6A2-.x6A29	Anniversaries, special celebrations, etc.

.xA1-.xA4	Serials
.xA5	Directories
.xA7-.xZ	General works

        For biography, see KDZ-KH2 300+ ; KDZ-KH3 28.4+

.xA2-.xA29	Journals
	Class here journals restricted to bar association activities
	For journals devoted to legal subjects, either wholly or in part, see K1+
.xA3-.xA39	Proceedings. Annual reports
.xA4	Incorporating statutes. Constitutions and bylaws. By date
.xA43	Regulations. Rules. By date
.xA45-.xA459	Other documents. Special meetings, etc.
.xA7-.xZ	General works. History

.xA3	Autobiography. By date
	Letters. Correspondence
.xA4	General collections. By date of publication
.xA41-.xA49	Collections of letters to special individuals. By correspondent, alphabetically
	For correspondence on a particular subject, see the subject
.xA8-.xZ	Biography and criticism

KDZ-KH7—
KDZ-KH18

| .x date | By date |
| .xA-.xZ | By editor |

.A2-.A29	Legislative documents
	Legislation
.A295-.A299	Serials
.A3	Monographs. By date
.A5-.A59	Decisions. By court, agency, etc.
.A7-.A79	Miscellaneous documents
.A8-.Z	General works

.xA2-.xA29	Legislative documents
	Legislation
.xA295-.xA299	Serials
.xA3	Monographs. By date
.xA5-.xA59	Decisions. By court, agency, etc.
.xA7-.xA79	Miscellaneous documents
.xA8-.xZ	General works

.x   General (Table K12)
.x2A-.x2Z   Particular cases, A-Z

0	General (Table K11)
0.1	Trade practices. Antitrust measures. Price policy (Table K11)
0.2	Economic assistance. Price supports (Table K11)
0.3	Sanitation. Plant inspection. Product inspection (Table K11)
0.4	Standards. Grading (Table K11)
0.6.A-Z	Particular companies, A-Z
	Subarrange each by Table K12

A

Bond issues
  Public finance: KDZ-KH1 906+, KDZ-KH2 4570+, KDZ-KH3 405.7, KDZ-KH4 76.3
Bonding
  Contracts: KDZ-KH2 939
  Surety and fidelity insurance: KDZ-KH2 1276
Bonds
  Business corporations: KDZ-KH1 339, KDZ-KH2 1357+
  State and local finance: KDZ-KH2 4843
  State finance: KDZ-KH2 4858
Bonus system
  Labor law: KDZ-KH2 1888+
Book industries and trade
  Regulation: KDZ-KH2 4014.B66
Books
  Export trade: KDZ-KH2 4073.B64
Bottomry and respondentia
  Ship mortgages: KDZ-KH2 1418
Boundaries
  Real property: KDZ-KH2 619, KDZ-KH3 47.5
Boycotts
  Collective labor disputes: KDZ-KH1 446, KDZ-KH2 1845+, KDZ-KH3 162
Brand inspection
  Livestock industry and trade: KDZ-KH2 3882.B7
Brands
  Livestock industry and trade: KDZ-KH2 3882.B7
Brazilian "private wills"
  Civil law: KDZ-KH2 680.6
Breach of contract
  Obligations: KDZ-KH2 791+
    Government contracts: KDZ-KH2 865.B73
Bribery
  Criminal law: KDZ-KH1 966.M57, KDZ-KH2 5657
Bridges: KDZ-KH2 3303
Broadcasters
  Regulation: KDZ-KH2 4459.B76

Broadcasting rights
  Literary copyright: KDZ-KH2 1597.3
  Musical copyright: KDZ-KH2 1603.3
Brokers
  Commercial law: KDZ-KH1 236, KDZ-KH2 1091+, KDZ-KH4 21.5.B74
Budget
  Public finance: KDZ-KH1 903, KDZ-KH2 4560, KDZ-KH3 405.4, KDZ-KH4 76.2, KDZ-KH5 16.5, KDZ-KH6 .x2F54
  State and local finance: KDZ-KH2 4842
    Local finance: KDZ-KH2 4902
    State finance: KDZ-KH2 4856
Building: KDZ-KH1 652+, KDZ-KH2 3350+, KDZ-KH3 328+, KDZ-KH5 8.5+, KDZ-KH6 .x2Z64
Building accidents
  Negligence: KDZ-KH2 985, KDZ-KH4 20.5.B84
Building and construction
  Contracts: KDZ-KH2 898.B84
Building and loans associations: KDZ-KH2 1154.B84
Building laws: KDZ-KH1 655, KDZ-KH2 3354+, KDZ-KH3 328.5, KDZ-KH4 48+
Bullfighting: KDZ-KH2 3527, KDZ-KH4 57, KDZ-KH6 .x2S67
  Recreation: KDZ-KH5 10.5.B84
Burden of proof
  Civil procedure: KDZ-KH2 2641+
Burial and cemetery laws: KDZ-KH2 3405, KDZ-KH3 337, KDZ-KH4 51.5
Bus lines
  Regulation: KDZ-KH2 4191.B86, KDZ-KH5 13.8+
Business associations: KDZ-KH1 320+, KDZ-KH2 1295+, KDZ-KH3 101+, KDZ-KH4 25+
Business corporations: KDZ-KH1 328+, KDZ-KH3 104+, KDZ-KH4 25.5+
Business education: KDZ-KH2 3585
Business enterprises
  Commercial law: KDZ-KH2 1069+

INDEX

Economic planning: KDZ-KH2 3702+, KDZ-KH3 358

Economic policy: KDZ-KH2 3702+, KDZ-KH3 358

Economic protection: KDZ-KH4 61.2+

Economics of law practice: KDZ-KH2 224+, KDZ-KH3 23.6+

Education: KDZ-KH1 710+, KDZ-KH2 3540+, KDZ-KH3 352+, KDZ-KH4 58+, KDZ-KH5 11
Air Force: KDZ-KH2 5183+
Armed forces: KDZ-KH2 5123+
Army: KDZ-KH2 5143+
Indians: KDZ-KH2 2210.E38
Navy: KDZ-KH2 5163+
Notarial profession: KDZ-KH2 256

Education and training (Physicians): KDZ-KH2 4447.E37

Education of teachers: KDZ-KH4 58.5.E37

Educational exchanges: KDZ-KH1 726, KDZ-KH2 3641

Ejidos: KDZ-KH2 3813+, KDZ-KH3 367.5, KDZ-KH4 63.55

Election districts: KDZ-KH2 3059, KDZ-KH3 280.5

Election law: KDZ-KH1 585+, KDZ-KH2 3053+, KDZ-KH3 280+, KDZ-KH4 38.8+

Election law and congressional representation of territories: KDZ-KH2 3054

Elections: KDZ-KH5 7.2, KDZ-KH6 .x2E43

Electoral courts: KDZ-KH2 3061

Electric engineering
Contracts: KDZ-KH2 898.E43

Electric industries
Collective labor agreements: KDZ-KH1 440.E43
Collective labor disputes: KDZ-KH2 1850.E43+
Regulation: KDZ-KH2 4012.E43

Electric industry
Wages: KDZ-KH2 1896.E43

Electric installations
Building laws: KDZ-KH2 3356

Electricians
Regulation: KDZ-KH2 4459.E43

Electricity
Power supply: KDZ-KH1 857, KDZ-KH2 4136+, KDZ-KH3 386.5, KDZ-KH4 71.5.E44, KDZ-KH5 13.75.E43, KDZ-KH6 .x2E45
Taxation: KDZ-KH2 4763.E43

Electrification
Taxation: KDZ-KH2 4668.E44

Electronic commerce
Taxation: KDZ-KH2 4763.E44

Electronic data processing
Legal research: KDZ-KH2 152+

Elementary education: KDZ-KH2 3572+, KDZ-KH3 353, KDZ-KH4 58.6+

Elements of crime
Criminal law: KDZ-KH2 5435+

Emancipation
Minors: KDZ-KH1 136.M54
Peonage: KDZ-KH3 269.5

Embezzlement
Criminal law: KDZ-KH2 5620

Emergency economic legislation: KDZ-KH2 4950+, KDZ-KH3 440+, KDZ-KH4 87+

Emergency legislation
Rural leases: KDZ-KH2 3854.E45

Emergency medical services: KDZ-KH2 3439.E5

Emergency powers: KDZ-KH1 603, KDZ-KH2 3127+, KDZ-KH3 287

Emergency tax: KDZ-KH2 4665

Eminent domain: KDZ-KH1 645, KDZ-KH2 3325, KDZ-KH3 322, KDZ-KH4 45.75, KDZ-KH5 8.2, KDZ-KH6 .x2P82

Emphyteusis
Real property: KDZ-KH2 624

Employee leasing (Table B): KDZ-KH2 894.S83

Employee ownership
Incentive wages: KDZ-KH2 1888+

Employees' copyright: KDZ-KH2 1590

Employees' inventions
Patent law: KDZ-KH2 1650

INDEX

Force against, resistance to, or
disrespect for public authorities or
officers
Criminal law: KDZ-KH2 5664
Foreclosure
Real property: KDZ-KH2 642.F65
Foreign arbitral awards
Conflict of laws: KDZ-KH3 34.6.F65
Foreign banks: KDZ-KH2 1154.F65
Foreign business associations: KDZ-
KH2 1298.F65
Foreign corporations: KDZ-KH1 341,
KDZ-KH2 1362, KDZ-KH3 106.2,
KDZ-KH4 25.65.F65
Foreign currency debts
Obligations: KDZ-KH2 782
Foreign exchange and regulations
Public finance: KDZ-KH2 4555+,
KDZ-KH3 405.3
Foreign exchange regulations: KDZ-
KH1 902
Foreign insurance companies: KDZ-
KH2 1224, KDZ-KH3 97.5.A34
Foreign investments
Economic legislation: KDZ-KH1 744,
KDZ-KH2 3725, KDZ-KH3 360,
KDZ-KH4 61.3
Income tax: KDZ-KH1 924, KDZ-KH2
4648, KDZ-KH3 409
Foreign investors, Works for: KDZ-KH1
101.B87, KDZ-KH2 333.B86, KDZ-
KH3 32.6.B87
Foreign judgments
Conflict of laws: KDZ-KH1 116.F65,
KDZ-KH2 351.F65, KDZ-KH3
34.6.F65
Foreign licensing agreements
Patent law: KDZ-KH2 1661
Foreign relations
Constitutional law: KDZ-KH2 2962+
Foreign service: KDZ-KH2 3149+
Foreign source income
Taxation: KDZ-KH2 4648, KDZ-KH3
409
Forensic psychology
Civil procedure: KDZ-KH2 2636,
KDZ-KH3 233

Forensic psychology
Criminal procedure: KDZ-KH2 5877
Forest reserves
Public land law: KDZ-KH2 3335
Forestry
Regulation: KDZ-KH1 765+, KDZ-
KH1 800, KDZ-KH2 3781+, KDZ-
KH2 3886, KDZ-KH3 367+, KDZ-
KH3 369.7, KDZ-KH4 65.7
Foresty
Regulation: KDZ-KH4 63+
Forfeiture
Criminal law: KDZ-KH2 5475
Forfeiture of concessions (Mining):
KDZ-KH2 3943
Forged checks: KDZ-KH2 1137.F65
Forgery
Criminal law: KDZ-KH2 5616, KDZ-
KH3 445.F7
Forgery of documents: KDZ-KH2 5726
Forgery of postage stamps: KDZ-KH2
5724
Forgery of seals: KDZ-KH2 5724
Forgery of stamped paper: KDZ-KH2
5724
Form of government
Constitutional law: KDZ-KH1 550,
KDZ-KH2 2926
Form of juristic acts and their proof:
KDZ-KH2 436
Form of wills
Civil law: KDZ-KH2 680+
Formalities
Conflict of laws: KDZ-KH2 348.F65
Copyright: KDZ-KH2 1584
Formation of contract: KDZ-KH2 845
Formation of contract
Obligations: KDZ-KH2 830+
Formation of islands
Real property: KDZ-KH2 580
Forwarding agents
Regulation: KDZ-KH2 4368
Foundations
Juristic persons: KDZ-KH2 472, KDZ-
KH3 42.3
Franchises
Retail trade: KDZ-KH2 4088

M

Mistake of law: KDZ-KH2 356.I35
Mixed contracts: KDZ-KH2 827.5
Mixed leases
  Contracts: KDZ-KH2 885
Modalities of juristic acts: KDZ-KH2
  437+
Mode of remuneration
  Labor standards: KDZ-KH2 1887+
Modus
  Wills: KDZ-KH2 688.6
Monarchs: KDZ-KH2 3122
Monetary unions
  Pubic finance: KDZ-KH1 901
Money
  Public finance: KDZ-KH1 901, KDZ-
    KH2 4552+
Money orders
  Postal service: KDZ-KH1 880.5
Monopolies: KDZ-KH1 759, KDZ-KH2
  3753+
  De facto: KDZ-KH2 3758
Moral and religious education: KDZ-
  KH2 3578
Moral rights
  Copyright: KDZ-KH2 1588
Moratorium
  Emergency economic legislation:
    KDZ-KH2 4960.D42, KDZ-KH4
    87.5.M65
  Insolvency and bankruptcy: KDZ-KH2
    1516.M65
Mortgage bonds
  Business corporations: KDZ-KH2
    1358.M65
Mortgage guaranty insurance: KDZ-
  KH2 1280
Mortgage loan banks: KDZ-KH2
  1154.M65
Mortgages
  Real property: KDZ-KH2 641+, KDZ-
    KH3 48.6, KDZ-KH4 15.5.M65
Mosquito abatement
  Public health: KDZ-KH2 3418
Motion pictures: KDZ-KH2 3623+, KDZ-
  KH4 59.6, KDZ-KH5 11.7.M66, KDZ-
  KH6 .x2M66
  Copyright: KDZ-KH2 1610

Motor carriers
  Regulation: KDZ-KH1 865, KDZ-KH4
    72.3
Motor fuels
  Taxation: KDZ-KH2 4763.M65
Motor vehicles
  Insurance: KDZ-KH2 1263
  Regulation: KDZ-KH4 72.2+
  Taxation: KDZ-KH2 4763.M66
Multinational business enterprises:
  KDZ-KH2 1363
Multinational corporations: KDZ-KH1
  342, KDZ-KH2 1363
Municipal bonds: KDZ-KH2 4903, KDZ-
  KH4 85.15
Municipal civil service: KDZ-KH1 618,
  KDZ-KH2 3224+, KDZ-KH3 299, KDZ-
  KH4 42.5, KDZ-KH5 7.6, KDZ-KH6
  .x2M84
Municipal contracts
  Obligations: KDZ-KH2 863
Municipal corporations: KDZ-KH1 613+,
  KDZ-KH2 3182+, KDZ-KH3 294+,
  KDZ-KH4 41.2+
  Torts: KDZ-KH2 995
Municipal courts: KDZ-KH3 217
Municipal debts: KDZ-KH2 4903, KDZ-
  KH4 85.15
Municipal government: KDZ-KH1 613+,
  KDZ-KH2 3182+, KDZ-KH3 294+,
  KDZ-KH4 41.2+
Municipal licenses and franchises:
  KDZ-KH5 12+
Municipal officials: KDZ-KH1 614, KDZ-
  KH2 3187+, KDZ-KH3 295
Municipal services: KDZ-KH2 3182+,
  KDZ-KH3 294+, KDZ-KH4 41.2+
Municipal taxing power: KDZ-KH2
  4905+, KDZ-KH3 437.3+
Munitions
  Air Force: KDZ-KH2 5195
  Armed forces: KDZ-KH2 5135
  Army: KDZ-KH2 5155
  Navy: KDZ-KH2 5175
  Public safety: KDZ-KH1 696, KDZ-
    KH2 3500, KDZ-KH3 347.3, KDZ-
    KH4 56.3+

INDEX

INDEX

S

INDEX

INDEX

Wildlife protection: KDZ-KH1 649, KDZ-KH2 3338+, KDZ-KH3 325.5, KDZ-KH4 46.6

Wills

Civil law: KDZ-KH1 189+, KDZ-KH2 672+, KDZ-KH3 53.3

Wills made in lucid intervals

Civil law: KDZ-KH2 676

Wine and wine making

Liquor laws: KDZ-KH3 345.6.W54

Wine and winemaking

Liquor laws: KDZ-KH1 693, KDZ-KH2 3492.W54

Witchcraft

Trials: KDZ-KH2 133.H45

Withholding essential information

Insurance fraud: KDZ-KH2 1229

Withholding tax: KDZ-KH2 4672

Witnesses

Civil procedure: KDZ-KH1 512+, KDZ-KH2 2651+, KDZ-KH4 33.5

Criminal procedure: KDZ-KH2 5885

Witnesses to wills

Civil law: KDZ-KH2 683

Women

Capacity and disability: KDZ-KH2 462.W64

Citizenship: KDZ-KH3 274.5.W64

Civil law: KDZ-KH1 136.W64, KDZ-KH3 40.6.W62, KDZ-KH4 11.6.W64

Human rights: KDZ-KH2 3009.W64

Labor law: KDZ-KH2 1946, KDZ-KH4 27.73

Nationality and citizenship: KDZ-KH1 562.W64, KDZ-KH2 2980.W64

Suffrage: KDZ-KH2 3057.W64

Women lawyers: KDZ-KH2 210.W64

Women and social insurance: KDZ-KH2 1985.W64

Work rules

Labor standards: KDZ-KH2 1933+

Workers' compensation

Maritime social insurance: KDZ-KH2 1444+

Social insurance: KDZ-KH1 465, KDZ-KH2 1991+, KDZ-KH3 184+, KDZ-KH4 28.3.W67

Works councils

Labor standards: KDZ-KH2 1935

Works of art and photography

Copyright: KDZ-KH2 1605+

Wreck

Maritime law: KDZ-KH2 1426.A83

Writ of security

Civil procedure: KDZ-KH2 2762

Wrongful acts: KDZ-KH2 438+

Y

Youth services

Social legislation: KDZ-KH2 2048, KDZ-KH4 28.6.C48

Z

Zoning: KDZ-KH1 652+, KDZ-KH2 3350+, KDZ-KH3 328+, KDZ-KH4 48+, KDZ-KH5 8.5+, KDZ-KH6 .x2Z64

GPO U.S. GOVERNMENT PRINTING OFFICE: 2008–330–111/60008